YODHA-I

ILLUSTRATED MILITARY HISTORY OF INDIA

The Epics (BCE) to The Uprising (1857)

For my mother, Usha
Who not only followed the Drum
But also inculcated in me
A sense of our multifaceted history

YODHA-I

ILLUSTRATED MILITARY HISTORY OF INDIA

The Epics (BCE) to The Uprising (1857)

SHIV KUNAL VERMA

THE BROWSER | FAUJI DAYS

Yodha-I: Illustrated Military History of India—
The Epics (BCE) to The Uprising (1857)
by Shiv Kunal Verma

978-93-92210-31-0
First edition 2024, Second print run

Published by:
JGS Enterprises Pvt Ltd
Imprint: The Browser | Fauji Days

Publisher's Address:
SCO 14-15, FF, Sector 8-C, Chandigarh 160 009

Website: thebrowser.org
Email: service@thebrowser.org

Printed in India

Layout and Cover Design © 2024 by 99 beagles
99beagles.com

THE BROWSER
thebrowser.org
Publishers & Booksellers

FAUJI DAYS
faujidays.com
Oral History & Military Publishing

CONTENTS

Shiv Kunal Verma

Introduction

Thirteen years had passed since independence. My father, Ashok Kalyan Verma, then a captain, was posted at Walong, and though he was on the road trying to get to my mother, Usha, he was not by her side when I arrived on this planet. In those days, getting into or out of the North-East Frontier Agency (NEFA) region was a massive exercise that could take days, if not weeks, and India, then, was a very different country from what it is now. Yet, there is a timeless side to our history that is a part of our collective DNA, which goes back hundreds of years. For most of us, our grandparents' generation is, perhaps, as far back as we can see.

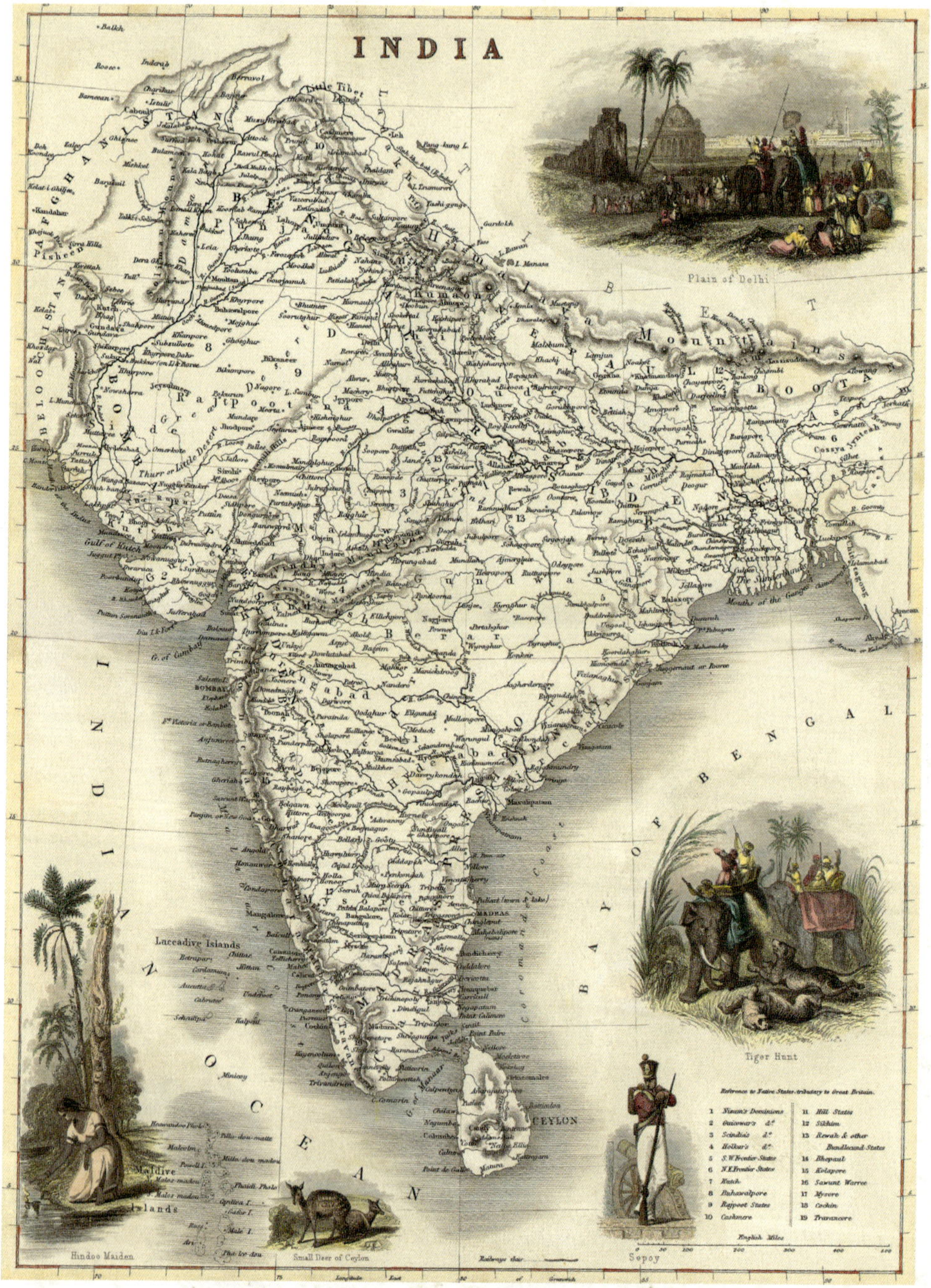
INDIA
Plain of Delhi
Tiger Hunt
Hindoo Maiden
Small Deer of Ceylon
Sepoy
BAY OF BENGAL
INDIAN OCEAN
CEYLON
Laccadive Islands
Maldive Islands
Reference to Native States tributary to Great Britain.
1 Nizam's Dominions
2 Guicowar's d.°
3 Scindia's d.°
4 Holkar's d.°
5 S.W. Frontier States
6 N.E. Frontier States
7 Kutch
8 Bahawalpore
9 Rajpoot States
10 Cashmere
11 Hill States
12 Sikhim
13 Rewah & other Bundlecund States
14 Bhopaul
15 Kolapore
16 Sawunt Warree
17 Mysore
18 Cochin
19 Travancore
English Miles

India's military history is a complex subject. The subcontinent, as the name implies, is physically vast, perhaps too vast a canvas for individuals to relate too easily. Forget about an Apatani or an Adi in Arunachal, even an Assamese living in Guwahati has little or no knowledge of what is happening in say, Trivandrum, Poona, or Calcutta, and if I may hasten to add, vice versa! With the emergence of an India that belonged to all of us, regardless of which part we were in, the creation of West and East Pakistan, combined with the abrupt appearance of China on our northern borders, made the situation even more complicated.

For a start, it is vital for all of us—be we students or ageing grandparents—to first try and understand the geography of our surroundings. The subcontinent binds us together in a manner which is amazingly unique. The great mountain chains to the west, north, and east box us in, while the Bay of Bengal and the Arabian Sea hem in the main peninsula that juts out towards the south. Only when we can see the larger geographical picture each and every time in our minds' eye, will we be able to relate to the way life has played out through the generations before us.

When we look at any battle or period in history piecemeal, we come away with a picture that is quite different from what we see if we view the same event against the larger framework. Even after independence, besieged as we were with the problems we inherited in the post-colonial vacuum, India's military history, unfortunately, was never given its due for various reasons. Much that happened over the last 2,000 years and more was left buried in the sands of time. On the contrary, we were led to believe that British and Mughal history, the two immediately preceding periods, were all that we needed to concern ourselves with. To be fair, a lot that we now know was not available then. If we got the dates and the chronology that Barbur's son was Humayun whose son was Akbar who then fathered Jehangir and then rattled off the names of Shah Jahan and Aurangzeb, we were considered to have mastered the system. It would take us the better part of six decades to realise that we were, on the contrary, standing at the bottom of an incredible ladder. Like in the story of Jack and the Beanstalk where Jack climbs up a very tall magic beanstalk, this compilation, too, is like a climb up the magic vine, for only then can we come across the

'hen that lays endless golden eggs'—a wealth of valuable insights and knowledge!

There are three factors that we need to keep in mind when we embark on this incredible journey. First, in the immediate post-colonial period we tended to see everything through the prism of European eyes. If you chanced across the name of Khanoji Angre, the great Maratha admiral, you were told he was a 'pirate' who traumatised British and Portuguese ships, or that primitive headhunters from the Naga and Lushai Hills came down and raided the tea gardens of Assam, or that all maharajas and rajas were despotic and vile characters, from whose clutches we were spared thanks to the 'British system' that was just and honourable.

Second, in the case of the subcontinent, the line between mythology (even the use of the word mythology is considered to be an affront by some) and ancient history is blurred at best. When given a religious twist, this becomes even more complex. The Vedic literature (1500–1000 BCE), the two epics, the Ramayan and the Mahabharat (1000–600 BCE), Kautilya's Arthashastra (ca. fourth century BCE) and Banabhatta's Harshacharita (ca. seventh century CE), are all key texts regarding life in ancient India. The same is also true for Tibet in the north and Sri Lanka in the south. The great Sangam poets of South India have also left their mark in the telling of the narrative.

Third, there was nothing peaceful or romantic about warfare in ancient times. War was the chief means by which territory was annexed and rulers defeated. This continued to be the case in medieval and colonial times as well. The very concept of a king meant he had to have superior military skills. The concept of *digvijaya*, prominent among Hindu kings, allowed for *dharma yudha* so that a ruler could become a *chakravarti samrat.* The same was the case for devout Jains and Buddhist kings who also, more or less, followed the same principles. Even among their own families, among the ancient dynasties, quite a few of them have instances of patricide and fratricide. Once we enter the medieval period, the same terms apply, perhaps a little more frequently, with *dharma yudha* being replaced by *jihad.*

In this book, which acts as a window into the subcontinent's military history up to the 1857 uprising, it is not even remotely possible to cover each and every battle, some of which were of great significance to a region. Having worked closely with the Armed Forces for almost three decades, I have been exposed to some of the remotest corners of the country and have drawn on that exposure to try and make this book as comprehensive as possible. While photographing temple walls with stories in stone, it became evident that many paintings and historical evidence had been systematically removed. Amazingly, almost every district in India has a museum, and in them, there still exists a plethora of work that helps us piece together what happened.

By the time one goes through this book, one is left with a feeling of bewilderment as to just how we could have, as people, allowed ourselves to be so terribly subjugated. The main objective here is not to be judgemental but to just put the facts for the readers to get the big picture against this humungous platform that spans across both time and space.

Popular art in Kerala draws endless inspiration from the Ramayan ▸

Ramayan

The Ramayan is an ancient Indian epic, passed down orally from as long back as 1500 BCE, although it is generally agreed that the sage Valmiki composed the Sanskrit text of the Ramayan around 500 BCE. A relatively lengthy poem with over 24,000 couplets in 50,000 lines of verse, it is traditionally referred to as the *Adi Kavya* (adi=original, first; kavya=poem), though in the West it is read under the category of epic literature. The main plot involves palace politics and conflicts with demon tribes, but there are also sections of the story that discuss philosophy, ethics, and duty. The Ramayan leans more towards an ideal state of affairs than the other Indian epic, the Mahabharat, in which the characters are shown with all their human follies and failings: Ram is the ideal son and king, Sita the ideal wife, Hanuman the ideal devotee, Lakshman and Bharat, the ideal brothers, and even Ravan, the demonic antagonist, is not entirely abominable.

The climax is the decisive Battle of Lanka, where Ram, with his brother Lakshman and an army of monkeys and bears, fights against Ravan. Numerous fierce fights occur involving Ravan, his brother Kumbhakaran, and his son Indrajit, all formidable warriors in the epic. Ravan is the last to fall on the tenth day, marking the victory of good over evil, celebrated as Vijayadashami even today.

Over the centuries, the story was extended, and regional details were added; explanations and excuses were made for passages that cast the hero, Ram, in a less than heroic light during the years of retellings. Several vernacular versions exist – in the southern regions of India, the *Ramavataram* was written by the Tamil poet Kamban in the twelfth century CE. The *Ramacharit Manas,* written by the Awadhi poet Tulsidas, is well known in the north. In

The climax is the decisive Battle of Lanka, where Ram, with his brother Lakshman and an army of monkeys and bears, fights against Ravan.

A sculpture of Ram and Sita at the Madras Museum at Egmore, Chennai ►

◂ Ram breaking the bow of Lord Shiv in the court of Raja Janak at Mithila

Raja Ravi Varma's painting of Ravan carrying off Sita despite the vulture Jatayu's valiant effort to stop him

Bengali, Malayalam, Telegu, Kannada, and other Indian languages, there are more variations.

Hinduism and India are the epic's original settings, but throughout the ages, the tale has been performed in a variety of ways using different techniques and artistic mediums. In Java, there are Muslim variations, and in Thailand, there are Buddhist equivalents. The story is depicted in dances, plays, and ceremonial reenactments all over India, as well as in temple sculptures and shadow plays in Indonesia and Cambodia. The text is preserved in painted boxes in North India and Ola leaf books in Sri Lanka. Throughout the subcontinent, Ram is worshipped as an incarnation of the god Vishnu, and it is not uncommon to find a Ram temple in almost every other neighbourhood in the country, especially in the Gangetic

◂ Kumbhakaran, brother of the demon Ravan, was tricked by the gods into asking Brahma for the boon of interminable sleep. Ravan built him a lavishly adorned palace, where he slumbered for one hundred years until being awakened by his demon attendants in the episode shown here. They are alerting him that Ram and Lakshman, together with their monkey and bear armies, have attacked the city of Lanka

Scenes from the Thai Royal Palace in Bangkok ▾

belt. In countries across Southeast Asia, such as Cambodia, Indonesia, and Malaysia, the story of Ram continues to be told through intricately crafted shadow puppet shows.

Sita represents the furrow goddess, Ram represents Indra, and Ravan's conflict can be linked to the ancient Indra-Vritra myth from the Rigveda. There are arguments in favour of and against the claim that the epic is based on fictional characters. However, it is widely accepted that Ram was a real person who belonged to the royal Iksvaku house of Ayodhya and whose achievements both in war and peace left a deep impression upon the popular imagination.

Mahabharat

The Mahabharat is an ancient Indian epic where the main story revolves around two branches of a family – the Pandavs and Kauravs – who, in the Kurukshetra War, battle for the throne of Hastinapur. Numerous shorter stories about real or imagined persons and philosophical discussions are woven throughout this narrative. It was written by Krishna-Dwaipayan Vyas, who is himself a character in the epic; according to mythology, he spoke the lyrics as Ganesh

The Mahabharat is the longest epic poem ever written and is one of the most significant works of ancient Indian, and even world, literature since it also contains the Bhagavad Gita.

The rakshas Putana tries to kill the infant Krishna by smearing poison on her breasts ▶

recorded them. It is the longest epic poem ever written, with 100,000 verses, and it is generally accepted that it was penned in the 4th century BCE or earlier. The Indian subcontinent and its neighbouring regions form the backdrop for the events in the epic. A disciple of Vyas first told the story at the sacrifice of a snake for the great-grandson of one of the main characters. The Mahabharat is one of the most significant works of ancient Indian, and even world, literature since it also contains the Bhagavad Gita.

This illustration is from a translation of the ***Harivansh,*** which describes the origins of the cosmos and the legendary history of kings leading up to the birth and life of Lord Krishna. It is associated with the Mahabharat. The translation was done in about 1590. In this episode Krishna drags his uncle Kansa, the tyrant king of Mathura, by his hair from his throne. He then kills him

Draupadi being dragged from her chambers by Dushasan after she was lost in a game of dice by the eldest Pandav, Yudhishter. Her attempted disrobing and humiliation by the Kauravs would result in the Battle of Mahabharat being fought

▲Karna joins the battle on the Kaurav side

▼ Dronacharya being attacked by Arjun

▲ The dialogue between Arjun and his charioteer-guide Krishna

The Mahabharat has undergone numerous revisions since it was written two millennia ago to include fresh concepts that address the contemporary issues of different periods of time. There are thousands of handwritten Sanskrit versions of the manuscripts, and no two are alike. The story was told almost as frequently as it was read. At one level, the Mahabharat is a story relevant to today's world. The ancient Indian epic's story is about political corruption, bad behaviour, and battle. In the Mahabharat, inequality and human suffering are universal truths. The work provides insightful angles and vantage points for contemplating how many injustices manifest in the modern world as well.

The Mahabharat gives its readers a wealth of philosophy and ethics, especially regarding the nature of human suffering as a constant threat to any moral system.

◂ A Kangra painting showing the clash of the two armies. In the Indian context, the line between ancient history and mythology is often blurred

At one level, the Mahabharat is a story relevant to today's world. The work provides insightful angles and vantage points for contemplating how many injustices manifest in the modern world as well.

Copper plates depicting various war scenes from the Mahabharat in a museum in Pudukkotai, a former princely state in Tamil Nadu

The Buddha in meditation (from the Kushan period ca. 2 CE, Indian Museum, Kolkata) ▸

Advent of Buddhism

Buddhism is a philosophy and moral discipline that has its roots in India's sixth and fifth centuries BCE. A non-theistic religion (it does not believe in a creator god), it was established by Siddharth Gautam, often referred to as the Buddha, who lived from around 563 to 483 BCE and was believed to have been a Hindu prince.

Siddharth enjoyed a comfortable life as a noble with his wife and family until he became deeply aware of human suffering and worldly sorrows. He felt compelled to discover a means to lessen people's suffering by embarking on a spiritual journey to enlighten himself. He practised hard spiritual disciplines in order to become an enlightened being who could finally break free from the cycle of misery, rebirth, and death, known as Samsara. Having achieved a desired state of spiritual attainment, he began preaching to spread his message to the world. He expressed his view on the nature of life in his Four Noble Truths after becoming enlightened.

Born as Siddharth Gautam to royal parents of the Sakhya Clan in Lumbini which is now in Nepal, most of the subcontinent's documented history starts with the records kept by Buddhist monks who meticulously recorded events as they unfolded thereafter.

The Noble Eightfold Path—right belief, right determination, right speech, right behaviour, right activity, right effort, right mindfulness, and right samadhi—or meditation—was provided by the Buddha as a means of achieving these objectives. Buddhist doctrine holds that liberation from Samsara, the cycle of rebirth and sorrow, can be achieved by pursuing the Noble Eightfold Path.

Soon, he acquired many followers, and as the word spread, more and more people joined in, thus giving birth to a faith or way of life called Buddhism. As a philosophy, Buddhism refers to a spiritual path leading to insight into the nature of reality. Buddhist techniques such as meditation are ways to transform oneself so that one grows in awareness, kindness, and knowledge.

Many critics refuse to accept it as a new faith or religion since it doesn't accept the philosophy that identifies a creator god in other faiths. The resistance during the initial period was even greater. Resultantly, up until the reign of Ashoka the Great and the Mauryan emperors, who accepted and propagated the idea, it remained confined to a small region. These kings then spread it throughout India and Central and Southeast Asia. It found a great following in China, Ceylon, and Southeast Asia. Even though there existed a conflict between Hinduism and Buddhism, the latter did spread rapidly before it went into a phase of decline, both due to the resurgence of Hinduism and the arrival of Islam in the subcontinent.

Pillar reliefs at Sanchi depict Bimbisāra with his royal cortege issuing from the city of Rājagriha, on a visit to the Buddha ▶

Bimbisara

545–492 BCE

King of the Magadha kingdom, Bimbisara (545–492 BCE), is credited with achieving the first imperial control of the Indian subcontinent. He was the son of a minor monarch named Bhattiya and was known as Bimbisara in Buddhist tradition and Sreika or Seniya in the Jain scriptures. He belonged to the Haryanka Dynasty. The stories of different Indian monarchs before the Haryanka Dynasty are based on legends not conclusively supported by archaeological findings.

Bimbisara's reign coincided with a very distinguished period in the subcontinent's history as both Gautam Buddha and Mahavir Vardhaman, the respective founders of Buddhism and Jainism, embarked on their respective spiritual journeys at the time. Given that Bimbisara supported both these religions, he has received a lot of attention in early Buddhist and Jain literary works. Girivraja, also known as Rajagriha, the location from which he reigned, is now known as Rajgir in the current state of Bihar. It is reported that Bimbisara personally created the city of Rajagriha. Five hills surrounded the city on all sides, forming a natural defence. Bimbisara's son, Ajatashatru, filled in the gaps with stone walls, thereby giving the city a formidable protective system.

Though Bimbisara now acts as a marker in ancient history, obviously, there were thriving kingdoms before and all around him at the time. Four great kingdoms were also rising during that period—Kosala, Avanti, Vatsa, and Magadha. While the ancient Magadh Empire roughly corresponds to the modern states of Bihar, Jharkhand, some portions of West Bengal, Odisha, Uttar Pradesh, Nepal, and Bangladesh, the ancient Kosala Empire covered the modern state of Uttar Pradesh. Avanti was based in the state of Madhya Pradesh.

A young Bimbisara had witnessed his father leading a fruitless military campaign against the Anga king Brahmadatta. On assuming authority at the young age of 15, his first priority was to exact revenge on Brahmadatta. During his first-ever military expedition, he was able to easily defeat the Anga

In an almost identical scenario, Ajatashatru's royal procession where the king is flanked by his ministers and the women watch from balconies ▸

Bimbisara visiting Gautam Buddha and offering to place his kingdom at his feet. Painted by a Burmese artist, the clothing and overall attire reflects Burmese customs

soldiers due to his early training in ancient Indian warfare. He could access the Anga oceanic routes in this way, and his kingdom subsequently benefited from thriving international trade.

He was a capable and courageous military leader and possessed a balanced, logical mind. To cite an example, he preferred to seek marital alliances with powerful kingdoms that he could not conquer to expand his area of influence rather than confront them with lesser forces at his command. By marrying the sister of the Kosala kingdom's powerful monarch, Prasanajit, and by receiving the holy city of Kashi as a dowry, he added to his fortunes without shedding blood.

Sculpted walls at Borobudur in Java illustrating the life of the Buddha as narrated in the *Lalitavistara*

Kashi, one of the holiest locations in Hinduism and hence a major source of revenue, boosted Magadh's finances. Similarly, he married a Licchavi princess, Chellana, from the powerful confederation of the Vrijjis and another princess from the Madri clan of middle Punjab.

Even though Bimbisara had few military victories and conquests to his credit, his most important contribution to Magadh was establishing a government and administration that many of the dynasties that came after him adopted. Bimbisara established a structure of command among the officials to guarantee accurate taxation and collection. According to records, he controlled 80,000 villages, each with a headman in charge. High-ranked officials for the military, judiciary, and financial systems were also appointed (or fired) by Bimbisara.

Despite his shrewdness, Bimbisara also made typical errors made by kings. He blindly trusted his son, but Ajatashatru had ambitions from an early age and was encouraged to commit patricide by Devadatt, a relative of Gautam Buddha. Devadatt viewed Buddha's growing influence over Bimbisara as a hindrance to his desire for a place in the monarchy. He thus fooled Ajatashatru into usurping the throne by having him remove his father and put him to death. However, there is a counter legend that claims Bimbisara committed suicide after being imprisoned.

Vardhamana (ca. 599–527 BCE) better known as 'Mahavir' is the sage credited with founding of the nontheistic religion of Jainism, a belief system established in the 6th and 5th centuries BCE in India, which provided adherents with a disciplined path toward spiritual liberation. According to Jain tradition, however, he is not the founder of the religion but only the 24th *tirthankar* of the faith who inherited the vision from his predecessors and established it in its present form ►

Bodhisattva Vajrapani, Ajanta Caves, Gupta Period, 5th Century CE ▸

Early Indian Art

India has been referred to as the *Sone ki Chidiya*, or the Golden Bird, because of its extensive cultural legacy. The earliest types of Indian art date back to about 3500 BCE, and both cultural and religious factors have had a significant impact on their development. Whether they be paintings, sculptures, poems, or musical compositions, the diverse culture of the nation has left a lasting impression. India is recognised for being both spiritual and modern, having been incredibly gifted with both a beautiful landscape and a glorious past.

Illustrations of the rock cut temples of India including Khandagiri Hill, Cuttak and the Chaitya Cave, Ajanta

The earliest Indian art styles are thought to have originated during the Indus Valley Civilisation. Prehistoric rock art, like the Bhimbetka petroglyphs, was discovered in Central India and is thought to be at least 29,000 years old. The earliest known instances of these paintings date to around 7000 BCE. Indian art throughout the Indus Valley Civilisation, which roughly spans the years 3200 and 1200 BCE, is also seen to have been impacted by advancements in science and culture. Between 2500 and 1800 BCE, the inhabitants created the oldest known sculptures of Indian art that are still in existence today—terracotta and bronze sculptures of people and animals, including cows, monkeys, and dancing figures. Sometime during the sixth century BCE, stone and bronze sculptures were created by religious artisans. They also created spectacular examples of Indian cave art, including complete temples that were carved out of stone and embellished with sculptures.

The Satkunda Rock paintings—life in early historic and Neolithic art depicted animal figures and styled human beings. The richest paintings are reported from Vindhya range of Madhya Pradesh and their Kaimurean extension into Uttar Pradesh ►

Chandragupt Maurya (Indian Military Academy) ▸

Chandragupt Maurya 322–298 BCE

The Maurya Dynasty was founded by Chandragupt Maurya, who is referred to as Sandrakottos by the Greeks. He is credited with creating the first pan-Indian empire with the aid of his mentor and later minister Chanakya or Kautilya, who thoroughly documented in the *Arthashastra* the functioning, culture, military, and economy of the sizable and centralised empire. The Mauryan dynasty began in 322 BCE when Chandragupt Maurya overthrew the final Nanda emperor. He succeeded in unifying politics by taking control of all of north India, including the Gangetic Valley. Previously, there was an oligarchical and republican system of administration, which the Mauryans supplanted with a monarchy. They established Pataliputra, now popularly known as Patna in Bihar, as their capital city.

The history of Chandragupt is obscure. The oldest sources, those from Greece, mention him as having no warrior ancestry. The Hindu scriptures also claim that he was Kautilya's student of low birth, while many Buddhist scriptures claim that he was a Kshatriya. However, it is generally acknowledged that he was an orphan born into a poor family and then raised by Kautilya.

After Alexander gave up on conquering India in 324 BCE, Chandragupt took over some of the Greek-ruled territories within a year. The overall plan for such conquests, through overt wars as well as deceit, was invariably scripted by Kautilya and carried out by Chandragupt. Together, they had built up their own mercenary army to achieve their aims. In 321 BCE, they made their way into Magadh to the east, where he defeated Dhana Nanda in a series of conflicts, laying the cornerstone for the Maurya Empire. In fact, Kautilya used his '*war by other means*' tactic after realising that a battle with Magadh would require much more than a large army. He used a variety of intrigues, counter-intrigues, plots, and counter-plots to weaken Dhana Nanda by displacing his most important allies, adherents, and followers, most notably his chief minister, Rakshasa. Chandragupt eventually succeeded in regaining the throne at Pataliputra by using both military and non-military methods.

Chandragupt signed a deal with Seleucus Nicator in 305 BCE, resulting in his gaining control over Baluchistan, eastern Afghanistan, and the area to the west of the Indus. He also wed the daughter of Seleucus Nicator, who was given 500 elephants in exchange. This development meant the avoidance of war and bloodshed, which was the hallmark of Kautaliya's art of diplomacy.

With the exception of a few regions like Kalinga and the far south, Chandragupt pursued an expansionist agenda and unified nearly the entirety of modern India during his long rule between 322 and 298 BCE. Chandragupt and Chanakya adopted a number of significant economic and political reforms after unifying much of India. From Pataliputra, Chandragupt built a powerful central government, and the principles of statecraft and dealing with the economy outlined in the *Arthashastra* were put into practice. There are a variety of historical, legendary, and hagiographic accounts about Chandragupt's rule in the literature of various Indian religions. Chandragupt had an *Amatya* (council of ministers), with Chanakya serving as his prime minister throughout his rule. The empire was divided into *Janapadas* (territories), regional power centres were *Durga* (fortified), and the *Kosa* (treasury) provided funding for government operations. Megasthenes recorded that three concurrent administrative systems characterised Chandragupt's tenure. One oversaw village affairs, ensuring irrigation, keeping track of property ownership, keeping an eye on the supply of tools, enforcing rules pertaining to hunting, wood products, and forests, and resolving conflicts. A different administrative system oversaw all city concerns, including trade, commerce, foreign visitor traffic, harbours, roads, temples, markets, and factories. Additionally, they enforced uniform weights and measurements and collected taxes. The third administrative body supervised the military, its training, its supply of weaponry, and the needs of the soldiers.

▲Chanakya (375–283 BCE) (Indian Military Academy)

The empire developed a robust economy thanks to a well-developed network of highways, irrigation systems, and temples. Ancient epigraphic evidence reveals that Chandragupt began and finished a number of irrigation reservoirs and networks across the Indian subcontinent to ensure food supply for the civilian population and the army. His dynastic successors continued this practice. The empire of Chandragupt also established mines, factories, and commercial networks. Under his dominion, the Indian subcontinent's land routes were constructed for the transportation of goods. Roads appropriate for carts were expanded, and it is widely accepted that the Mauryan emperors were great road builders. Following the building of a 1,000-mile roadway connecting Chandragupt's capital, Pataliputra in Bihar, to Taxila in the northwest, other strategic networks connected Pataliputra with Nepal, Kapilavastu, Dehradun, Mirzapur, Odisha, Andhra, and Karnataka.

He left the throne in favour of his son Bindusara and travelled to Karnataka with Bhadrabahu, a Jain monk, having embraced Jainism. According to Jain tradition in Shravanabelagola, it is claimed that he starved himself to death.

In 326 BCE, King Porus and Alexander's armies engaged in the pivotal Battle of Hydaspes ▼

Porus vs Alexander
326 BCE

In 326 BCE, King Porus (sometimes spelt Poru or Paurava) and Alexander's armies engaged in the pivotal Battle of Hydaspes (The Greek name for the Jhelum River – the site is now in Pakistan). The Macedonian Army won the battle, allowing ancient Greek political and social influences to spread across the Indian subcontinent.

Earlier, in 327 BCE, Alexander had launched a fresh campaign to expand his kingdom farther into India after he routed the last of the Achaemenid kingdom's armies the previous year. Alexander's main army came through the Khyber Pass after deploying 10,000 troops to garrison Bacteria (modern-day Afghanistan). A smaller force

Alexander and Porus as depicted by the French painter Charles-André Van Loo. After his defeat, when asked how he wanted to be treated, King Porus replied, "Treat me as a king would treat another king." Alexander was impressed and allowed him to retain his lands

under Alexander's personal command travelled through the northern route, taking the fortress of Aornos (modern-day Pir-Sar) along the way. Despite having a somewhat larger army, in the fight with Porus, it is thought that 40,000 infantry and 5,000 cavalry made it across the Jhelum in time to face the opposition. Compared to his prior battles, Alexander sustained significant losses during this conflict.

Early in the spring of the next year, Taxiles (also known as Ambhi Kumar), the ruler of Taxila, and Alexander forged an alliance against Porus, who was preparing for war despite Alexander's order for him to submit. Porus enjoyed a formidable reputation, but through deceit, Ambhi Kumar managed to wean away Porus' friends who had promised to fight for him. Having weakened the opponent, Alexander moved ahead. On the right bank of the river, close to the village of Jhelum, Alexander established his camp. To prevent any crossing, Porus gathered on the Jhelum's southern bank. Any effort to cross the Jhelum River would most likely end in disaster for the attacking force because it was so deep and swift.

In order to counter the Macedonian cavalry, the Indians had deployed cavalry on both flanks, fronted by chariots and infantry in the centre, with war elephants stationed every fifty feet in front of them. The heavily armoured elephants carried *howdahs* that had a squad of archers and javelin warriors. The Pauravan soldiers wore garishly coloured clothing, steel helmets, and colourful scarves and carried axes, lances, and maces. Instead of fighting from a chariot, as was then customary for Indian rulers, Porus, wearing chain mail armour, was seated atop his largest war elephant.

Alexander opted to attack with his cavalry first on the flanks, holding back his phalanx until Porus' cavalry had been eliminated. The defending soldiers outnumbered the Macedonian heavy infantry phalanx 1:3. The latter was also at a severe disadvantage in close combat because of their lack of armour and their adversaries' long *sarissas*. The slick terrain made even their massive armour-piercing arrows ineffective, whereas the Indians' lighter armour benefited from the muddy terrain.

Porus ordered his elephants forward as his flanks came under attack. The Macedonian phalanx sprang up to meet the war elephants as they advanced toward the cavalry. The strong animals killed many Macedonian foot soldiers, stomping and dispersing their tight ranks while impaling many with their steel-clad tusks and lifting some of them into the air before smashing them on the ground.

However, the Macedonian infantry withstood the attack while the cavalry struck from behind in a classic 'hammer and anvil' manoeuvre, routing the entire Paurava Army as the Macedonian infantry finally locked shields and pushed against the disorganised mass of Porus' men. Finally, it was a victory for Alexander, but he had lost more than 10,000 men. Alexander's army then reached the Hyphasis (modern-day Beas), which brought him close to the Nanda Empire's borders. His soldiers argued that they should go back to the West since they were worn out from the constant fighting and worried about the possibility of encountering yet another enormous Indian army. Feeling the pulse of his men, Alexander separated his army and travelled along the Indus River to Persia. Four of his generals were left in command of the four northwest Indian provinces. Alexander left Persia and travelled to Babylon, where he passed away on 10 or 11 June 323 BCE due to a horrible sickness.

A portrait of Ashoka at the Indian Military Academy ▸

Ashoka 268–232 BCE

Ironically, despite the existence of his edicts, the Mauryan emperor Ashoka had almost been wiped out of Indian history. Most information pertaining to Ashoka surfaced only after the decipherment of the ancient Indian Brahmi script that was in use around the third century BCE but was subsequently lost. In the nineteenth century, the decipherment of Brahmi became the focus of the Asiatic Society of Bengal in Calcutta, and the script was deciphered by James Prinsep, the secretary of the society.

Ashoka's inscriptions, when deciphered, were found to be mainly focused on the topic of *dhamma* and provided little information regarding other aspects of the Mauryan state. However, much of the information about Ashoka comes from Buddhist legends that present him as a great, ideal emperor. These legends appear in texts and are recorded by Buddhist authors who were not contemporary to Ashoka and probably relied on oral records where myth and reality may have gotten blurred. Among modern scholars, opinions range from downright dismissal of these legends as mythological to acceptance of historical portions that seem plausible.

The Buddhist legends about Ashoka exist in several languages, including Sanskrit and Pali, and these legends can be traced to two primary schools: the North Indian tradition preserved in the Sanskrit-language texts such as the *Ashokavadana* and the Sri Lankan tradition preserved in Pali-language texts. There are several significant differences between the two traditions. For example, the Sri Lankan tradition emphasises Ashoka's role in convening the Third Buddhist council and his dispatch of several missionaries to distant regions, including his son Mahinda to Sri Lanka. However, the North Indian tradition makes no mention of these events. It describes other events not found in the Sri Lankan tradition, such as a story about another son named Kunala.

▾ The emperor with his wives as depicted in the Sanchi engravings

Until the Kalinga War, which was a watershed in his thinking and led to his renouncing armed conflicts, Ashoka's early years were marked by several military campaigns.

Ashoka was the third Mauryan emperor, and today, he is reputated as one of the greatest Indian emperors, being referred to as 'Ashoka the Great'. His reign is significant not only for the vast extent of the Mauryan Empire but also for his transformation from a ruthless conqueror to a compassionate and enlightened monarch. The exact date of Ashoka's birth is not certain, but it is believed he was born in 304 BCE and ascended to the throne around 269 BCE after a series of wars following his father Bindusara's death.

In the four years between Bindusara's death and Ashoka's coronation, he faced multiple challenges to his authority. There were uprisings and rebellions in various parts of the empire, and Bindusara's erstwhile ministers and generals were vying for power and influence. However, Ashoka was skilled enough to deal with the situation, and he quickly consolidated his power and stabilised the huge Mauryan Empire.

Ashoka was deeply influenced by the teachings of the Buddha and became a patron of Buddhist monasteries and established several religious institutions. Until the Kalinga War, which was a watershed in his thinking and led to his renouncing armed conflicts, his early years were marked by several military campaigns. However, unlike his predecessors, he often resorted to diplomacy and persuasion to win wars

rather than brute force, often sending emissaries to neighbouring kingdoms to establish peaceful relations. During his reign, the empire was facing threats from the emerging Shunga dynasty, and the subsequent decline of the Mauryas led to a period of political instability. India remained divided for nearly 600 years till the Gupta dynasty took over.

The Odisha State Museum credits Emperor Kharvela for restoring Kalinga's pride after the devastation caused by Emperor Ashoka two decades earlier. Karuvaki is the only queen of Ashoka who finds mention in his own inscriptions and it is most likely that her reginal name was Tishyarakshita

Scenes from the Mahabharat depicted as sculptures for the first time during the Gupta period (National Museum) ►

Guptas 320–467 CE

Between 320 and 550 CE, the Gupta Empire spanned across much of northern, central, and southern India. The achievements of the time are celebrated in the fields of philosophy, religion, science, architecture, and the arts. The Gupta realm started rising under Chandragupta I (320–335 CE), the first sovereign ruler of the lineage. It signalled the conclusion of 500 hundred years of provincial power dominance and unrest that followed the fall of the Mauryas. More significantly, it

◂ Coins depicting Samudragupta and Chandragupta II.

▾ War elephants

marked the start of a time of general prosperity and expansion that lasted for the following two-and-a-half centuries and was referred to in Indian history as the 'Golden Age'. However, its origin lay in 240 CE when Srigupt, who was then simply a provincial ruler, planted the seeds of the empire.

The most reliable sources of information pertaining to the early Guptas are the travelogues and writings of Buddhist monks who frequently visited this region. In this context, the journals of Fa Hien (Faxian, ca. 337–422 CE), Hiuen Tsang (Xuanzang, 602–664 CE), and Yijing (I Tsing, ca. 635–713 CE) are invaluable. During Srigupt's reign (about 240–280 CE), the Gupta kingdom only included Magadh and perhaps a small portion of Bengal. Srigupt governed from Pataliputra, a region close to modern-day Patna, like the Mauryas and other Magadh monarchs before him. In the period between 280 and 319 CE, Srigupt's son Ghatotkach replaced him as king.

The Gupta monarchs learned the value of cavalry from the Kushans, and Chandragupt I, the son of Ghatotkach, effectively evolved new tactics for his large army. He also acquired ownership of rich mines full of iron ore through his marriage with the Licchhavi Princess Kumaradevi. As metallurgy had already advanced, forged iron added a fortune to his treasury. It is believed that the Gupta Empire's borders had reached Allahabad by the conclusion of his rule.

Samudragupt (ca. 335–375 CE) was a military prodigy, and he turned his attention to South India. By the end of his southern campaign, he had added some of it to his kingdom. The Gupta Empire is accepted to have extended from Balkh, Afghanistan, in the west to the Brahmaputra River in the east, from the Himalayas in the north to the mouth of the Krishna and Godavari rivers in the south during his reign. He made significant financial contributions to a range of charitable causes, including the advancement of education. He was a poet and musician in addition to being a brave king and competent administrator.

His son, Chandragupt II (r. 380–414 CE), was a capable administrator and wise leader. He furthered the reach of his empire to the Arabian Sea by overthrowing the satrap of Saurashtra. His valiant efforts earned him the name Vikramaditya. In order to more effectively govern the large empire, Chandragupt II established his second capital in Ujjain. He also raised a naval fleet. As a result, the seaports of Tamralipta and Sopara became active centres of maritime trade. A major supporter of culture and the arts, his court was graced by some of the greatest academics of the day.

Following the death of Chandragupt II, Kumaragupt I (ca. 415–455 CE) exercised shrewd and capable administration over the enormous kingdom. He was able to keep the peace and even hold off fierce challenges from the Pushyamitra tribe and, later, from the Huns. His capable son Skandagupt, the last of the Gupta dynasty's suzerain kings (455–467 CE), assisted him. Skandagupt's demise set into motion a domestic conflict that ended the glorious empire.

Asit Kumar Haldar, the grand-nephew of Rabindranth Tagore, in his depiction of Prabhavatigupt, the queen and regent of the Vakataka dynasty, conducting her court with her son, Divakara Sena on her lap. Prabhavatigupt was the daughter of Chandragupt II and queen Kuberanaga. She was the first woman recorded to have held court in India

Early Southern India

Though it is popularly believed that the history of ancient South India dates back several centuries, even prior to the common era, we only have authentic archaeological evidence that goes back to about 600 BCE. While there are three Sangam stages in the ancient history of South India, the 'Third Stage' is considered by historians as the 'Sangam period'. The Sangam literature has been dated from the third

century BCE to the third century CE based on literary, archaeological, and extraterritorial evidence. Some major works of Sangam literature are *Ettutogai, Pattuppattu, Silappathikaram, Manimegalai, Pathinenkilkanakku,* and *Ettutogai*. In these records, there are intricate details about ancient South Indian history, including the people, their culture, and their ruling dynasties. The ancient history of South India saw many outstanding contributions to the economy, social development, and religion in the region.

Interestingly, the corresponding literature composed to the north of the Vindhyas does not give any cognizance to the region to the south despite the fact that during the reign of Ashoka (268–232 BCE) the three Tamil dynasties of the Chola, Chera, and Pandya were known to be ruling in the south. The *Mahavamsa*, the meticulously kept historical chronicle of Sri Lanka written in the style of an epic poem in the Pali language talks of the Chola prince Ellalan invading the Rajarata kingdom of Sri Lanka and conquering it in 235 BCE with the help of a Mysore army. Their history is then divided into a second period, known as the interregnum, which spans between the fall of the Sangam Cholas and the rise of the Imperial medieval Cholas under Vijayalaya (ca. 848 CE). The Chola dynasty, known for its military conquests and administrative efficiency, was one of the longest-ruling dynasties in the region.

Running parallel to the Cholas, the Pandya dynasty, on the other hand, was known for its maritime trade, literature, and architecture. The origin and the exact timeline of the Pandya dynasty are difficult to establish, but the early Pandya chieftains ruled Pandya Nadu from the Sangam period. Their capital was the city of Madurai, where the Sangam scholars are known to have congregated, and some of the poets

A stone relief showing a Pallava king at the Vaikuntha Perumal Temple in Kanchipuram

were also from the royal lineage. The early historic Pandyas faded into obscurity upon the rise of the Kalabhra dynasty in South India.

The territory of the Chera dynasty during this pre-Pallava period consisted of the present-day northern-central Kerala and Kongu region of western Tamil Nadu. The rest of Kerala was under the Ay dynasty (southern tip of Kerala) and the Mushika dynasty (northern tip of Kerala). After the fifth century CE, the Chera family's political prestige and influence declined considerably. The Pallava dynasty had come onto the political landscape by 275 CE, and they would be major players until 897 CE, ruling a significant portion of the Deccan, also known as Tondaimandalam. The Pallavas played a crucial role in shaping, in particular, the southern Indian history and heritage. The dynasty rose to prominence after the downfall of the Satavahana Empire, whom they had formerly served as feudatories.

The Pallavas played a crucial role in shaping, in particular, the southern Indian history and heritage.

A plethora of smaller kingdoms also flourished along the coastal region. Here, the death of a naval hero is celebrated in a hero stone off Goa. In the upper panel, apsaras welcome him to the other world ▸

South India's early history, unlike other parts of the country, has been partly preserved thanks to the large number of temples that were not damaged or destroyed by the vagaries of time. Paintings not only depict forms of warfare but

also events that were often brutal in the extreme, as was the heinous murder of Jain Munis who were crucified at Madurai by a Pandian king for not abandoning their religion. These are Pandya paintings from the Meenakshi Temple in Madurai

Elephant riders carved on stone wall inside the 7th century temples in Pattadakal, formerly known as Raktapura, in the Bagalkot District of North Karnataka ▸

Chaulakyas

6th to 12th CE

An important landmark in the history of the Indian subcontinent and that of Karnataka is the rise of the Chalukyas. They governed as three distinct but linked dynasties; they are known as the Badami Chalukya, the Eastern Chalukyas, and the Western Chalukyas. With the emergence of the Badami Chalukyas, the political landscape in South India catapulted itself from localised kingdoms into the league of vast empires. A South Indian dynasty had seized power and united the whole area between the Kaveri and Narmada Rivers for the first time in history.

Though historians disagree on the Chalukyas' early roots, they generally agree that the empire's founders were natives of what is now the Karnataka region. One hypothesis holds that the Pallavas of Kanchi were descended from the 'Seleukia' tribe of Iraq and that the Chalukya's fight with them was a reenactment of the ancient Seleukia vs. the 'Parthians', who were thought to be the Pallavas' progenitors. Many academics have criticised this hypothesis since it aims to create lineages based only on similar-sounding clan names. Although another hypothesis has been proposed, it has not been able to explain the discrepancy in lineage. It claims that they are derived from a chieftain named Kandachaliki Remmanaka, who was a feudatory of the Andhra Ikshvaku (from an Ikshvaku inscription from the second century). While Chalukya inscriptions refer to themselves as Harithiputras of Manavyasagotra, which coincidentally matches their early overlords, the Kadambas of Banavasi, the Kandachaliki feudatory refers to themselves as Vashisthiputras of the Hiranyakagotra. They are hence thought to have descended from the Kadambas. The region that the Kadambas had previously ruled was seized by the Chalukyas.

Pulakesin II stopped Harsha's southerly advance by defeating him on the banks of the Narmada River, and in the southeast Deccan, he then vanquished the Vishnukundins.

From the sixth until the twelfth centuries, the Chalukya dynasty dominated a sizable portion of southern and central India. Beginning around the middle of the sixth century, the oldest dynasty known as the Badami Chalukyas ruled from their capital city of Badami. The Badami Chaulakyas gained prominence during Pulakesi II's reign, having started to assert their independence after the decline of the Kadamba kingdom of Banavasi. In the eastern Deccan, the Eastern Chalukyas emerged as an independent state following Pulakesi II's demise. Up until roughly the eleventh century, they reigned from their capital at Vengi. The Chalukyas of Badami were supplanted in the western Deccan by the Rashtrakutas in the middle of the eighth century, and their descendants, the Western Chalukyas, brought them back in the late tenth century. From Basavakalyan till the end of the twelfth century, those Western Chalukyas dominated.

In the sixth century, significant changes occurred in the region south of the Vindyas, namely the Deccan and Tamilaham, with the fall of the Gupta dynasty and their immediate successors. In 550 CE, Pulakesin I founded the Chalukya dynasty and established Vatapi (Badami in the district of Bagalkot) as his capital. Pulakesin and his lineage are hence referred to by historians as the Chalukyas of Badami. They governed over an empire that included the majority of Andhra Pradesh in the Deccan and the whole state of Karnataka.

Possibly the greatest monarch of the Badami Chalukyas was Pulakesin II, also known as Immadi Pulakesin.

Pulakeshi II routed the Pallava king Mahendravarman I at Pullalur and holding court in Vatapi

Kadamba Devi, his queen, was a princess of the Alupas Dynasty. With the Alupas of South Canara and the Gangas of Talakad, they kept tight family and marriage ties. Pulakesin II stopped Harsha's southerly advance by defeating him on the banks of the Narmada River, and in the southeast Deccan, he then vanquished the Vishnukundins. Pulakesin, however, would meet his end in the hands of the Pallavas, whom he had dominated in the early part of his reign in the Battle of Vatapi in 642 CE.

The Chalukyas are credited with stopping Harshvardha's further expansion ▼

The Pallavas assumed the title of Vatapikonda (conqueres of Vatapi) and retained control till 652 CE. The Chalukyas restored their rule shortly thereafter and the conflict between both dynasties continued for many more years ►

Battle of Vatapi

642 CE

The Chaulakya king Pulakeshin II had repeatedly harassed and defeated the Pallava monarch Mahendravarman I and advanced as far south as the Kaveri River, which marked the northern boundary of the Cholas and was fertile rice-growing land. Unable to physically occupy the land, the Chalukyas had retreated to their capital, Vatapi. After Narasimhavaram I replaced his father in 630 CE, he not only finished the

Pulakeshin was defeated and killed, and the Pallavas then occupied the Chalukya capital, from where they transported a huge amount of war booty to Kanchipuram.

shore temples that were being built but tried to steady the Pallavas militarily as well. Having learnt their lessons from the previous defeat at the hands of the Chalukyas, the Pallavas bolstered their defences and bided their time.

A few years later, Pulakeshin once again invaded the Pallava kingdom after subduing the Banas, who were the Pallavas' feudatories. However, Narasimhavarman, along with his general, Paranjothi, defeated the Chalukyas in three successive battles fought at Pariyala, Suramana, and Manimangalam, the last just twenty miles to the east of Kanchipuram. Encouraged by his victory, Narasimhavarman decided to go on the offensive and in 642, the pivotal conflict occurred in the vicinity of Vatapi. Pulakeshin was defeated and killed, and the Pallavas then occupied the Chalukya capital, from where they transported a huge amount of war booty to Kanchipuram. Narasimhavarman, in honour of his triumph, built the Mallikarjuna Temple in Vatapi and also took on the title 'taker of Vatapi', or 'Vatapi-kondan'. At the Teggina-Irappa temple at Vatapi, he etched an inscription on the walls commemorating his triumph.

Plagued by constant warfare, sculptures in the temple complexes are a rich repository that tells its own story. A mounted soldier in Kanchipuram ▼

Medieval Cholas

848 CE

The ancient Cholas literally disappeared from South India's map around 300 CE. This period was caused by what is known as the Kalabhra Interregnum, wherein the Kalabhras overthrew the Cholas, Cheras, and Pandyas and ruled Southern India. Since their origins are not clear, historians refer to this period as the 'dark' age of Tamil history, which came to an end with the ascendancy of the Pandyas and the Pallavas in 590 CE.

◀ Though the early Chola Dynasty, according to the Tamil Sangam poets, dates back to 300 BCE, their re-emergence dates back to the mid-ninth century when Vijayalaya Chola defeated both the Pallavas and the Pandyas to take control of the southern region

During the reign of Simhavishnu, also known as Avanisimha (575–600 CE), the Pallavas struck a decisive blow against the Kalabhras. With the Pandyas following suit, the Tamil country was divided between the Pallavas in the north and the Pandyas in the south. According to some historians, the Pallava was founded by the Chola Prince Ilandiraiyan, even though the first Pallava monarch in recorded history was Simhavarman I, who reigned from 275–300 CE. Ironically, it was the Cholas who drove the Pallavas away from Kanchipuram in the mid-fourth century, but then they, too, were defeated by the Kalabhras.

Vijayalaya Chola came out of virtual obscurity, revived the Chola dynasty, and founded the Imperial Chola Empire in 847 CE. Making use of the opportunity during a war between the Pandyas and Pallavas, Vijayalaya Chola conquered Thanjavur from Elango Mutharaiyar, who was the final ruler of the Mutharaiyar dynasty, a feudatory of the Pallavas who had been governing the Thanjavur, Trichy, and Pudukottai regions. Five years later, Vijayalaya Chola clashed with the Pandyas and defeated them as well. With the Cholas quickly becoming powerful, it set the alarm bells ringing, and the Pallavas and the Pandyas jointly moved against Vijayalaya Chola, forcing him to become a feudatory to the Pandyas.

Vijayalaya was succeeded by his son Aditya Chola I, who is considered to be the founder of the Imperial Chola Dynasty. In 885 CE, the Pallava king Nripatunga, supported by the Pandyan Varagunavarman II, faced his step-brother Aparajitavarman in a war of succession. Aditya Chola and Prithvipathi I, the king of the Western Ganga Kingdom, threw in their lot with Aparajita, who went on to win the Battle of Thirupurambiyam, which would completely change the existing dynamics in Southern India.

This battle resulted in Varagunavarman II renouncing his throne and leading an ascetic life, which reduced the Pandyas to a shadow of their

Vijayalaya Chola (847-871 CE), under whom the Cholas came to power and went on to become the Imperial Cholas ▼

◄ Rajaraja Chola as depicted in a mural in the Brihadisvara temple

former self. The grateful Aparajita not only allowed Aditya Chola to keep the territories won by his father, Vijayalaya Chola but also gave him jurisdiction over some extra lands that had been acquired from the defeated Pandyas.

Aditya Chola, however, was not satisfied with Aparajitha's magnanimity. Extremely aggressive and wanting to take the battle to others, he bided his time and then attacked and invaded the Pallava Empire in 897 CE. In the battle, Aditya singled out Aparajitavarman while he was mounted on an elephant and killed him. That marked the end of the Pallavas, and their entire kingdom was absorbed into the Chola territory.

Successive Chola kings continued to build their empire. Parantaka Chola I ruled for forty-eight years, annexing most of the remaining Pandya territory by defeating Rajasimhan II and then expanding northwards into the Deccan, winning the Battle of Vallala against the Rashtrakutas which happened around 916 CE. The fighting against the Rashtrakutas would continue, and the Cholas suffered a major setback when they were defeated in the Battle of Takkolam in 949 CE, where the crown prince Rajaditya was killed. This would have severe repercussions as there were at least five kings that followed Parantaka I.

After three decades of instability, the Chola kingdom had shrunk while the Pandyas had again become powerful. Parantaka II met Vira Pandya's army at Chevur and won a bloody contest. The twelve-year-old crown prince, Aditya Karikalan, who accompanied his father, is reputed to have taken Vira

Pandya's head. The Pandya king had the Sinhalese king Mahinda IV as his ally, which led to the not-so-successful Chola invasion of Lanka.

Rajaraja I reigned from 985 to 1014 CE, and at the time of his ascension, his empire included vast regions of not just Pandya and Chera country, but parts of northern Sri Lanka also. Successful campaigns against the Western Gangas and the Western Chalukyas extended the Chola Empire as far as the Tungabhadra River. On the eastern coast, he battled with the Telugu Chola king Jata Choda Bhima for the possession of Vengi. During his reign, the northern kingdom of Vengi became a Chola protectorate, and the Chola influence on the eastern coast extended as far as Kalinga in

◄ Rajendra Chola I with his guru, Karuvuvar. During his reign, the Cholas sent their forces up to the Ganges in the north and Sumatra across the Bay of Bengal

the north. Apart from his military conquests, Rajaraja also ensured that his was a well-administered empire that possessed not just a strong army but also a navy. A naval campaign led to the conquest of parts of the Malabar Coast, and also some of the Lakshadweep and Maldives Islands, which were essential to the Chola control over trade with Southeast Asia and with Arabia and Eastern Africa.

In the Thanjavur inscriptions, a number of regiments, divided into elephant troops, cavalry, and infantry, are mentioned. A series of murals in the Brihadisvara Temple behind the main complex depict various scenes from the period. Rajaraja died in 1014 CE and was succeeded by his son Rajendra Chola I, during whose reign the Chola Empire reached its height in military prowess.

Rajendra Chola's three-decade-long reign saw an endless amount of warfare, with some of the largest and bloodiest conflicts being fought. The Chalukya Wars were fought from 992 CE onwards, the largest being the Battle of Maski (1019–1020 CE), where Rajendra Chola led an army of 900,000 and defeated Jayasimha II. The Cholas also annexed the entirety of Sri Lanka, making Kassapa VI their puppet ruler. Apart from defeating the Chera and Pandyas and multiple clashes with the Western Chalukyas, the Cholas also embarked on a three-year expedition that traversed through the kingdoms of Vengi, Kalinga, Madhya Pradesh, Jharkhand, Odisha, Bengal, Bihar, and Uttar Pradesh, culminating with their arrival at the Ganges. The main reason for the expedition was ostensibly to get water from the holy river. The Chola victory over the Pala king Mahipala I is considered to be the climax of the expedition.

In 1023 CE, Rajendra Chola turned his attention overseas in what was probably an attempt to establish trade relations or maybe just to add lustre to his crown, and his fleet of ships with Chola warriors was sent to Palembang in southern Sumatra, then a part of the Srivijaya kingdom. In his inscription after the event, Rajendra Chola claimed he had 'despatched many ships in the midst of the rolling sea' and conquered more than a dozen cities altogether in Sumatra and the Malay Peninsula. The Chola fleet, then sailing south to north, attacked the adjacent settlement of Malaiyur and the island of Bangha before it captured Pannai and Ilamuridesam in eastern and northern Sumatra. The Cholas then sailed to

Malaysia and captured Vallaipandur and Kadarem. From there, Rajendra's forces sailed north and attacked the adjacent settlements of Ilankasokam, Mathamalingam, and Thalaitakkolam in Thailand, after which the fleet returned to Chola country in 1025, capturing en route Manakkavaarem in the Nicobar Islands and Magpapaalam in Burma.

Perhaps what is even more fascinating is that the Chola expeditions (the second was in 1070 CE) may have been the result of complex geopolitics that involved the developing trade between the Fatimids of Eygpt and the Song Dynasty of China. The Imperial Cholas, who were positioned at the centre of the Indian Ocean trade route, then clashed with the Sriviajayans, who until then had complete hegemony over the Straits of Malacca, considered even then to be the gateway to the lucrative Chinese market. Excavations in both Gangaikonda and Nagapattinam also point towards a thriving trade between the Chinese and the Cholas that existed until the Pandyas razed the Chola cities to the ground in the thirteenth century.

Mounted cavalry charge

Most of the Chola 'warships' were probably merchant vessels acquired by Rajendra Chola. However, it is beyond doubt that the Cholas were extremely advanced in sea-faring skills, their knowledge of nautically relevant celestial bodies and navigational skills being extremely sophisticated, with a fair knowledge of routes to be followed. In addition, the Cholas also had a complex system in place to handle logistics that included provisioning, ports of departure, and ship-building centres.

Rajadhiraja Chola was made co-regent by his father in 1018 CE when he was only 24, and for the next twenty-six years, they would rule together, the son being at the forefront of most of his father's military campaigns. When Rajadhiraja finally became the monarch, he appointed his brother, Rajendradeva Chola, also known as Rajendra Chola II, as his co-regent. Rajadhiraja's reign, like his successors, would be spent quelling rebellions in Sri Lanka or in fighting with the Pandyas and Western Chalukyas. Rajadhiraja would be the first Chola monarch to be killed on the battlefield during the Battle of Koppam, which was fought with the Chalukya king Someshvara I in 1054 CE.

The Chola expeditions may have been the result of complex geopolitics that involved the developing trade between the Fatimids of Eygpt and the Song Dynasty of China.

Perhaps the only exception to the rule was Kulottunga, who reigned from 1070 to 1122 CE. Kulottunga avoided unnecessary wars and evinced a true regard for the well-being of his subjects. He had a long and prosperous reign of 52 years, characterised by unparalleled success that laid the foundation for the well-being of the empire for the next 150 years. He also simultaneously ruled as the emperor of the Eastern Chalukya between 1061 and 1118 CE.

Ever since the Cholas got the better of the Pandyas, they continued to go from strength to strength, with a series of rulers who remained extremely aggressive in their outlook. However, despite their 'take-no-prisoners' attitude and an uncompromising approach to warfare, they could not decisively eradicate the Pandyas or the Western Chalukya dynasties, or for that matter, quell Sinhala resistance in Sri Lanka over the years. Continuous wars meant

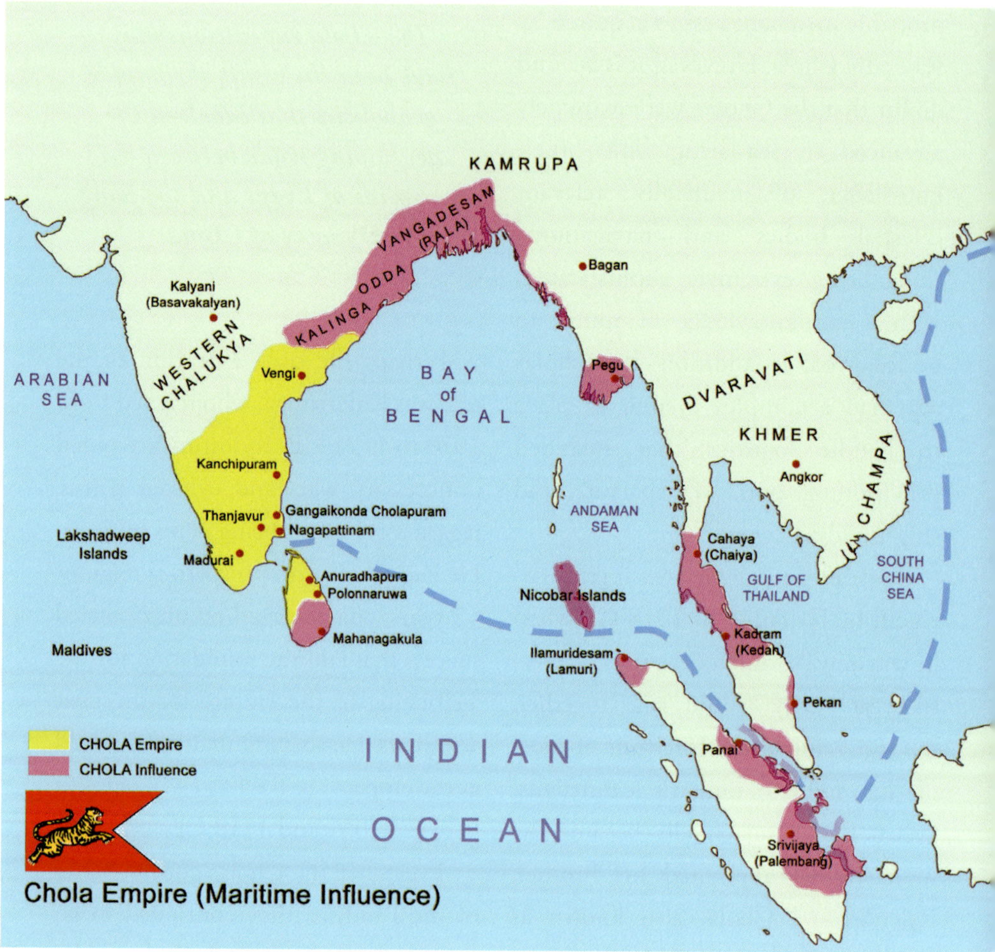

Chola Empire (Maritime Influence)

high taxation, and the Chola system of granting land to landlords as per the 'devadaanam' meant the farmers were the ones who suffered. They, in turn, were in a constant state of unrest.

Though the year 1279 CE marked the end of the Chola Dynasty under Rajendra Chola III who was defeated by Maravarman Kulasekara Pandyan I, their decline had begun in 1216 CE with the defeat of Kulottunga Chola III at the hands of Maravarman Sundara Pandyan I who was the one who laid the foundation for the resurgence of Pandyas rule. Years of frustration manifested themselves as

'he extent of the Chola Empire and its influence across Southeast Asia. In 1023 CE, after ,endra Chola's conquest of Kadram, he assumed the name 'Kadaremkondaan', and his ·ndson who led the expedition was bestowed the title 'Kadaremkonda Chola', which meant e Chola who captured Kadarem'

▲ Rajendra Chola I conquered Chera, Pandya, and Sinhala and annexed them into his kingdom. He defeated the Western Chalukyas in several battles and destroyed their capital but could not achieve complete victory over them. His first military campaign was against Bengal from the eastern seaboard, defeating the kings of Kalinga

▼ Being blessed by Shiva

most of the Chola cities were razed to the ground by the Pandays.

The Pandya Empire, too, was plagued with endless conflicts. The Delhi Sultanate had already been in power for nearly a century by then. After the death of Maravarman Kulasekhara in 1310 CE, his sons Vira Pandya IV and Sundara Pandya IV fought a war of succession for control of the empire. Unfortunately, the Pandya civil war coincided with Alauddin Khalji's general Malik Kafur's raids in South India. Taking advantage of the political situation, the neighbouring Hoysala king also invaded the Pandya territory but had to retreat post haste when Kafur invaded his kingdom at the same time. After subjugating the Hoysalas, the Khalji forces invaded Pandya territory in March 1311 CE. The Pandya brothers fled, and the Khaljis pursued them unsuccessfully. By late April, the Khaljis returned to Delhi with the plunder. Vira and Sundara Pandya resumed their conflict. Sundara Pandya was defeated and sought help from the Khaljis. Subsequently, there were two more expeditions from the Sultanate, which, along with the family disputes, shattered the crumbling Pandyan Empire beyond repair.

A bas-relief from the Bayon in Khmer country (Cambodia) showing warships of the time in action

Kulottunga Chola I reigned from 1070–1122 CE and was also the Eastern Chalukya monarch between 1061–1118 CE; Jatavarman Sundara I ruled the Pandyan Empire between 1250–1268 CE. The Pandyan revival saw them wipe out the Cholas by 1279 CE

Chola soldiers in combat

Hoysala Dynasty

1006–1346 CE

The Hoysala rulers originally lived as hill peoples of Malnad, an elevated region that is a part of the Western Ghats. The earliest record of a member of the Hoysala dynasty is dated 950 CE and names Arekalla as their chieftain.

In the early twelfth century, taking advantage of the internecine warfare between the ruling Western or Kalyani

◂Temple walls tell the story of the Hoysala armies in intricate detail. Panels on temple walls that date back to the Hoysala period give a fair indication of what South Indian armies looked like

Chalukya and Kalachuri kingdoms that had come up in the Karnataka-Maratha region, they annexed parts of what is today Karnataka and the fertile areas to the north of the Kaveri delta, their boundaries extending up to the Chola kingdom that lay beyond the river. By the thirteenth century, they had expanded northwards and controlled most of what is today Karnataka, parts of Tamil Nadu, and Andhra Pradesh.

The empire, at its zenith, extended across the valleys of three main rivers, the Krishna, the Tungabhadra, and the Kaveri. The kingdom flourished, and successive Hoysala kings invested large sums of money in the import of horses, elephants, and other armaments for the Hoysala armies. Members of the royal family and other important personage were protected by special bodyguards, whose loyalty was considered to be so fierce that

they would commit suicide en masse when their principal died.

The king Vishnuvardhana ascended the Hoysala throne in 1108 CE. Apart from defeating the Cholas, Vishnuvardhana also managed to defect the other powerful rulers of the Nilgiri region, such as the Chengalvas, the Kongalvas, and the Nidugal Chola ruler Irukkavela.

Carvings at Halibed, Belur, and other Hoysala locales depict various arms of the army. During the reign of Vishnuvardhana (1108–1152), Hoysala art reached its zenith

Ahoms 1228 CE

The Ahom Dynasty, commonly known as the Ahom Kingdom, ruled over the present-day Assam region for an incredible six centuries. Founded in the thirteenth century by a Tai prince, Chaolung Su ka Phaa, who had crossed the Patkai mountains to enter the Brahmaputra Valley, it saw the development of a strong state that extended its influence over adjacent lands. The Ahom kings were renowned for their military strategy and administration.

◄ Crossing the Naga-Patkai from Mong Mao on the Burma-Chinese border, Su Ka Phaa headed for Upper Assam where his intention was to permanently settle. Joined by various Tai groups en route, he arrived in the subcontinent in 1228 CE with approximately 9,000 followers and was responsible for converting the undulating alluvial forest and marshy plains into flat rice fields able to hold water for rice cultivation via a network of embankments

The Ahom chronicles meticulously record Su Ka's passage into India. His first domain was in the Kham-Jang Valley with the Nongyang Lake or the 'Valley of the Shining Lake', which lies below the Pangsau Pass on the Patkai Hills. During the Ahom rule, many smaller Tai ethnic groups sought refuge with them, having fled the torture inflicted by the Burmese king Alamfra and others. These were the Tai Khamti, Tai Phake, Tai Khamyang, Tai Aiton, and Tai Turung. The initial Ahom kings were credited with introducing the wet rice growing technique, which allowed them to settle down in Charaideo in 1253 CE.

The Ahoms subdued the earlier Bhuiyan political order, or landlord system, and established a sizable state by the 1530s. During the sixteenth century, they annexed the kingdoms of the Chhutiyas in 1523 and Koch-Hajo in 1581 CE. The Ahoms also conquered other tribes.

Ahom society was divided into clans or *khels*, each controlling several villages; among them were a few castes of artisans in the Ahom areas who later made their way to the nearby kingdoms. All able-bodied men belonging to the settlements under individual *khels* were supposed to fight as part of the imperial army as and when any conflict took place. Interestingly, village communities would grant lands to anyone joining the *khel* from other areas. Even the king couldn't cancel or take back such allotments without the consent of the community concerned. As a result, some of the densely populated areas were relieved of their excess population, while the countryside saw many villages flourishing across its

length and breadth. However, a system of forced labour did exist wherein every village was required to send a pre-decided number of labourers, called *paiks*, to the capital by rotation.

The Ahom kings profoundly affected Assam's socio-cultural landscape. They also took a keen interest in architecture, which led to the construction of some spectacular monuments, including temples, palaces, and forts. They were also instrumental in advancing the regional language, literature, and religious customs by fusing native rituals with practices from other neighbouring civilisations.

▲ The symbols that represented the Ahom that were carried by Chaolung Su Ka Pha are on display at Sibsagar; a rich tradition of art adorns temple walls across Assam ▶

Muhammad of Ghor 1186–92 CE

Shihab ad-Din Mu'izz ad-Din Muhammad, also known as Muhammad of Ghor or Mohd Ghori, was born in 1149 CE. He ruled over the Ghurid Empire from 1202 to 1206. However, he started leading military campaigns of his brother's army in 1173. He is credited with having established Muslim rule in the subcontinent. At his peak, his family reigned over parts of modern-day Afghanistan, Bangladesh, Iran, Northern India, Pakistan, Tajikistan, and Turkmenistan.

In 1186, he attacked and annexed the Punjab, prompting many North Indian Hindu princes to form a confederacy to take him on under the command of Prithvi Raj Chauhan. Five years later, the combined army defeated Ghori in the Battle of Tarain near Delhi. His life, however, in an act of great magnanimity, was spared by the Rajput King.

In 1192, Ghori returned yet again with a massive army that defeated the Hindu Army in the Second Battle of Tarain. That allowed Ghori to establish the first Muslim foothold in Ajmer in India. He then returned to Ghazni, leaving his general, Qutb ud-Din Aibak, to continue his conquests in India. In 1193, Aibak captured Delhi and Meerut.

Muhammad Ghori's campaigns in India left an indelible mark on the subcontinent's history. He had no progeny and was succeeded by his slave generals, whom he groomed into first-rate soldiers and administrators, then giving them enough experience under him to make them able rulers in the future. Another ward of Ghori, Muhammad bin Bakhtiyar Khalji, added to Ghor territory by capturing Bengal and its surrounding regions.

Muhammad Ghori's long military career was dotted with constant warfare. When he succeeded his brother and ascended the throne in 1202, his native kingdom of Ghor itself came under severe attacks by the Turkic-Mamluk-origin Khwarazm Empire. The latter delivered a decisive defeat to Ghori in 1203. That setback prompted many erstwhile Indian rulers to rise in revolt against Ghori. By 1206, Ghori had brutally suppressed a massive revolt from the Ghakkars or Khokkars, a martial community of Punjab, thus establishing his sway over the complete tract of territory between Ghazni and Delhi.

He then left Indian affairs under Aibak and embarked on a return journey. However, while returning to Afghanistan, somewhere in Punjab, he was apparently murdered by assassins from the Khokkar community, though it has also been inferred that a rival Islamic sect might have assassinated him. There are also parallel claims that his assassination was at the hands of Prithvi Raj Chauhan, whom he had blinded, or his death could have been caused because of the wounds sustained during the Battle of Jhelum. As his kingdom subsequently broke up and most of it was taken by the Khwarazms, the territory in India was divided by different slave rulers among themselves. Aibak, with his control over Delhi and adjoining areas, founded an independent kingdom that came to be known as the Delhi Sultanate.

The Second Battle of Tarain in 1192 fought some 70-odd km from Delhi between Prithviraj Chauhan's Rajput Confrederation and the invading Ghurid forces ▸

Delhi Sultanate
1192–1526 CE

In the immediate vicinity of Delhi, the fierce Rajput armies were a formidable obstacle to the marauding Islamic warlords and their mercenary armies, who were perennially looking towards India mainly with the intention of gathering whatever loot they could lay their hands on.

The Delhi Sultanate was an Islamic empire based in Delhi which covered major parts of the subcontinent during the medieval period. The foundation of the Delhi Sultanate was

laid by Qutb ud-Din Aibak in 1206. It all begins with the second battle of Tarain, fought between Muhammad Ghori and Prithviraj Chauhan in 1192 CE. After winning, Ghori left his kingdom to his trusted lieutenant and former slave Qutb ud-Din Aibak, who started the Slave or Mamluk Dynasty. After the rule of the Mamluk Dynasty, there were four more dynasties in the Delhi Sultanate, namely Khaljis, Tughlaqs, Sayyids, and Lodis. They ruled Delhi as their capital from 1206 to 1526 CE.

Qutb ud-Din Aibak ▼

Aibak expanded the Ghurid power in northern India by conquering and raiding several places in the Chahamana, Gahadavala, Chaulukya, Chandela, and other kingdoms. After the assassination of Muhammad Ghori in March 1206, Aibak fought with another former slave-general, Taj al-Din Yildiz, for control of Ghurid territories in north-western India. During this campaign, he advanced as far as Ghazni, although he later retreated and set up his capital at Lahore. Aibak was succeeded by Aram Shah and then by his former slave and son-in-law Iltutmish, who transformed the loosely-held Ghurid territories of India into the powerful Delhi Sultanate. His rule was challenged by a series of wars.

During the first half of the 1220s, Iltutmish neglected the Indus River Valley, which was contested between the Mongols, the Khwarazm kings, and the Qabacha. Post the decline of the Mongol and the Khwarazmian threat, the Qabacha took over the region, but Iltutmish invaded his territory during 1228–1229 CE. He also defended his empire from attacks by the Mongols and the Rajputs. Iltutmish's son Nasiruddin Mahmud, who had been governing Bengal since 1227 CE, died unexpectedly. Taking advantage of the situation, an officer of Illtumish, Malik Balkha Khalji, usurped the authority in Bengal. Iltutmish invaded Bengal and defeated him in 1230 CE. Iltutmish also re-annexed many states which had declared independence after the death of Aibak, such as Ranthambore, Gwalior, Ajmer, Bayana, Jalor, Mander Kalinjar, and Thangir.

Sultana Razia Begum (1236-39) who was the first and only woman to rule the sultanate

In 1231 CE, Kanauj and Benaras were reoccupied. He annexed Malwa and Ujjain to his empire in 1239 CE. He died in 1236 and was succeeded by his daughter Razia Sultana, as he did not consider his sons equal to the task. She was the first and last Muslim woman to rule Delhi. Her first military campaign was the invasion of Ranthambore, whose Chahamana ruler had asserted his sovereignty after Illtumish's death. She also sent a force to re-assert Delhi's control over Gwalior. During her reign, the Shias revolted against the Sultanate, but it was suppressed. The nobles who supported Razia intended her to be a figurehead, but she increasingly asserted herself. Along with her husband, Altunia, she led an army against Bahram and was defeated on 14 October

One of the first Islamic monuments to be built in India by Hindu craftsmen. They laid blocks of stone horizontally and rounded the sides of individual stones to create the curve. The screen was ornately decorated with carved calligraphy and repeating scroll-like designs. The iron pillar on the right-hand side of the lower photograph carries a Sanskrit inscription. This records that it was erected by King Chandra, a devotee of the god Vishnu. The king has now been identified as Chandragupt II (375-413 CE) and the pillar is dated to the 4th century ▼

These photographs taken 157 years ago by Samuel Bourne, show the back view of the screen or 'Great Arch' of the Quwwat-ul-Islam mosque. The other side has ornate decoration and an inscription stating that it was built in 1199 by Qutb ud-Din Aibak. The central arch is 6.7 metres wide and 16 metres high. On the right-hand side is the Qutb Minar, the tower from which the daily call to prayer was made. It is the highest stone tower in India and tapers from a base diameter of 14.32 metres to 2.75 metres at the top. It too was begun in 1199. Only the first storey was built during the lifetime of Qutb ud-Din Aibak. The next two storeys were built by his successor, Shamsuddin Iltutmish, who also built what was the fourth and final storey. When this was destroyed by lightning, Firoz Shah Tughlug (1351–1388) added the two storeys seen here ▶

1240. The next day, she was killed by a group of Hindus. Ghiyasuddin Balban ascended the throne two decades after Razia and maintained an army of 12 lakhs consisting of varied castes. During his reign, he led military campaigns, including the Mongol siege of Uch under Masud Shah and Mayo. The Mayos were the people of Mewat who used to plunder the people of Delhi even in daylight. He also unsuccessfully laid siege to the fortress of Ranthambore but did recapture Gwalior from the Rajputs. In 1247 CE, Balban suppressed the rising of the Chandela Chief of Kalinjar.

▲ During his reign, Ghiyas-ud-Din Balban (1266–87 CE) routed the people of Mewat and reconquered Bengal, all while fending off the Mongol threat. Balban strengthened his line of defence by building and reinforcing forts at Bhatinda, Sunam and Samana to check any Mongol advance beyond Beas. In 1270, he ordered the fort of Lahore to be rebuilt, and appointed architects to rebuild the city ▶

The Khalji dynasty was the second dynasty that ruled the Delhi Sultanate between 1290 and 1320 CE and was founded by Jalaluddin Firuz Khalji, who had fought the Mongols on several occasions. After the death of Balban in 1286 CE, there was confusion in Delhi since there were no successors, and there was a good deal of opposition and resentment at the attempt of Turkish nobles to monopolise high offices. Khalji's coming to power was welcomed by non-Turkish sections of the nobility. During his six-year reign, some of the commanders of the Mamluk dynasty revolted. The revolt was suppressed, and the commanders executed. Jalaluddin led an unsuccessful expedition against Ranthambore and repelled a Mongol force on the banks of the river Sind with the help of his nephew Alauddin Khalji. After the planned assassination of Jalaluddin Khalji, Alauddin rose to power and became the Sultan of Delhi. During his reign of 20 years, he conquered Rajputana, attacking and seizing the states of Jaisalmer, Ranthambhor, Chittorgarh, and Malwa. He also conquered Gujarat and plundered the wealthy state of Devagiri during his raids in the south. He also withstood two Mongol raids.

▲ Alauddin Khilji (1296-1316)

Alauddin's lieutenant, Malik Kafur, captured Warangal, overthrew the Hoysala Empire south of the Krishna River, and raided Madurai in Tamil Nadu. He then looted the treasury in capitals and from the temples of south India. Among these loots was the Warangal loot that included one of the largest known diamonds in human history, the Koh-i-Noor. Malik Kafur returned to Delhi in 1311 CE, laden with loot and war booty from the Deccan peninsula, which he submitted to Alauddin Khalji. This made Malik Kafur, born in a Hindu family and who had converted to Islam before becoming Delhi Sultanate's

The seige of Ranthambore in 1301 preceded the attack on Chittor two years later. Alauddin Khilji's westward consolidation of his empire would more or less be the path followed by the Mughal emperor Akbar two centuries later

army commander, a favourite of Alauddin Khalji.

In 1311 CE, Alauddin ordered a massacre of Mongols in the Delhi Sultanate wherein between 15,000 and 30,000 Mongol settlers who had recently converted to Islam were killed after Khalji suspected them of plotting an uprising against him. Alauddin Khalji died in January 1316 CE. Thereafter, the sultanate witnessed chaos, coups and a series of assassinations. Malik Kafur became the sultan but lacked support from the amirs and was killed within a few months.

The Tughlaq dynasty was the third dynasty to rule over the Delhi Sultanate. Its reign started in 1320 CE in Delhi when Ghazi Malik assumed the throne under the title of Ghiyath al-Din Tughlaq. His eldest son, Jauna Khan, who was later known as Muhammad bin Tughlaq, plundered the Hindu kingdoms of Arangal and Tirang, looted all the wealth and state treasury, and renamed it Sultanpur. The Tughlaq army plundered Jajnagar in Odisha. East and South Bengal were incorporated into the sultanate, while North Bengal remained a vassal state under Nasirudddin Ibrahim.

Court of Muhammad bin Tughlaq (1325–1351), who was the eighteenth Sultan of Delhi and the son of Ghiyath al-Din Tughlaq who founded the dynasty after taking control of the Sultanate from Khusrao Khan in 1320 ►

The sultan died in 1325 CE due to the collapse of a wooden pavilion built in his honour, after which his son Muhammad bin Tughlaq became the sultan of Delhi. He undertook a policy of conquest and sent expeditionary forces to Khurasan, Nagarkot, Qarajal, Mewar, Telangana, and Malabar. With the best of intentions, the sultan's experiments were grand failures. His reign witnessed dissent and rebellions. The governors of the northwestern province and Bengal were given harsh punishments. Independent kingdoms came into existence, such as Malabar, Vijayanagar, and the Bhamani Sultanate. At the time of his death in 1351 CE, the disintegration of the Delhi Sultanate had already begun.

The army of the Delhi Sultanate consisted of four types of soldiers. First, there were the soldiers who were recruited by the centre for the army of the sultan. The army which was constituted by these soldiers was called *Khasah-khail*. Alauddin Khilji kept a large standing army at the centre, which included 4,75,000 horsemen besides the infantry. Ghiyas-ud-din Balban and Muhammad bin Tughlaq also kept standing armies at the centre. But the rest of the sultans, before or after them, failed to keep such standing armies at the centre. This army was looked after by the *Diwan-i-ariz*, who was responsible for its recruitment, organisation, maintenance, salaries, etc. There was no regular course of training for these soldiers. Every soldier was responsible for improving his talents as he desired.

The second category of soldiers was those who were employed on a permanent basis by nobles and provincial governors. It was expected that the nobles and governors would place their armies before the sultan for inspection every year, but this rule was normally not observed. They brought their armies to the service of the sultan only when ordered.

The third category was those soldiers who were recruited only in times of war on a temporary basis and were paid only for that period. Lastly, there were the Muslim soldiers who joined the army as volunteers at times of war against the Hindus. They considered such wars as 'holy wars', which were known as *jihads*. They were not paid for their services but were given a share of the booty captured in the war.

The army of the Delhi Sultanate primarily consisted of cavalry, infantry, and elephants. The backbone of the army was the cavalry. There were two types of cavalrymen: one, the *sawar*, who maintained a single horse and the other, the *do-asga*, who kept two horses. The trained war elephants were the second most important part of the army. Only sultans had the privilege to keep elephants. There was a separate department for the training and maintenance of elephants. They were also armoured during the course of battles.

The third part of the army was the infantry. The foot soldiers were called

◄ Firoz Shah Tughlaq

payaks. They were armed with swords, spears, and bows and arrows. The sultan maintained a large number of boats as well, primarily for transport purposes but for fighting as well. All the rulers of the Delhi Sultanate mostly pursued the same tactics in war. Spies were sent out to find out the movement of the enemy, and the advance guard was sent to test its strength. The army was divided into four parts at the time of conflict: the Center Division, the Left Division, the Right Division, and the Reserve Division. The sultan kept permanent armies in every fort and at all strategic points within his kingdom.

The defeat of Ibrahim Lodi in the First Battle of Panipat at the hands of Babur ended the Delhi Sultanate, which had lasted 334 years across five different dynasties. Not only had the Delhi Sultanate not evolved new military tactics, Ibrahim Lodi had repeatedly failed as a military commander, losing time and again to Rana Sangha, which severely dented his prestige in the eyes of his nobles and subordinate commanders. In addition, Ibrahim Lodi had become increasingly arrogant, insisting on bestowing a demi-god status to himself, having declared that 'kingship knows no kinship'.

With a fragmented and divided army, Ibrahim Lodi perhaps did not quite appreciate the threat posed by the Mughal Army of Babur, who, on the

other hand, commanded an army of absolute loyalists. The Delhi Sultanate had lived by the sword and met its end by it as well.

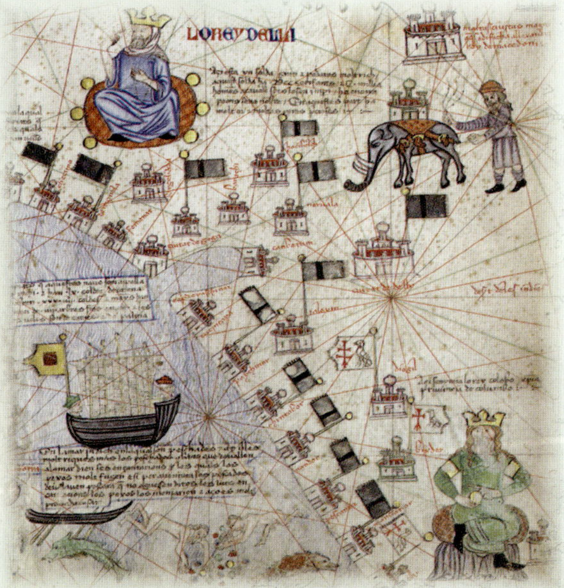

The Catalan Atlas was produced by the Majorcan cartographic school, possibly by Cresques Abraham, a Jewish book illuminator who was described by a contemporary as a master of the medieval world map, or the *mappae mundi*, as well as of compasses, during the reign of Firoz Shah Tughlaq, the 19th ruler of the Delhi Sultanate. The atlas was in the royal library of France by 1380, during the reign of King Charles V, and is still preserved in the Bibliothèque Nationale de France

Krishnadevaraya (1509–29 CE) ►

Vijaynagar Empire 1336 CE

Vijayanagar, meaning 'city of victory', was the imperial capital of the last great Hindu empire to rule South India. Established in 1336 and named after its capital, the Vijayanagar empire expanded and prospered throughout the next century. In 1565, this impressive city was sacked by armies from the Deccan sultanates and never rebuilt. Now known as the 'Group of Monuments at Hampi', the site represents the empire's finest and highest concentration of

Enterance to Kalyana Mandappa ▸

▴ Various buildings including the elephant stables ▸

First photographed in 1856, these early images of Hampi were only published in 1910. The Garuda shrine, Maha Mandapa and Eastern Gopura, Vitthala temple complex ▾

architecture. Classified into religious, courtly, and military buildings, its pillared audience halls and towering gateways are its stylistic hallmarks. Many secular buildings bear Islamic features, displaying the city's cosmopolitan inception. Some of its religious complexes remain in use today.

The group of Monuments at Hampi represent the empire's finest and highest concentration of architecture. Classified into religious, courtly, and military buildings, its pillared audience halls and towering gateways are its stylistic hallmarks.

The Vijayanagar Empire covered most of South India, controlling the lands of the modern states of Karnataka, Andhra Pradesh, Tamil Nadu, Kerala, Goa, and some parts of Telangana and Maharashtra. It was established in 1336 by the brothers Harihara I and Bukka Raya I of the Sangama dynasty, members of a pastoralist cowherd community that claimed Yadava lineage. The empire rose to prominence as the bulwark against the

Shiva temples on Hemukuta Hill ▼

▲ Everyday scenes from the outer walls of the Hazara Rama temple and painted ceiling, Virupaksha Temple

Watchtower ▼

Perso-Turkic Islamic invasions of the Deccan and the Deep South by the end of the thirteenth century. At its peak, the Vijayanagar dynasty subjugated almost all the well-established South Indian ruling families and pushed the sultans of the Deccan beyond the Tungabhadra-Krishna River doab region, in addition to annexing the Gajapati Kingdom in Odisha till the Krishna River, thus becoming a notable power. It lasted until 1646, although its power declined after a major military defeat in the Battle of Talikota in 1565 by the combined armies of the Deccan sultanates.

Known as the 'King's Balance', an oblique view of a freestanding, ornate post and lintel squared arch around which are a number of figures ▼

Prataparudra Deva of the Gajapati Empire, who was at loggerheds with the Vijaynagar kingdom. Though the Odisha kingdom failed to defeat the Vijaynagar army, historians feel they succeeded in weakening the kingdom, resulting in the eventual defeat of Rama Raya in 1565 CE ▼

▲The Vijayanagar rulers produced a new style of architecture known as the Provida style. Architecture included constructions of temples, monolithic sculptures, palaces, official buildings, cities, irrigation works such as step wells, tanks, etc.

Gajapati Empire (Odisha) 1434 CE

Gajapati literally means 'elephant army'. The rulers of the Gajapati Dynasty were believed to have more than 200,000 pachyderms in their stable when the dynasty, founded by Emperor Kapilendra Deva or Kapilendra Gajapati, was at its peak. After deposing the former king, Bhanudeva IV of the Eastern Ganga Dynasty, he took the

The Vijayanagar armies defeated Prataparudra Deva at the Battle of Panchalingeswar, which resulted in the loss of several lands. Kakharua Deva, the last ruler of the Gajapati Dynasty, ruled only for one year. In 1541 CE, he was killed in battle by Govinda Vidyadhara, who then founded the Bhoi Dynasty in Odisha.

throne in 1434 CE. As a competent military tactician, Kapilendra Deva made multiple conquests to increase the size of his realm.

Kapilendra Deva established his rule over a significant portion of Odisha by successfully repelling the attacks of the Delhi and Bahmani Sultanates. The successors of Kapilendra Deva upheld the prestige of the Gajapati Dynasty, which had other famous emperors—Purushottama Deva, Prataparudra Deva, and Mukunda Deva. These kings promoted the arts, literature, and architecture while physically enlarging their kingdoms. Kataka-Pattana (the present-day Cuttack) served as the empire's administrative centre.

During Purushottama Deva's rule, Quli Qutb Shah, the sultan of Golconda, invaded the kingdom in 1520 but was beaten back by the Gajapati Army. However, during the following decades, the Vijayanagar Empire's ascent to power presented the Gajapati dynasty with significant challenges during Prataparudra Deva's rule. The Vijayanagar armies defeated Prataparudra Deva at the Battle of Panchalingeswar, which resulted in the loss of several lands. Kakharua Deva, the last ruler of the Gajapati Dynasty, ruled only for one year. In 1541 CE, he was killed in battle by Govinda Vidyadhara, who then founded the Bhoi Dynasty in Odisha.

A watchman keeping guard in an outpost in Bengal (watercolour by George Chinnery) ▸

Bengal Sultanate I

1342 CE

Bengal again asserted its independence from the Delhi Sultanate. In 1342, Shams al-Din Ilyas Shah wrested Bengal free from Delhi's grip and established the Ilyas Shahi Dynasty, the first of several dynasties that would remain independent from the Delhi Sultanate for the next two and a half centuries. The break with Delhi was marked by a shift of the Ilyas Shahi capital from Lakhnauti, the provincial capital throughout the age of Delhi's hegemony, to the new site of Pandua, located some twenty miles to the north.

Initially, Delhi did not allow Bengal's assertions of independence to go unchallenged and in 1353, Sultan Firuz

Tughlaq moved with a huge army down the Ganges to punish the breakaway kingdom. Although Firuz slew up to 180,000 Bengalis and even temporarily dislodged Shams al-Din Ilyas Shah from his capital at Pandua near Gaur, he failed to reannex the delta. Six years later, Firuz made another attempt to restore the delta under Delhi's authority, but he was again rebuffed, this time by Shams al-Din's son Sikandar Shah. These inconclusive invasions of Bengal and the successful tactics of the two Bengali kings to elude the North Indian armies by fading into the interior finally persuaded the Delhi Sultans of the futility of trying to hold onto the distant province, and after 1359, Bengal was left undisturbed by North Indian armies for two centuries.

Bengal's emergence as one of the richest regions dates back to this period, when Bengal's economy first become thoroughly monetised and the rulers minted *tankas* (coins) from the silver looted from the defeated Hindu kingdoms of Sonargaon and Kamrup, among others. These circulated in large numbers throughout the region from the thirteenth century onwards, making the control of Bengal extremely lucrative.

The Agna Mahal, part of the Nawab of Bengal's palace at Murshidabad with boats on the Hoogly in the foreground ▼

Breaking off from the Delhi Sultanate, Alauddin Bahman Shah (1347–58 CE) was the first sultan of the Bahmani Sultanate. In all there were fourteen sultans who ruled over the entire Deccan region

Bahmani Sultanate

1346 CE

The Bahmani Sultanate, which ruled over the Deccan region from 1347 until 1518, is regarded as South India's first Islamic kingdom, its society being dominated by Persians, Afghans, and Turks. The Bahmani Sultanate was established in 1347 by the monarch Alauddin Bahman Shah, a Turkish officer in service of the Delhi Sultanate, who was aided in his uprising against Muhammad bin Tughlaq, the sultan of Delhi, by a number of warlords and rulers of other states.

The Deccan was known for its lawlessness, and it was left to Muhammad Shah I (1358–75 CE), the son of Alauddin Bahman Shah, to bring a semblance of law and order to the region. Ironically, the sultans themselves plundered at will, Alauddin having picked up a thousand singing and dancing girls from the northern Carnatic region. While the Bahmani Sultanate was at odds with the Vijayanagar Empire from the very outset, Muhammad Shah I also got into a conflict with the Warangal Empire, then ruled by the Kapaya Nayak. In a raw display of wanting to spread Islam by the sword, he let loose an orgy of violence against the Hindu populations in the Carnatic, killing over five lakh people, according to some estimates.

Between 1347 and 1425, Asanabad (present-day Gulbarga) served as the capital of the Bahmani Sultanate. Thereafter, the capital was moved to Muhammadabad (present-day Bidar). The emergence of Urdu as the court language and many architectural monuments like Golconda Fort in Hyderabad, Golgumbaz at Bijapur, and Jama Masjid at Gulbarga owe their existence to this sultanate.

During the period 1466–1481, Muhammad Shah III ascended the throne. Barely nine years old, Mahmud Gawan ruled as the *vazir* under Makhduma-e-Jahan Nargis Begum, and under his watch, the Bahmani Sultanate attained the height of its power. He continually expanded and governed the entire Deccan region, including the Konkan and the Krishna River basin and expanded the Bahmani kingdom from the Bay of Bengal in the east to the Arabian Sea in the west. In 1470 CE, the threat from the Gajapati Empire was also neutralised.

The Bahmani kingdom was eventually partitioned into five inheritor states known as the Bahmani Deccan Sultanate in 1490. These were the *tarafs* of Golconda, Bidar, Ahmednagar, Bijapur, and Berar. Many historians have attributed such a development to a compulsion arising from the fact that the Muslim sultans ruled a predominantly Hindu populace. Numerous cooperative commissions and a culture of non-interference among the various religious societies made it easier for the Shia Muslim sultans to exercise political and radical dominance in the region with such a demographic profile.

A total of fourteen sultans ruled over the sultanate during its long rule. However, while the Bahmani Sultanate was going through its ups and downs, the Vijayanagar Empire was also going through a similar see-saw of events. All the sultans fought everlasting wars with the Vijayanagar Empire. Krishnadevaraya of the Vijayanagar Empire finally defeated the last remnant of the Bahmani Sultanate in 1518.

The independent Nizam Shahi Sultanate was founded by the son of the regent of Muhammad Shah II, Nizam-ul-Mulk Bahri ▼

◀With his eyes on the Ottoman Empire, Timur, unlike earlier invaders, had no intention of ruling over the Sultanate. Instead, he was focused on loot and plunder

Timur 1398 CE

Timur was a Turco-Mongol conqueror and the founder of the Timurid Empire in Persia and Central Asia. He was given the title 'Taimur Lang', as one of his legs was wounded on the battlefield and compelled him to walk with a limp. After conquering Central Asia, he set his eyes on India, which was considered to be 'The Golden Bird'. Unfortunately, during this period, India was ruled by weak rulers, and there was complete chaos and disharmony among the people.

He entered the subcontinent and arrived unopposed at Multan after crossing the Indus and Chenab Rivers in September 1398; he let his 90,000-strong army loose on the city. Moving eastward, his spies informed him of a combined army of Rajputs and Muslims inside the fort of Bhatner (present-day Hanumangarh) in Rajputana. The Hindu King,

Dulachand, sought an audience with Timur and offered peace through surrender. Dulachand's own brother, enraged by the prospect of such a surrender, refused to let Dulachand enter the fort. After a brief resistance, the fort finally fell to the Timurid Army; it was plundered mercilessly, and all men were put to the sword. What followed was a ceaseless orgy of rapes, plunder, and slaughter through the vast terrain between Bhatner and Delhi. Central Asian warlords who made up Timur's fighting force inflicted unimaginable atrocities on the local populations. Some feeble opposition by the Jat peasants was also crushed without remorse. About 100,000 had been taken prisoners before the Timurid Army could even reach Delhi. Timur ordered them to be slaughtered to reduce his baggage and to nip any possibility of a revolt in the bud.

By mid-December 1398, Timur was knocking at the gates of Delhi. The joint armies of Sultan Nasir ud-Din and Mallu Iqbal faced the invaders. The elephants lined up by the defenders were armoured with chain mail and had poison on their tusks. Timur ordered his men to dig a trench in front of their positions. He then ordered his camels to be loaded with as much wood and hay as they could carry. Timur set the hay on fire when the war elephants charged, but they were met by flaming camels howling in pain. Timur had understood that elephants were easily panicked. Faced with the strange spectacle of camels flying straight at them with flames leaping from their backs, the elephants turned around and stampeded back toward their own lines. Timur capitalised on the subsequent disruption in the opposing forces, securing an easy victory. Nasir ud-Din Mahmud Shah Tughlaq fled with remnants of his forces.

The city of Delhi was sacked and reduced to ruins, with the population enslaved. After the city's fall, uprisings by its citizens began to occur, causing a retaliatory bloody massacre within the city walls. After three days of citizens uprising within Delhi, it was said that the city reeked of the decomposing bodies of its citizens, with their heads being erected like pyramids and the bodies left as food for the birds and animals. Timur then ordered the destruction of crops and granaries in and around Delhi before turning back. It is believed that this part of the subcontinent took almost a century to recover from the damage caused by the Timurid Army.

Among the various monuments built by the Sultans, the Muhafiz Khan Mosque (top), built in 1465, stands out for its Mughal style of architecture ▶

Gujarat Sultanate

1394 CE

Even in ancient times (1000 to 750 BCE), Gujarat had a flourishing history of trade, with links with Egypt and other littoral states in the Persian Gulf. Multiple dynasties ruled over the region, and various battles were fought as the Mauryas, then the western satraps, were challenged for supremacy by the Satavahana dynasty when Gautamiputra Satakarni conquered parts of Gujarat in the second century CE. Three hundred years later, the Gupta Empire included both the Saurashtra and Anarta regions.

Mohammad Bin Qasim's conquest of Sindh was followed by an Arab thrust into the subcontinent in what were the Caliphate campaigns in India but they were defeated by a collation of Hindu rulers from the Chalukya, Guhila, and the Gurjara-Pratihara dynasties in a battle fought on the west bank of the Indus River. Between 960 to 1243 CE, the Chalukyas reigned supreme with their capital at Anhilwara (Patan) and Gujarat was a major player in maritime trade. The Vaghela dynasty was in power in 1297 when the vastly superior forces of Alauddin Khaliji came calling. Karandev would become the last Hindu ruler, for after his defeat, Gujarat became an important part of the Delhi Sultanate.

Henceforth, two of the richest provinces that filled the coffers of the Delhi Sultanate were Bengal and Gujarat. Both were rich provinces on account of their fertile land and flourishing seaports. In a long line of governors who administered Gujarat, Zafar Khan was appointed by Firoz Shah Tughlaq in 1391 CE and, from the beginning, exercised independent power. After Timur's invasion left the Delhi Sultanate in tatters, in 1407 CE, Zafar Khan proclaimed himself the ruler of Gujarat and took the title Muzaffar Shah. He founded the Muzaffarid Dynasty, and in 1411 CE, he was succeeded by his grandson, Ahmad Shah I, who then shifted his capital to Ahmedabad. The Muzaffarid Dynasty would retain control of the Gujarat Sultanate for the next 167 years before Akbar would defeat Muzaffar Shah III and bring it back into Mughal control.

The Jama Masjid in Ahmedabad that was built in 1424 by Sultan Ahmad Shah I, who is also the founder of the city ▼

Portuguese

1498 CE

On May 20, 1498, the Portuguese explorer Vasco da Gama arrived in Calicut, an important seaport in southwest India. He had sailed around Africa via the Cape of Good Hope and thus became the first European to land in India. Notably, he fared better than his Spanish counterpart Christopher Columbus, who, while on a similar mission, had ended up discovering America only four years previously.

▼ The first Portuguese ships to arrive off Calicut were the ***Nau St Raphael*** and the ***St Gabriel*** under the command of Vasco da Gama. An Arab navigator, Ahmad ibn Majid helped Vasco da Gama find his way from Africa to India ►

While the Portuguese excelled in trade and metallurgy, and their churches patronised visual arts, uncalled-for religious intolerance the was one thing that blemished their innings in India.

Vasco was given a warm reception by the Hindu ruler, the Zamorin of Calicut, who also granted him a few privileges when he was told by the former that his sea voyage had aimed to open a maritime route for trade between Europe and the subcontinent.

Incidentally, the arrival of the first Portuguese sea vessel in India coincided with the imperial proclamation of the Chinese Ming emperor, which restricted the range of Chinese ships in the Far East. Consequently, by 1525 CE, the most powerful naval power in the world had destroyed more than 3,500 ships of its own. That left the Indian Ocean in the hands of Arab sailors who were dominating the sea

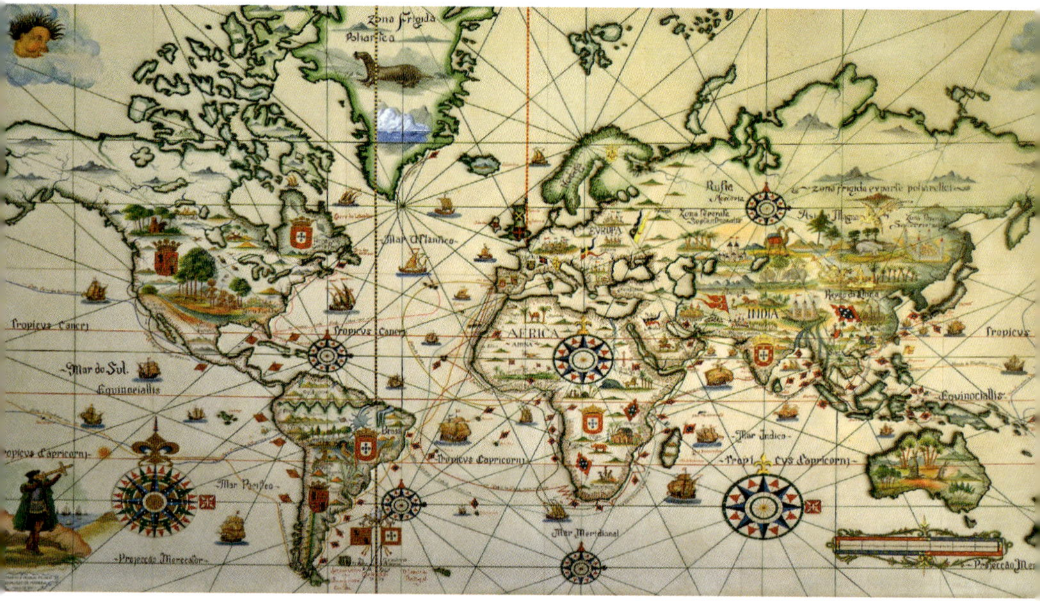

▲ At the Portuguese Maritime Museum in Lisbon, the map of the world with Portuguese colonies marked

trade routes. However, the Portuguese were more organised, cohesive, and battle-ready than the Arabs, who were traders with no military power. In contrast, the Portuguese ships had canons, and most ships had multiple decks and were strappingly built. Every ship had a self-defence mechanism in the form of prows and sterns to prevent the storming of ships.

Early Portuguese ships were technically superior to their British, Dutch, Spanish, and French counterparts. The Iberian Peninsula, constantly in a state of conflict in the thirteenth to fifteenth centuries, was way ahead of other European countries when it came to ship design. Initially, the emergence of the *carvel* opened up new possibilities, for these were capable of going into open seas

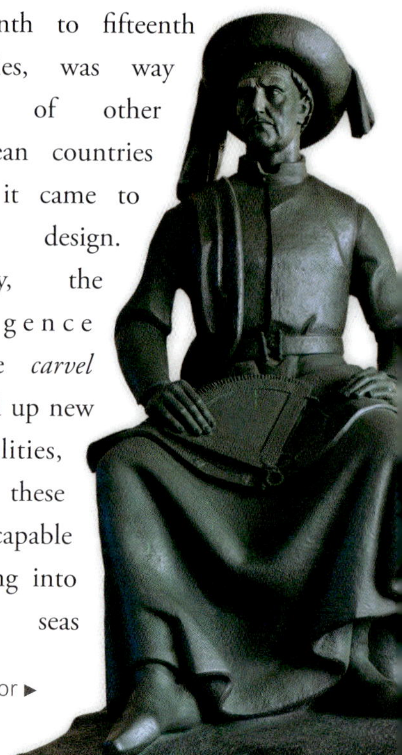

Prince Henry the navigator ▶

and were also large enough to carry cargo. By the end of the fifteenth century, the Iberian ship designers had improved on the *carvel* and developed the *carrack*, which had a three-masted six-sail configuration (bowsprit, foresail, mainsail, mizzen sail, and two topsails), as was the case with *Nau São Gabriel* that carried da Gama to India. The Portuguese *carracks* were usually over 1000 tons displacement. Interestingly, the Arabs, the Gujaratis, and the Bengalis at the time also used ships similar to the Portuguese and Spanish *carracks*.

In the decades following the landing of Vasco da Gama, the Portuguese kept gaining strength. By the middle of the sixteenth century, they controlled the sea lanes serving most of India's west coast between Gujarat and Thiruvananthapuram. Daman and Diu, Mumbai, Goa, Mangalore, Cannanore, Cochin, and Calicut were some of their naval strongholds. Their influence soon expanded to the east coast, where they built their settlements in Chennai, Nagapattinam, and Hooghly. They were the first traders to touch Puducherry, almost a century

Vasco da Gama meeting the Zamorin of Calicut ▼

◄ The sword and symbol of the Kunjali Marakkars who looked after the Zamorin's maritime interests. Kunjali Marakkar (alternatively spelled Kunhali Marakkar) is the title inherited by the Admiral of the fleet of the Samoothiri (Zamorin), the king of Kozhikode (Calicut), in present-day Kerala, India. There were four Marakkars whose war tactics defended against the Portuguese invasion from 1520 to 1600. The Kunjali Marakkars are credited with organizing the first naval defense of the Indian coast

before the Dutch, Danes, and finally, the French joined the competition in that coastal town.

While the Portuguese excelled in trade and metallurgy, and their churches patronised visual arts, uncalled-for religious intolerance was the one thing that blemished their innings in India. After capturing any piece of geography, the choice given to the natives would be between conversion and carnage. Their insolence toward religious issues was especially cruel to Indians, whose religious open-mindedness was the custom. Portuguese also engaged in disorder and vicious treatment of others. Moreover, the missionaries mixed up work and pleasure, and the merchants' attention had been drawn away from trade because of a free-for-all scenario. As a result, they fell behind in terms of shipbuilding proficiency due to technical developments happening elsewhere.

Battle of Cochin

1503 CE

Vasco da Gama left Indian waters in December 1502. By then, the Portuguese had established a healthy trade relationship with Trimumpara, the king of Cochin. A few Portuguese were left in Cochin to run a factory that Trimumpara had granted to them. The Zamorin of Calicut, however, disapproved of such a relationship between the two. He, therefore, gathered a large army of 50,000 men to seize

Cochin. At that time, the Portuguese were also at war with Arab Moors, who had close ties with the Zamorin. Another expedition from Portugal was on its way to India, but rough seas made their voyage troublesome.

In the meanwhile, Trimumpara raised whatever force he could to resist the impending invasion. However, he was beset by further difficulties because many of his subjects and tributary chiefs had deserted to the Zamorin. As the large force from Calicut attacked Cochin, they were thwarted by a spirited defensive battle by Trimumpara's small army. The fighting continued through the summer of 1503. Unable to penetrate Cochin's defences, the Zamorin bribed the chief of Trimumpara's army and captured Cochin through treachery. Trimumpara, taking the Portuguese along with him, fled to an island that had a formidable defence potential. A stalemate ensued, during which the expedition force from Portugal arrived. Cochin was retaken as the Zamorin and his men fled back to Calicut. Trimumpara got Cochin back, and the defence of his territory was taken over by a small force of 100-odd Portuguese with 5,000 native soldiers under command.

A Portuguese carrack ship off Cochin. They were the mainstay of the Portugese Navy and dominated the smaller maritime vessels that were at the disposal of the Zamorin and the Arab traders ▼

▼ Portuguese traders

Against this backdrop, a series of battles were fought between the 50,000-strong army of Calicut supported by Moors and lords of Malabar, including those of Tanur, Bespur, Cotugan, and Corin and a handful of Portuguese with Cochin soldiers in tow between March and July of 1504 CE. Also referred to as the Second Siege of Cochin, the fighting saw a spirited fight put up by the Portuguese under Pacheco, even while Trimumpara's soldiers continued to switch sides. Many pitched battles were fought on land and sea throughout the period. The sea component had more than 380 cannons, 100 large ships, 110 paraos, and eighty pinnaces to support the attack by the ground forces. And yet, Pacheco didn't allow the Zamorin Army to take over Cochin again. The attackers employed all kinds of tactics during a five-month-long campaign but to no avail. By July 1504, the Zamorin had lost nearly 20,000 of his men and many of his naval assets. Frustrated, he withdrew to Calicut, after which a peace treaty was signed between Cochin and Calicut.

The Raja of Cannanore had, in 1501, invited the Portuguese to set up their factory and trade with him instead of the Zamorin. Almost immediately, the Portuguese started to fortify their position by constructing the stone St. Angelo's Fort. However, their barbaric behaviour once again came to the fore when bodies of women and children, along with an Indian ship's crew that had been stitched into a sail and thrown into the sea on the grounds that the ship was not carrying a *Cartaz* (pass issued by the Portuguese to ships), led to the Seige of Cannanore when the Cannanore and the Zamorin's forces attacked the Portuguese in 1507.

The Second Siege of Cochin saw a spirited fight put up by the Portuguese under Pacheco, even while Trimumpara's soldiers continued to switch sides. Many pitched battles were fought on land and sea throughout the period.

▼ The Zamorin's Nair army

▲ St Angelo's Fort (top and right) in Kannur was built by the first Portuguese Viceroy in India, Don Francesco de Almeida in 1505 ▶

◂ Afonso de Albuquerque, a Portuguese general, admiral, and statesman was appointed as the viceroy of Portuguese India from 1509 to 1515, during which he expanded Portuguese influence across the Indian Ocean and built a reputation as a fierce and skilled military commander

Portuguese and Mamluk carracks clash off Diu ▸

Battle of Diu

1509 CE

In the listing of battles that influenced events not just in the Indian subcontinent but also in the shaping of the new world order, the naval battle fought off Diu on 3 February is perhaps among the most important. On the one side was the great Indian/Arab Alliance that not only had the Sultan of Gujarat, the Zamorin of Calicut, and the Mamluk Burji Sultanate of Egypt supported by the Republic of Venice and the Ottoman Empire, while on the other was the Portuguese

Navy that was trying to stamp its dominance in the Arabian Sea ever since they had arrived in India in 1498. The battle, which was eventually won by the Portuguese ships, ensured that Western European dominance over the Indian Ocean would become the defining factor for the next four centuries.

The final naval engagement was the culmination of events that had begun with the massacre of the Portuguese in Calicut in 1500. The Arab and Gujarati traders had their established trade routes that linked them to the markets of Europe through Egypt and the Venetians, and the arrival of the Portuguese threatened their very livelihood. In December 1504, the Portuguese intercepted and destroyed the Zamorin's annual merchant fleet, which was bound for Egypt laden with spices.

Anticipating an Arab backlash, King Manuel I of Portugal, on receiving

(Left) King Manuel I of Portugal
(Right) The Sultan of Eygpt & Syria, the Mamluk Al-Ashraf Qansuh al-Ghuri, whose help was sought by the Sultan of Gujarat & the Zamorin of Calicut to fight the Portuguese

the news of these developments, gave express orders to Dom Francisco de Almeida to not just safeguard Portuguese factories but also to curb hostile Arab shipping. Dom Francisco's fleet of twenty ships departed from Lisbon in March 1505. His twenty-year-old son, Dom Lourenço, was nominated *capitão-mor do mar da Índia* or captain-major of the sea of India. Meanwhile, both the Sultan of Gujarat and the Zamorin sent ambassadors to the Sultan of Egypt for immediate help to take on the Portuguese.

The Egyptians, mostly an agrarian society with little ties to the sea, had a formidable land army, but their naval strength, especially when compared to the Europeans, was relatively weak. The Mamluk Sultanate was, at the time, the main bridge between the spice-producing regions of India and buyers in the Mediterranean, mainly in Alexandria. From there, the Venetian traders sold the spices in the rest of Europe at a huge profit. Their monopoly threatened, the Venetians were quick to break off ties with Portugal and threw in their lot with the Mamluks.

To combat the Portuguese, Venice decided to equip the Mamluks with Mediterranean-type carracks and war galleys that were to be manned by Greek sailors and included Turkish, Nubian, and Ethiopian mercenaries plus Mamluk gunners. In Alexandria, the ships were dismantled and taken across to the Suez, where they were reassembled. The fleet, with 1,100 men under the command of Amir Hussain Al-Kurdi, a Kurdish Mamluk, and the former governor of Jeddah, set sail for India in November 1505.

The fleet arrived at Diu only in September 1507, which was a thriving port of the Gujarat Sultanate under Mahmud Shah I, or Mahmud Begada, the name given to him after he had at a very young age, captured the forts of Pavagadh and Junagadh. His governor was Malik Ayyaz, who was a former slave of East European descent and ruled Diu with a fair degree of autonomy. The arrival of the Mamluk fleet was viewed by Ayyaz with a fair degree of apprehension, for he was pragmatic enough to realise that the fleet had severe limitations to take on the Portuguese ships. The Mamluk galleys could, at best, deploy their cannons fore and aft, but not along the gunwales because the guns would interfere with the rowers. The dhows that made up the Gujarat Sultanate's own fleet had sewn wood planks that

A Portuguese ***nau***, the backbone of its dominant navy; Mamluk soldiers, who were far more proficient in land-based campaigns than out at sea ▼

could carry only very light guns. In addition, other than the Zamorin, none of the other Indian rulers seemed to be interested in fighting the Portuguese.

Nevertheless, in March 1508, Hussain, with a somewhat reluctant Ayyaz in tow, sailed south and caught the Portuguese fleet under the command of Lourenço in the harbour of Chaul, a Portuguese settlement in the Konkan. Not familiar with the silhouette of the approaching Mamluk ships, the Portuguese were caught by surprise and lost their flagship with Lourenço on board. Though prisoners were taken, the bulk of the Portuguese navy managed to get away mainly due to Ayyaz hanging back. In the euphoria of having scattered the Portuguese fleet, and despite reservations about Ayyaz's future intentions, the fleet returned to Diu, from where Hussain sent a message back to Sultan Al-Ashraf Qansuh al-Ghawri in Cairo, claiming a major victory.

The Mamluk galleys could, at best, deploy their cannons fore and aft, but not along the gunwales because the guns would interfere with the rowers.

Hussain, however, had stirred up a hornet's nest without having gained any strategic advantage. Dom Francisco de Almeida, reinforced with the arrival of Afonso de Albuquerque's fleet from Portugal, sailed northwards from Cochin on 9 December 1508 in the hope of catching the Zamorin's fleet, but it had already departed for Diu. At Anjadiva (off Karwar), the Portuguese were attacked by oar ships from Dabul, a part of the Bijapur Sultanate, which was then the next port of call. A landing party was ambushed, and the captain of the *São Miguel* was ambushed and killed. Two days later, after routing the defenders, de Almeida ordered the razing of Dabul. All civilians, including animals, were killed.

At Bombay, Ayyaz's envoy met de Almeida, and in a tone of appeasement, it was conveyed to the Portuguese governor that all prisoners were alive and well looked after. On 2 February, as the lookouts in Portuguese crow's nests sighted Diu, Ayyaz withdrew from the town leaving it in the hands of Hussain. The fighting was brutal, with the Mamluk-Gujarat-Calicut coalition fighting fiercely, but the Portuguese, with their modern ships manned by seasoned sailors, more cannons and better gunners, armour-plated infantry, arquebuses, and a type of clay grenade filled with gunpowder were far more proficient.

Ayyaz, deft in diplomacy, would retain his position, returning the Portuguese prisoners to de Almeida after the battle. Hussain, having fought till his flagship went down, made it back to Cairo, where he survived long enough to be given another command against the Portuguese, but was murdered by his own Turk second-in-command. The rest of the Mamluks were not so fortunate, as de Almeida had them blown from cannons, hung, or torn apart as revenge for his son's death. Diu would be seized yet again in 1538, but for then, was let alone.

▼In the post-Battle of Diu era, a Goan Indian soldier, a Portuguese man-at-arms, and a soldier in the 1580s and 90s

Five Deccan Sultanates 1518 CE

The Deccan sultanates were located on the Deccan Plateau between the Krishna River and the Vindhya Range and included Ahmednagar, Berar, Bidar, Bijapur, and Golconda. The Bahmani Sultanate's dissolution led to the sultanates' independence. The independence declarations of Ahmednagar, Bijapur, and Berar in 1490 provided the impetus for the five sultanates to come into being. In 1518, Golconda

◄ Despite their overall rivalry, the sultanates got together to reduce the Vijaynagar Empire to rubble. However, during their 200-year existence, they were mostly fighting each other, failing to present a united face against the Mughals or the Marathas

gained independence, followed by Bidar in 1528.

The founders of the five sultanates came from a variety of backgrounds and were mostly not originally Muslim. For example, a Deccani Muslim of Brahmin origin founded the Ahmednagar Sultanate; a Kannadiga Hindu Brahmin slave raised as a Deccani Muslim founded the Berar Sultanate; a Georgian slave founded the Bidar Sultanate; a Georgian slave bought by Mahmud Gawan founded the Bijapur Sultanate; and an Iranian Turkmen originally founded the Golconda Sultanate. However, all of them followed the Shia sect of Islam.

Ahmednagar Sultanate

Malik Ahmad Nizam Shah I was a well-known figure in Bahmani politics who headed the Deccani Muslim group at court. He was the son of Nizam ul-Mulk Malik Hasan Bahri, who was originally a Hindu Brahmin slave from Vijaynagar and was known by the name of Timapa before converting to Sunni Islam. Ahmad was made the governor of Beed and other districts near Daulatabad by Mahmood Shah Bahmani II. Operating from Junnar, he first captured the fort at Soonere and, through 1485, occupied Chavand, Lohgad, Tung, Kooray, Tikona, Kondhana, Purandar, Bhorop, Jivdhan, Kuhrdroog, Murud-Janjira, Mahuli, and Pali. He was camping in the Konkan coastal region in 1486 when he got the news of his father's assassination. Nizam-ul-Mulk had overseen the massive ethnic cleansing of Shia foreigners, especially the Turks and Georgian population in Bidar, by the orders of Mahmood Shah Bahmani. Shortly thereafter, the sultan sent General Jahangir Khan to bring Ahmad to book, but instead, the Bahami force was defeated by Ahmad, who then assumed the title of Nizam ul-Mulk Bahri from his father, and declared himself the sultan with dynastic control over his domain. Initially, his capital remained in Junnar, but in 1494, after a series of further skirmishes with Bahmani forces and his own relatives, the foundation was laid for the new capital, Ahmednagar, and five years later, the fortress of

Daulatabad was also under his control. Just before his death in 1510, Ahmad and his family adopted Shia Islam as their faith. Ahmad's seven-year-old son, Burhan Nizam Shah I, succeeded him and reigned for the next 43 years.

Berar Sultanate

Fathullah Imad-ul-Mulk, who was raised as a Muslim after being taken prisoner by Bahmani forces during an invasion against the Vijaynagar empire, was born a Kannadiga Hindu and went on to build the Berar Sultanate. Imad-ul-Mulk, the governor of Berar at the time, declared independence and established the Imad Shahi Dynasty of the Berar Sultanate in 1490 as the Bahmani Sultanate started to wane away. He fortified Gavilgad and Narnala and established the capital at Achalpur (Ellichpur). Ala-ud-din, Imad-ul-Mulk's eldest son, succeeded him after his death in 1504. Ala-ud-din, with the aid of the Gujarat Sultan Bahadur Shah, repelled Ahmednagar's assault in 1528. In an effort to stop Bijapur from attacking him, Darya Imad Shah, the third sultan of Berar, initially made an alliance with Bijapur to prevent the aggression of Ahmednagar, but was unsuccessful. His young son, Burhan, succeeded him in 1562, but one of Burhan's ministers, Tufal Khan, stole the throne in 1574. Berar was annexed by Ahmednagar's Sultan Murtaza I to his sultanate the same year. Burhan, Tufal Khan, and Shamshir-ul-Mulk, the son of Khan, were brought to Ahmednagar and imprisoned in a citadel, where they all eventually perished.

◄ Muhammad Quli Qutb Shah was the fifth sultan of the Qutb Shahi dynasty of Golkonda and founded the city of Hyderabad and built its architectural centerpiece, the Charminar

◄ Ahmednagar Fort

Yusuf Adil Shah, the founder of the Bijapur Sultanate, is shown seated and being handed the key of legitimacy by Shah Ismail I of Safavid Iran, symbolising the unwavering allegiance of the Adil Shahi dynasty to the Shia creed of Islam. All subsequent nine Adil Shahi sultans are depicted in the painting in a dynastic assembly. Yusuf Adil Shah was constantly at war with the neighbouring Vijaynagar Empire, and he was killed at Koilkonda when he was thrown off his horse in a conflict with Krishnadevaraya. Shortly prior to that, Yusuf Adil Shah had been defeated by the Portuguese, who then established Estado da Índia at Goa ▼

▲The Golconda Fort, which is but one of the many fortifications that dominate the entire Deccan Sultanate. All five sultanates were the direct result of the crumbling Bahmani Empire

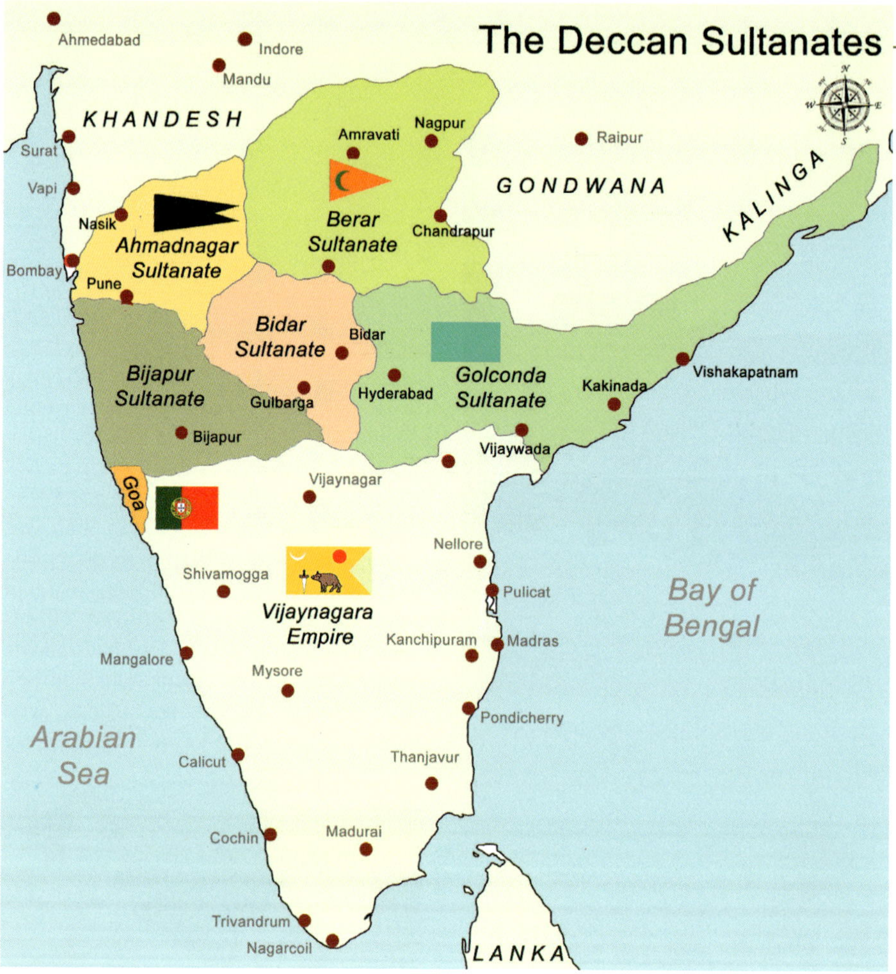

Bidar Sultanate

Out of all the five Deccan sultanates, Bidar was the smallest. Georgian-born Qasim Barid I, who had been taken as a slave by the Turks, established the sultanate. He began serving as a *sar-naubat* (commander) in the Bahmani Sultanate under Mahmud Shah Bahmani. Later, he rose to the position of *mir-jumla* (governor). While Sultan Mahmood Shah Bahmani and then his son, Ahmed Shah Bahmani II, continued to be the official rulers of the Bahmani Sultanate until 1528, in 1492 itself, Qasim Barid had taken on the role as the Bidar Sultanate's de facto ruler.

In 1425, the Bahmani Sultanate had shifted its capital to Bidar from Gulbarga, and hence, the power behind the Bahmani kingdom was also Qasim Barid, who ran the sultanate while Mahmood Shah Bahami enjoyed a life of indulgence. Qasim Barid died in 1504 and was succeeded by his son Amir Barid I, who was the prime minister of the Bahmani Sultanate. He, too, became the de facto ruler like his father, and in 1520, he proclaimed Alauddin Shah Bahmani II as the sultan, who reigned from 1520 and 1523. Alauddin planned to assassinate Amir Barid on one of their monthly visits. However, when Amir Barid arrived, one of the assassins in the inner quarters of the house sneezed, alarming him and giving away the conspiracy. Alauddin was imprisoned and put to death in 1523. He then proclaimed Wali-ullah the sultan, but he, too, was caught in a conspiracy against the prime minister and was put to death. Amir Barid proclaimed his brother Kalimullah the new Sultan. Kalimullah fled to Bijapur in 1527 and later to Ahmednagar but was not welcomed by either of the sultanates and spent the rest of his life as a prisoner.

Amir Barid did not elect another puppet monarch and continued to rule until 1542. However, he never assumed royal titles.

Golconda Sultanate

In the early sixteenth century, Quli Qutb-ul-Mulk travelled to Delhi from Persia with a few of his family members and friends. Subsequently, he moved to the Deccan and worked as a servant with Mohammed Shah Bahmani. Following the fall of the Bahmani sultanate in 1518, Quli Qutb-ul-Mulk acquired control of Golconda and assumed the role of governor of the Telangana province. He soon proclaimed his independence and established the Qutb Shahi dynasty.

Bijapur Sultanate

The Adil Shahi dynasty controlled the Bijapur Sultanate, which was situated in Southwestern India and stretched across the Western Ghats in Southern Maharashtra and northern Karnataka. Yusuf Adil Shah, the dynasty's founder, was probably a Georgian slave that Mahmud Gawan bought from Iran. Originally serving as province governor within the Bahmani Sultanate, Ismail Adil Shah founded an independent sultanate following the dissolution of the Bahmani Kingdom in 1518. Several monuments were added to the capital city of Bijapur by Ismail Adil Shah and his successors. Ibrahim Adil Shah I changed his identity to that of a Sunni, removing Shia leaders from their positions. He abolished Shia dominance and elevated Sunni Muslims to authority in Bijapur.

A portrait of Babur at the Indian Military Academy ▸

Babur

1526–1530 CE

Zahir-ud-din Mohammad Babur was a Timurid from Fergana in Central Asia. Born on 14 February 1483 in the Uzbekistan city of Andijan, he ascended the throne in 1494 after the death of his father, Omar Sheikh; he was only 11 years old at that time. He was a descendant of Timur (on his father's side) and Genghis Khan (on his mother's side). In 1497, Babur invaded Samarkand, an Uzbek city, and took control of it. However, a rebellion back home robbed him of

Fergana, and while he rushed to crush the rebels, his own army deserted him, resulting in the loss of Samarkand. Not the one to give up, he gathered his army and recaptured both the regions before losing Samarkand again in 1501. He raised a new army over the next three years and captured Kabul in 1504.

Now established as a ruler of a prosperous kingdom, he undertook many campaigns to regain his home and capture Persian lands to the west. A series of victories, rebellions, and losses kept him busy for two decades, after which he started looking east because he failed to make any considerable gains in the north and west. Heading south, he took over Lahore in 1524 before abandoning it in the face of a strong warlord of Punjab and a

◂ The Mughals entering Samarkhand

◄ In the Battle of Khanwa, Babur defeated the battle-hardened Rana Sanga on 16 March 1527. Rana Sangha's defeat has largely been attributed to Babur's artillery

minister of Ibrahim Lodi, Daulat Khan. Interestingly, it was Daulat Khan who, having become disgruntled as a minister of Ibrahim Lodi, had first invited Babur and then turned against him. A year later, Babur was back in Punjab and recaptured Lahore in 1525. It was now time to challenge Lodi. Despite having a much larger force under his command in the ensuing First Battle of Panipat, Ibrahim Lohi was killed by the rampaging Mughals, who were the first to deploy artillery guns in India when the two sides met on 20 April 1526. The death of Ibrahim Lodi ended the Delhi Sultanate and paved the way for the Mughal Dynasty, which would hold sway over most of the subcontinent till the beginning of the eighteenth century, officially ending with the exile of Bahadur Shah Zafar in 1858.

As the Mughals came from Central Asia, they brought the Central Asian military tradition along with them. A new style of combat was adopted due to the arrival of gunpowder; with that, a new kind of tactics was also employed. This was not the case earlier since fighting predominantly revolved around using horses and elephants with weapons like bows, arrows, swords, and shields. But from now on, a new phase of military combat was adopted that focussed on using artillery and muskets, bombs, etc. This contributed to the change in battlefield tactics and the evolution of military strategy. New organisations were created with civilian administrative institutions to support the new setups. As far as the structure was concerned, the Mughal Army consisted of cavalry, infantry, and artillery. Among these, artillery held a subordinate position compared to that of the infantry and cavalry. In addition, elephants continued to be used. Under the Mughals, the emphasis was on the numbers and quality of the horses in an army. However, with the passage of time, the use of artillery kept increasing to break through enemy forces and defeat them.

Babur's artillery was of two kinds, the heavy and the light, or, as they call the latter, 'the artillery of the stirrup'. The heavy artillery was called the *Kazan* or heavy cannon, which was able to fire balls of about 20–25 pounds in weight, while the lighter cannon was called *Zarbzan*, which was mobile and could be moved to different places and was able to fire three to four-pound projectiles. The *Kazan* were big guns and were used against forts and fortified positions. Besides, there was also a third kind called *Firingi* or Frankish canon, which was much smaller than the *Zarbzan*. The last kind of Babur's artillery consisted of a heavy siege gun that fired about 100 pounds or more projectiles.

After the Battle of Panipat, Babur continued to expand his empire, conquering much of northern India, including present-day Delhi, Agra, and Lahore. In terms of military organisation, he maintained a small well-trained standing army that was highly mobile and composed mainly of cavalry. His military campaigns were characterised by his tactical acumen and his ability to adapt to different terrain.

The new war tactics introduced by Babur were the *tulughma* and the *araba*. *Tulughma* meant dividing the whole army into various units, viz., the Left, the Right, and the Centre. The Left and Right Divisions were further subdivided into Forward and Rear Divisions. Through this, a small army could be used to surround the enemy

Babur entering the gates of Kabul; Babur during his second Hindustan Campaign travelling on a raft from Kunar to Atar; Fought on 20 January 1528, the Battle of Chanderi saw the Rajput women commit Jhauhar and the men eventually fell on their own swords. Babur had a tower of skulls erected in order to continue terrorizing his opponents in the manner of Timur

from all sides. The Centre Forward Division was then provided with carts (*araba*), which were placed in rows facing the enemy and tied to each other with animal hide ropes. Behind them were cannons protected and supported by mantelets, which could be used to manoeuvre the canons easily. These two tactics made Babur's artillery lethal. The guns and cannons could be fired without any fear of being hit as they were shielded by the bullock carts, which were held in place due to the hide ropes; the nozzle of the heavy cannons could also be easily changed as they could be manoeuvred by the mantelets which were provided with wheels. Using such tactics and battlefield manoeuvres, he was able to take native warriors, who were not accustomed to fighting in the face of such stratagems, by complete surprise. Among the most famous battles where he emerged a winner were the First Battle of Panipat against Ibrahim Lodi in 1526, the Battle of Khanwa against Rana Sanga in 1527, the Battle of Chanderi against Medini Rai in 1528 and the Battle of Ghagra against Mahmud Lodi (brother of Ibrahim Lodi) in 1529. But for his untimely death in 1530, he would have continued to expand his empire since age was on his side.

Having expanded his empire through numerous successful campaigns, Babur dedicated his later years to organising the finances and operations of his new empire and enhancing Agra, which he had made his capital. He encouraged art and introduced the technique of book engraving that he managed to bring from Byzantine. He also authored his memoir, *Baburnama*, written in Chagatai/Turkish. Despite his self-accolading accounts, he is remembered as a ruthless warrior who drew sadistic pleasure from torturing and killing his victims. Babur allegedly built the Babri Mosque in Ayodhya, on the site of a Hindu temple that marked Lord Ram's birthplace, in 1528.

Babur was not yet 50 when his son, Humayun, fell gravely ill. The royal medics tending to him saw no hope of the young kid's survival from a deadly disease that had infected his tender body. Devastated by the turn of events, Babur started fervently praying for his child. Babur expressed his desire to take Humayun's illness and pass away in his place in these prayers, which he uttered while he circled his son. The strange thing is that Babur's prayers were answered, and Babur succumbed to this illness at the age of 48. He was buried in Kabul.

Humayun
1530–1540; 1555–1556

Nasir al-Din Muhammad Humayun, the second ruler of the Mughal kingdom, was the elder son of Babur. He was born on 17 March 1508 CE in Kabul. He ascended the throne at a young age, in 1530, but was forced out of power within a decade. He regained his crown in 1555 but could rule only for one year before he died.

He was a trained military leader who, as a teenager, had been with his father when the Mughal Empire was founded after the

Battle of Panipat in 1526. Subsequently, he participated in the conquest of Agra before being assigned to restore peace in the Ganges Valley in the far east of the Mughal Empire. Thereafter, he was appointed the governor of Badakhshan in 1528, which, today, lies on the border between south Tajikistan and north Afghanistan. Badakhshan lay east of Kabul, the city that served as Babur's rear base throughout his conquests. However, at the time of Babur's death, the Mughal kingdom was far from stable as there were multiple threats and issues that needed to be tackled by the young Humayun.

His days as a king saw his half-brother, Kamran Mirza, plotting and conspiring against him even though he had shown much kindness towards the latter multiple times. He went to the extent of awarding the provinces of Punjab and Kabul to Kamran, who was also recognised as an independent ruler, but Kamran couldn't mend his ways and kept on needling him from time to time. However, his real nemesis was a duo—Sultan Bahadur Shah of Gujarat and Sher Shah Suri in Bihar, the latter getting assistance from Kamran Mirza on more than one occasion.

Simultaneously, under threat from the Portuguese and the Mughals, Sultan Bahadur Shah assembled an army to uproot the Mughals first. This event occurred in 1531 when Humayun was only six months into his rule. To counter the threat, Humayun besieged the fort of Kalinjar in Bundelkhand, achieved a decisive victory over the Afghans at Dahua and defeated the combined armies of Sultan Mahmud Lodi of Jaunpur and Bahadur Shah, who escaped and sought refuge with the Portuguese. After that, it was time to meet with Sher Shah Suri on the battlefield.

The Afghan—Sher Shah Suri—had had a great career. After joining the Bihar Sultan's service in 1522, he served Babur in 1527–1528, receiving land as

◀ Hamida Banu Begum was the wife of Humayun. Her Persian lineage played a role in helping Humayun regain his empire

payment. Unable to contain himself, he set out to annex Bihar and joined ranks with the Sultan of Bengal to create his own foothold. After tackling Gujarat, Humayun then marched towards Bihar and besieged the city of Chunar. In the meantime, Sher Shah, making a pincer move, rushed west and conquered a large chunk of the Mughal Empire, threatening Agra, the capital. As a result, Humayun retraced his steps but was defeated at the Battle of Buxar in June 1539. He lost his army and also his harem and barely escaped with his life.

In 1540, he raised a new army to fight Sher Shah, who, by now, had already created a kingdom in the north-eastern part of the subcontinent. The Battle of Kanauj saw Humayun biting the dust once again and fleeing first to Punjab and then to Sindh. It was in Sindh that he started planning the recapture of his kingdom. He understood that he wouldn't be able to make a dent unless he could manage the support of someone powerful.

In 1544, he went to Persia and convinced Shah Tahmasp I to lend him a strong military column. Between 1544 and 1549, he captured and lost Kabul on more than a couple of occasions. Finally, with Kabul under his grip, he began his journey back home. A number of battles were fought – Peshawar (1554), Lahore, Dipalpur, and Macchi Bhawan (1555) before he was back on the throne in Agra after a long gap of 15 years. Unfortunately, a nasty fall claimed his life on 27 January 1556. His wife, Biga Begum, got a mausoleum, Humayun ka Makbara, constructed in Delhi in 1570.

Despite his relatively short reign, in the field of painting and architecture, Humayun made groundbreaking progress. He was the first person to build the Din Panah citadel in Delhi. However, the building was destroyed during the reign of Sher Shah Suri. According to legend, Humayun set the groundwork for Mughal art and led the effort to integrate Persian art and culture into the native art forms. While he did pay attention to the kingdom's growth, he also focused on the development of literature and architecture. For this reason, his reign is regarded as having set the stage for the subsequent flourishing of Mughal art and architecture.

Mughal historians portray him as the most morally upright emperor and claim that he had pledged not to attack any Muslim. Though a Sunni himself, he allowed freedom of religion to Shias and Sufis. There is mention of both Shias and Sufis holding him in high esteem. However, his destruction of numerous Hindu temples and atrocities after his conquests tell a different story.

Humayun had inherited an unstable kingdom, and he handed Akbar a kingdom that was still unstable. However, even though Babur is regarded as the founder of the Mughal Dynasty in India, had Humayun not recaptured his territory, the Mughal history in the subcontinent would have been very different or non-existent.

The Bara Darwaza (big gate) at the Purana Qila (old fort) in 1864. The sixteenth century citadel is one of the oldest in Delhi and was believed to have been built under Humayun ▼

Sher Shah Suri founder of the Suri Empire in India ▸

Sher Shah Suri

1540–1545 CE

Sher Shah, born Farid Khan, was an Afghan who founded the Suri Empire. He had his capital at Sasaram in modern-day Bihar. Having served as the commander in the Mughal army under Babur, he went on to become the governor of Bihar. After the Battle of Surajgarh, which was fought between 1533 and 1538 CE, he overran the state of Bengal and, subsequently after the Battle of Kannauj in 1540

CE, established the Suri Empire with its capital in Delhi. He realised the importance of maintaining a powerful and a well-organised army at the very outset of his reign. His army consisted of 150,000 cavalry, 25,000 infantry, 5,000 war elephants, and a huge contingent of artillery. His cavalrymen, the Afghans, were trusted soldiers, but he also employed Hindus and other communities in his army. Sher Shah used to pay personal attention to the employment, training, discipline, and payment of the salaries of the soldiers.

Sher Shah appointed a military officer known as *Bakshi-e-Lashkar* to look after the military administration. There were several Bakshis in the empire to look after the army. The soldiers were provided matchlocks or bows and were commanded by trusted young officers appointed by Sher Shah himself. Besides the standing army which was under the direct command of the sultan, provincial governors, nobles, and subordinate rulers were also allowed to maintain their separate armies. Sher Shah was a past master in adopting successful war tactics. He knew fully well where to make a tactical retreat, when to strike at the enemy, how to sow dissensions in the army camp, how to make friends

In a painting now at the Allahabad Museum, a lion surrenders before Sher Shah Suri ▼

with the enemy of the enemy, and how to feign a retreat if required.

After taking control of the Mughal Empire, Sher Shah immediately conquered and seized Punjab from Kamran who was Humayun's brother. In 1542, he suppressed the restless Khokhars of the northern region of the river Indus and Jhelum and also annexed Malwa. Between the period 1543–1545, he attacked Raisin, a Rajput principality and besieged it. In 1543, Sher Shah Suri, with a huge force of 80,000 cavalry, set out against Maldeo Rathore, ruler of Mewar who, with an army of 50,000 cavalry, advanced to face Sher Shah's army.

Instead of marching to the enemy's capital, Sher Shah halted in the village of Sammel. After one month, Sher Shah's position became critical owing to the difficulties of food supplies for his huge army. To resolve this situation, he resorted to a cunning ploy. One evening, he dropped forged letters near the Maldeo's camp in such a way that they were sure to be intercepted. These letters falsely indicated that some of Maldeo's army commanders were offering assistance to Sher Shah. This caused great consternation to Maldeo, who immediately (and wrongly) suspected his commanders of disloyalty. Maldeo left for Jodhpur with his own men, abandoning his commanders to their fate. Sher Shah emerged victorious in the ensuing battle of Sammel (also known as the Battle of Giri Sumel) against a depleted army. After that, he turned towards Bundelkhand. While besieging the fort of Kalinjar, he died in 1545 in an accidental gunpowder blast.

Sher Shah Suri's brief reign saw him construct theSonargaon–Sind, Agra–Burhampur, Jodhpur–Chittor, and Lahore–Multan roads and the extension of the Grand Trunk Road from Chittagong in Bengal to Kabul in Afghanistan.

A Mughal on horseback attacking a man with a shield

Rama Raya

1542–1565 CE

Aliya Rama Raya was born in a Telugu family and was later married to the daughter of Sri Krishna Deva Raya, one of the greatest emperors of the Vijayanagar Empire. He was a capable administrator and a gallant general who led many successful missions and won many battles while fighting for his father-in-law. After the king's demise, Achyuta Raya, Krishna Raya's half-brother, became the emperor and was challenged by Rama Raya. As the power struggle peaked, Achyuta died, and his son, Sadasiva Raya, became the king. By then, however, Rama Raya had become very powerful and was the de facto ruler between 1542 and 1565.

Ali Adil Shah I of Bijapur; Hussain Nizam Shah I of Ahmednagar; Ali Barid Shah I of Bidar; and Ibrahim Quli Qutb-Shah of Golkonda

Wielding unbridled power, he removed all the loyalists of his father-in-law and appointed his own men to the court. Among those inducted were two Gilani brothers who switched sides at a crucial moment when Rama Raya's army was about to crush the combined armies of the Deccan sultans in the battle of Talikota in 1565. His enemies captured and beheaded him, after which they ransacked Hampi, the Vijayanagar Empire's capital city.

◄Rama Raya succeeded in keeping the Deccan Sultanate at bay as they were too busy fighting each other. In 1565, the four sultanates – Ahmednagar, Bijapur, Bidar and Golkonda formed an alliance and defeated him, after which Vijaynagar was ransacked

Akbar

1556–1605 CE

Abul-Fath Jalal-ud-din Muhammad Akbar, popularly known as Akbar the Great, was the third Mughal Emperor, who reigned from 1556 to 1605 CE. Akbar succeeded his father, Humayun, under a regent, Bairam Khan, who helped the young emperor expand and consolidate Mughal domains in the Indian subcontinent. Babur's empire did not last long, and the Mughal empire collapsed with the expulsion of Humayun,

◄ Akbar's army attacks Chittor in 1567

who fled westward to modern-day Sindh. Following chaos over the succession of Sher Shah Suri's son Islam Shah, Humayun reconquered Delhi in 1555, leading an army partly provided by his Persian ally Tahmasp I. A few months later, Humayun died. Bairam Khan concealed his death to prepare for Akbar's succession on 14 February 1556 amid a war against Sikandar Shah to reclaim the Mughal throne.

Soon the Afghan Sultan Mohammad Adil Shah's Hindu general, Hem Chandra (Hemu), led an Afghan army to seize Agra and Delhi. The Mughal army was driven out and after 350 years of Muslim imperialism, Hemu instituted Hindu authority in North India in 1556. Urged by Bairam Khan, who re-marshalled the Mughal army before Hemu could consolidate his position, Akbar marched on Delhi

Bairam Khan, a Shia, was not too popular with the Sunni courtiers in the Mughal court, and Akbar asked him to step down as regent and proceed to Mecca. Some say Bairam Khan was recognised by Hemu loyalists while Mughal court records claim he was killed by Afghans.

to reclaim it, and the Mughal forces faced Hemu and the Sur army on 5 November 1556 at the Second Battle of Panipat, 50 miles (80 km) north of Delhi. Hemu, having declared himself Samrat and taken the title Vikramaditya, had an army that was much larger than that of Akbar. Bairam

Khan led the Mughal army while the young Akbar was kept at a safe distance. Initially, Hemu's army was in a better position, but a stray arrow hit Hemu in the eye after which his army literally disintegrated. Bairam Khan then asked Akbar to cut off Hemu's head, which the 14-year-old did. Mughal records claim that Akbar refused, and it was Bairam Khan who beheaded Hemu. However, in the manner of the times, after Akbar entered Delhi, a pyramid of heads was created. Akbar's initial years were marked with brutal violence.

The Mughal forces then occupied Agra. Akbar stayed for a month in Delhi, and he and Bairam Khan then returned to Punjab to deal with Sikandar Shah, who had become active again. In the next six months, the Mughals won another major battle against Sikander Shah Suri, who then fled east to Bengal. Akbar and his forces occupied Lahore and then seized Multan in the Punjab. In 1558, Akbar took possession of Ajmer, the aperture to Rajputana, after the defeat and flight of its Muslim ruler. Late in the same year, a Mughal commander defeated Ibrahim, the last Sur prince, and annexed Jaunpur, the capital of the former Sultanate of Jaunpur in the eastern Gangetic valley. The Mughals

▲ Akbar's army attacks Chittor in 1567 and the women commit jauhar. In his early years, Akbar was extremely brutal in his dealings with defeated enemies as in Ranthambore

Battle between Akbar's forces and Muhammad Husain Mirza near Ahmadabad in 1573; Akbar's entry into Surat in 1572. Surat was defended by a former slave of Humayun, Hamzaban, who had joined the Gujarat Mirzas ▼

had also besieged and defeated the Sur forces in control of Gwalior Fort, the greatest stronghold north of the Narmada River. The flurry of victories put the vital cities and strongholds located between Lahore, Delhi, Agra, and Jaunpur under Akbar's control.

The Mughal Empire, founded by Akbar in 1556, proved more stable and enduring. Akbar restructured the army and introduced a new system called the *mansabdari* system. The Mughal army had no regimental structure. In this system, a military officer worked for the government and was responsible for recruiting and maintaining his quota of horsemen. His rank was based on the horsemen he provided, which ranged from ten (the lowest), up to 5,000. A prince had the rank of 25,000. This was called the *zat* and *sowar* system. An officer had to keep men and horses in a ratio of 1:2. The horses had to be carefully verified and branded, and Arabian horses were preferred. The officer also had to maintain his quota of horses, elephants, and camels for transportation, as well as foot soldiers and artillery. Soldiers were given the option to be paid either in monthly/annual payments or *jagir*, and many chose *jagir*. The emperor also allocated a *jagir* to *mansabdars* for

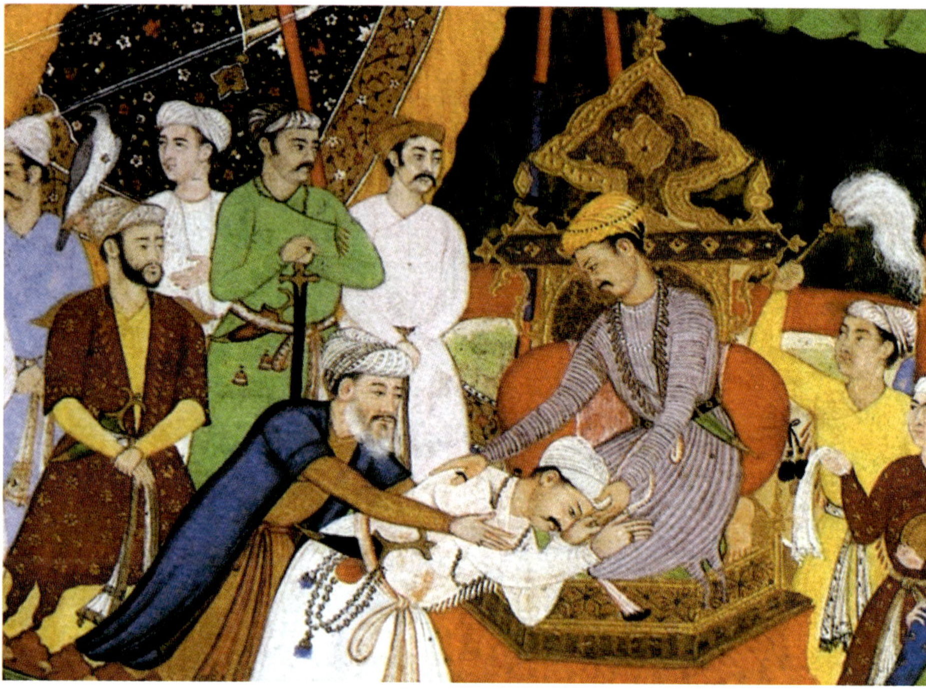

▲ Raja Rao Surjan Hada making submission to Akbar after surrendering the Ranthambore Fort in 1568

the maintenance of the *mansabs*. Akbar also took an interest in matchlocks and effectively employed them during various conflicts. He sought the help of the Ottomans, as well as Europeans, especially the Portuguese and Italians, in procuring advanced firearms and artillery. Akbar's vizier, Abul Fazl, once declared that 'with the exception of Turkey, there is perhaps no country in which its guns have more means of securing the Government than [India]'. Scholars and historians have used the term 'Gunpowder Empire' to analyse the success of the Mughals in India.

The Empire did maintain a fleet of warships that also consisted of transport vessels. The Mughal warships were characterised by their strength and their size, due to the shipbuilding skills of their Bengali shipbuilders. It is known from the standard survey of maritime technology in 1958, that Bengali expertise in shipbuilding was subsequently duplicated by the British East India Company in the 1760s, which led to significant improvement in the seaworthiness and navigation of European ships during the Industrial Revolution. The navy's main duty was controlling piracy, and it was sometimes used in war. The foundation of the salt water naval force of the Mughal Empire was established by Akbar in the late sixteenth century after he conquered Bengal and Gujarat. Akbar reorganised the imperial navy from a collection of civilian vessels with more professional institutions of naval administration, which is detailed in the *Ain-i-Akbari* document. This record identifies the institution's primary objectives, including the maintenance of transport and combat vessels, the retention of skilled seamen, the protection of civilian commerce, and the enforcement of tolls and tariffs. Akbar, thus, had full control of Hindustan, the old heartland of Muslim Turko-Afghan political and military power in India.

◂ Akbar's Imperial Mughal army led by Qutb ud-Din and Sharif Khan defeat Sultan Adam in the Battle of Gakkhar in 1563. Three of the top-ranking artists of the time—Tulsi, Bhawani, and Sanwala worked on the painting while A'bul Fazl wrote the text wherein he emphasised that no ruler from Hindustan had previously succeeded in capturing Gakkhar

During the reign of Akbar, the Sultan of Bengal, Daud Khan Karrani, had seized Fort Zamania, a frontier post of the Mughal Empire ▸

Bengal Campaign
1572–1575 CE

During the early Muslim period, the former Sena Hindu kingdom came to be known as the Sultanate of Bengal and Bihar, ruled intermittently by the Sultans of Delhi. This period was followed by chaotic shifts in power between the Afghan and Turkish rulers who briefly held sway. Their control over the Sultanate came to an end when the Mughal rule extended itself over Bengal during the sixteenth century. On

3 March 1575, Akbar's troops defeated the combined forces of the Sultanate of Bengal at the Battle of Tukaroi in what is now the Balasore district of Odisha.

During the reign of Akbar, the Sultan of Bengal was Daud Khan Karrani, who had seized Fort Zamania, a frontier post of the Mughal Empire. This gave Akbar the cause for war. Akbar prepared a fleet of elaborately equipped boats to proceed down the rivers towards Agra. Akbar, who was in Gujarat when he received the news of Daud's audacity, at once dispatched orders to Munim Khan and the representative of the imperial power in Jaunpur to chastise the aggressor. Munim, on receipt of his sovereign's

◂ Akbar moving by boat from the Agra Fort

◄ Often moving along the river, paintings indicate that the Mughals had an elaborate fleet of boats that could even carry elephants

instructions, assembled a powerful force and marched on to Patna where he was opposed by Lodi Khan, an influential Afghan chief who had placed Daud on the throne and now served that prince as minister. Munim Khan, who was then very old, had lost his energy and, after some skirmishing, was content to cease hostilities and grant Daud extremely lenient terms. Neither of the principal parties was pleased, and Emperor Akbar thought that the Munim Khan had been too easygoing whereas Daud was jealous of his minister, Lodi Khan.

The Emperor accordingly deputed Raja Todar Mal to take the command in Bihar handing over the Raja's civil duties as Diwan temporarily to Rai Ram Das. Daud treacherously killed his minister, Lodi Khan, and confiscated his property. Munim Khan, stung by his master's censure, returned rapidly to Patna and laid siege to the city. But he soon found the task of taking it to be beyond his powers and begged the Mughal

Emperor to come in person and assume charge of the campaign. Akbar, who had just returned to the capital after paying his annual visit to Ajmer, proceeded to Agra in March 1574 CE and prepared a fleet of elaborately equipped boats to proceed down the rivers.

The rainy season, being then at its height, was hazardous, and many mishaps occurred. After traveling for 26 days, Akbar reached Benares, where he halted for three days. He then proceeded to where the Gomti River joins the Ganges River. On the same day, the army, which had marched by land, arrived. The whole movement evidently had been thought out and executed with consummate skill in the face of tremendous difficulties due to the weather.

Although Daud had at his disposal 20,000 horses, a large park of artillery and many elephants, he came to the conclusion that he could not resist the Imperial power and decided to flee. During the night he slipped out quietly and went to Bengal. The garrison, which attempted to escape, suffered heavy losses. The capture of a city in the middle of the rainy season was an almost unprecedented achievement and a painful surprise to the Bengal Sultan. The battle led to the Treaty of Katak in which Daud ceded the whole of Bengal and Bihar, retaining only Odisha. The treaty eventually failed after the death of Munim Khan, who died at the age of 80. Sultan Daud Khan took the opportunity and invaded Bengal. This would lead to the Battle of Raj Mahal in 1576.

Raja Todar Mal (1500–1589) was the *Mushriff-i-Diwan* (Finance Minister) of the Mughal Empire during Akbar's reign. He was also the *Vakil-us-Sultanate* (Counsellor of the Empire) and Joint Wazir. As one of the premier nobles in the Mughal Empire, he was a *mansabdar* of 4,000 ▸

Haldighatti
1576 CE

In Akbar's scheme of things, a stable route to Gujarat through the kingdom of Mewar was strategically vital. When Rana Pratap ascended the throne in 1572, Akbar unsuccessfully sent a number of envoys, entreating the Rana to become a vassal like many other Rajput leaders in the region. Years later, the Mughals laid siege to Chittorgarh, and the Rana lost the fertile eastern belt of his kingdom. On 18

June 1576, the Battle of Haldighatti was fought between the Mughal forces led by Man Singh I of Amber and the Mewar kingdom led by the spirited Rana. Though the Rajputs were soundly defeated at Haldighati, and the city of Udaipur was also lost as a result. Maharana Pratap managed to escape, and the wooded regions of the hilly kingdom continued to be under the control of the Sisodias. Forced to sue for peace, Rana Pratap had to give his daughter Jodhabai to Hussain Khan, the Governor or Ajmer, in marriage, but by and by, after a series of skirmishes, Mewar became a part of the Mughal Empire.

Maharana Pratap of Mewar on his famous horse, Chetak, took on Akbar's forces led by Man Singh I of Amer, at Haldighatti, on 18 June 1576. In all probability, the Mughals outnumbered the Mewar forces by a factor of four to one ▼

Sultana Chand

1595–1599 CE

Chand Bibi, also known as Chand Khatun or Chand Sultana, was the daughter of Hussain Nizam Shah I of Ahmednagar. She was married to Ali Adil Shah of the Bijapur Sultanate. On the death of her husband, she served briefly as the regent of Bijapur on behalf of her husband's nephew, Ibrahim Adil Shah II. She then, again, stepped in as the regent of Ahmednagar (1595–1599 CE) and defended the Ahmednagar Fort against Akbar's army on two occasions.

In the anals of the Deccan's political quagmire, Sultana Chand Bibi would keep Akbar at bay

A portrait of the fourth Mughal emperor ▸

Jehangir 1605–1627 CE

The fourth Mughal emperor, Nur-ud-Din Muhammad Salim, better known as Jehangir, meaning the '*Conqueror of the World*', reigned at the helm of the Mughal Empire from 1605 CE until his demise in 1627. He was the third and last surviving child of Akbar and Mariam-uz-Zamani and was born to them on 31 August 1569. Salim Chishti, an Indian Sufi saint, was the inspiration for his name.

The Emperor Jehangir presenting Prince Khurram a turban and conferring on him the title 'Shah Jahan' at Mandu in 1617

He inherited the Mughal Empire at the age of 36 but faced a real challenge since he had to step into big shoes, having succeeded a legendary father. Jehangir was neither as accomplished a ruler nor as adventurous a warrior as Akbar, who has also been given the title by historians 'Akbar the Great'! However, he was rather adept at upholding the status quo, which he accomplished for over 20 years. While dividing most of his time between Lahore and Agra, Jehangir devoted his energies towards upholding the empire's central government, promoting the arts, and occasionally—though infrequently—slightly enlarging the Mughal Empire's frontiers. Soon after ascending the throne, he promulgated 12 edicts or ordinances for the empire's general welfare and better governance. Although these ordinances confirmed Jehangir's desire to continue with Akbar's liberal policies, in practice, they remained ineffective.

The first military campaign undertaken by Jehangir was against Rana Amar Singh, the son of Rana Pratap of Mewar. The expeditions sent against Mewar in 1606 and 1608–09 proved indecisive, but in 1613–14, the campaign led by Khurram (the third son of Jehangir) proved decisive, and Rana Amar Singh submitted to the Mughals in 1615. Jehangir offered extremely liberal terms to Mewar and thus ended the long struggle between Mewar and the Mughals. After conquering Mewar, Jehangir turned his attention towards South India. He was determined to conquer Ahmednagar, but despite his best efforts was not able to have complete control over regions like Ahmednagar, Bijapur, and Golconda. Bijapur's ruler successfully arranged a peace treaty between Jehangir and Malik Ambar, the Wazir of Ahmednagar. Due to this treaty, a few forts and the territory of Balaghat became a part of the Mughal Empire, but he was never able to completely conquer the region throughout his life.

The subjugation of the Kangra Fort was another feather in Jehangir's cap. The fort surrendered to the Mughals on 16 November 1620. Jehangir visited the fort the following year and had a mosque built there. However, he lost Kandahar to the Persians when Shah Abbas of Persia, who apparently professed friendship with the Mughals, conquered Kandahar in June 1622.

A lifelong user of opium and wine, Jehangir was frequently ill in the 1620s. He tried to restore his health by visiting Kashmir but decided to return to Lahore because of a severe cold. On the journey from Kashmir to Lahore, he died near Bhimber on 29 October 1627. Noor Jahan, his wife, prevented a family feud by delaying the news of his death to her kin. She had his entrails removed and had his body conveyed by palanquin to Lahore, where he was buried in Shahdara Bagh.

◄ Mughal armies moving by boat during one of the expeditions to the Deccan

Arrival of the Dutch 1596 CE

Ninety-eight years after the Portuguese first landed in India, the first Dutchman to set foot on Indian soil was Cornelis-de-Hartmann. Three ships bearing a cargo of silver, Dutch cloth, and trinkets were followed by others and the first settlement was set up at Masulipatam in Andhra

Pradesh in 1605. Five years later, they established themselves at Pulicat, which lay to the north of Madras and, in subsequent years, established factories in Surat and Bengal. The Dutch were a powerful European sea power, and they went on to have virtual control over the East Indies (Indonesia) where they established themselves in 1602. Subsequently,

The first merchant sent to India by the Dutch East India Company was David Van Deynssen who landed at Surat in 1606.

the Dutch East India Company on the Malabar Coast monopolised the pepper and spices trade, making them one of the richest countries in Europe at the time.

The first merchant sent to India by the Dutch East India Company was David Van Deynssen who landed at Surat in 1606. Unfortunately, his mission turned out to be a disaster as the Portuguese succeeded in setting the Mughal authorities against him. After being tortured by the latter and repeatedly threatened, he committed suicide, leaving all his merchandise in their hands. Apart from textiles, the items traded by the Dutch in India included precious stones, indigo, silk, saltpetre, opium in Bengal and pepper in Malabar. A lesser-known fact is that Indian slaves were also exported to the Spice Islands and the Cape Colony.

Johan van Oldenbarnevelt established the Verenigde Oostindische Compagnie (United East India Company) as a chartered company on 20 March 1602 ▸

▴ The cemetery at Pulicat, now situated in the Thiruvellur district of Tamil Nadu. The VOC would build their first factory at Masulipatnam, followed by the second at Pulicat where they also built Fort Geldria later ▸

King James I of England who was the monarch at the time ▸

Arrival of the British 1608 CE

In 1582, an English merchant named Ralph Fitch, inspired by the tales of wealth that existed in India, as narrated by Portuguese and Dutch sailors, set sail from Gravesend and made his way to Goa via Tripoli in Syria and the Straits of Ormuz. After being away for nine years, Fitch made his way back to London in 1591 and the report he brought back said that India was not only rich in pepper, ginger, cloves, nutmegs, sandalwood, and camphor but also in precious stones like amber, sapphires, rubies, diamonds, pearls and so on. There was no doubt that India was the country to trade with, but unfortunately, even a century after the Portuguese had found a way beyond the Cape of Good Hope, no English ship had been successful in finding a way thither.

Through the sixteenth century, in the wake of Vasco da Gama, Portuguese vessels went backwards and forwards, zealously guarding the monopoly bestowed to them by the secrets unlocked by their navigators. Portugal reigned supreme over the seas, wielding a dominance too formidable for any European nation to contemplate seizing by force what had been acquired through diligent study and unwavering dedication under the visionary leadership of Prince Henry the Navigator. Those who wanted Indian goods would have to come to Lisbon where the oriental markets were held.

In Elizabethan times, English sailors were not yet as deft at sea as their Portuguese counterparts. The British also had to contend with yet another Iberian sea power, which was Spain, who themselves were trying to obtain what Portugal was enjoying. A round trip to India fetched each merchant vessel approximately 60 times the profit when compared to the cost of each trip. However, things were changing. In 1577, Sir Francis Drake and then, in 1586, Thomas Candish successfully circumnavigated the globe, in the process also correcting many navigational errors that were being made by English ships. With the information brought back by Candish and additional knowledge gained from mother sources, the British were confident that they could now finally get to India. With the defeat of the Spanish Armada, the threat from Spanish vessels also lessened considerably.

There were many false starts over the next decade and a half, each expedition bringing back more valuable information. On 13 February 1601, James Lancaster, on his flagship, the 600-ton *Red Dragon*, set sail with four other ships from Woolwhich, their combined crews amounting to

480. Also under command were the *Hector* of 300 tons and 108 men; the *Ascension*, weighing 260 tons and manned by 82 sailors; the *Susan* of 240 tons and 88 men; and, finally, a victualling ship called the *Guift* with a displacement of 130 tons. Struck by scurvy and missing India's west coast altogether, this expedition, and another subsequent voyage involving the same ships, made it to the Nicobar Islands and the Indonesian Islands but failed to get to India. On the return leg, *Susan* would sink.

Despite the hardships and lack of success, on 1 April 1608, a third voyage would set off for India. Captain Keeling was in overall command on board the *Red Dragon*, while the *Hector* was under the command of Captain Hawkins. They, once again, went around the Cape of Good Hope and then as far to the northeast as Socotra, an island off Yemen, where they separated, with Keeling sailing to Bantam and Sumatra while the *Hector* arrived off Surat, the first EIC ship to make it to India.

Hawkins was carrying a letter from King James I addressed to the Great Mughal (Jehangir), and after despatching the *Hector* to join Keeling, Captain Hawkins made his way to Agra where he made a favourable impression on the emperor. Not only did it look

British ships off Surat where the EIC had obtained permission from the 'Great Mughal' to set up their first factory ▼

Just like the Portuguese and the Dutch before them, the British, too, surrounded themselves with all the pomp and show that they could muster. The Hector, under the command of Captain Hawkins, carried various English products as gifts for the Mughal emperor

as if the Mughals were open to trading with the English, Jehangir also asked Hawkins to stay on in his Imperial Court as the English representative at an annual salary of 3,200. This was accepted by Hawkins, but it invoked such a jealous reaction from the Portuguese and other Mughal officials that the emperor did a quick volte-face. Hawkins returned to Surat (minus the promised salary) where Keeling picked him up in the *Hector* as the *Red Dragon* had already been sent home directly from Bantam. The voyage was seen to be extremely successful for it had finally not only found the route to India, but the two ships also returned with goods that fetched a 234 per cent profit.

The Portuguese, having realised that the British were now serious rivals, decided that they must be met by force. The East India Company (EIC), on the other hand, was not going to turn away from such a lucrative trade without a fight. King James I was then petitioned by the Company for much greater powers. Even though the original charter granted by Queen Elizabeth was for 15 years and still had another six years to run, King James was quick to recognise that the number of ships and merchant adventurers needed to be increased substantially. Thus, in 1615, Jehangir's court received an appeal for further concessions for the Company from Sir Thomas Roe, who had been despatched by Emperor James I of England. Due to Roe's skill in diplomacy, the EIC was able to obtain a royal charter that allowed it to conduct business freely throughout the Mughal empire.

The Red Fort in Delhi that was built by Shah Jahan on the banks of the Jamuna River ▸

Shah Jahan 1628 CE

Shah Jahan, the son of Emperor Jehangir and his second wife, Jagat Gosaini (a Rajput noblewoman), was born in Lahore, Pakistan, in 1592 CE, as Prince Mirza Shahab-ud-din Muhammad Khurram. His grandfather, Akbar, gave him the Persian name Khurram, which means 'joyful' in English. Jehangir then bestowed the title 'Shah Jahan Bahadur' upon him due to his son's early military successes against various foes, including the kingdom of Mewar, the Lodis in the Deccan, and Kangra in the north. He was not just an astute military commander but also a gifted builder, as evidenced by the redesigning of several structures inside the fort at Agra. 'The Builder of the Marvels' was one of many titles he had acquired during his lifetime. However, the name Shah Jahan, which means the 'King of the World', was possibly an apt one for the fifth Mughal Emperor during whose reign the pinnacle of artistic and architectural prowess reached its zenith.

Shah Jahan's defining phase in history began in 1607 when he was 15 and was engaged to Arjumand Banu Begum, the young granddaughter of a Persian noble, who was just 14 at the time. After their marriage, in 1612, she was given the name Mumtaz Mahal, which means 'Jewel of the Palace,' after Shah Jahan found her to be the most attractive and admirable of all the women at the time. Although Mumtaz was not Shah Jahan's only spouse, his other wives 'had nothing more than the status of marriage', according to the official court chronicler Qazwini.

After Jehangir's death in October 1627, Shah Jahan defeated his youngest brother, Shahryar Mirza and crowned himself emperor in the Agra Fort. Under his leadership, the empire militarily expanded significantly and the number of nobles and their entourages nearly quadrupled, which resulted in a significant increase in taxation from the populace at large. In the south, Hussain Shah of the cash-rich Nizam Shahi Kingdom of Ahmednagar was imprisoned in the castle at Daulatabad,

Shah Jahan astride a horse, maintained one of the most powerful armies ever in the subcontinent ▸

▲ Shah Jahan receiving a delegation

Maharashtra, which the Mughals had taken in 1632. Following Bijapur's submission in 1636, Golconda also followed suit in 1635. Shah Jahan then named one of his sons, Aurangzeb, the viceroy of the Deccan, which included Khandesh, Berar, Telangana, and Daulatabad.

During his rule, the Mughal Empire grew gradually as his sons held command of sizable armies on many fronts. He devoted his time to assembling a sizable army. It is said that Shah Jahan had 185,000 horses and over 911,400 troops in his army. He also undertook mass production of cannons. Shah Jahan built his empire into a well-oiled military machine during the course of his 30-year rule. When Shah Jahan and his sons conquered Kandahar from the Safavids, in 1638, the Persians, under Abbas II of Persia, responded by retaking the city in 1649. The Mughal armies were unable to recapture it despite repeated sieges during the Mughal–Safavid War. On the religious front, Shah Jahan was particularly harsh towards the Jesuits, who were found to be converting peasants. He got the church at Agra demolished and gave a tough time to the Portuguese.

Mumtaz passed away in 1631, while giving birth to their fourteenth child, and Shah Jahan decided to build the most stunning mausoleum in the world in her honour. This monument, which also subsequently housed his own remains along with those of Mumtaz Mahal, was dubbed '*Taj Mahal*' and was constructed over the course of 22 years by 22,000 workers.

He is credited with the building of numerous stunning monuments across North India's landscape. Shah Jahan founded Shahjahanabad in Delhi as well. Modern estimates place the price of the beautiful Takht-e-Taus (Peacock Throne), which he had made for himself, in millions of dollars.

Shah Jahan became ill in 1657, and Dara Shikoh, Mumtaz Mahal's eldest son, took control of his father's throne. His other son, Aurangzeb, accompanied by his younger brothers Shuja and Murad, marched upon Agra to stake his claim to the throne. They defeated Dara's armies, declared their father Shah Jahan incompetent to rule, and put him under house arrest in the Agra Fort, where he died in captivity in 1666. The former ruler of all of India and other lands had passed away while he was being held captive by his own son. The state's noblemen planned to carry her father's body in a parade throughout Agra at the request of Princess Jahanara Begum so that the people might bid their beloved emperor a fond farewell. Aurangzeb, however, was not in the mood for such a lavish funeral.

Finally, Sayyid Muhammad Qanauji and Kazi Qurban removed Shah Jahan's body from the prison, cleaned it, and placed it in a sandalwood coffin. The coffin was subsequently transported over the river to the Taj Mahal, where he was buried next to Mumtaz, the love of his life.

◂ The first instance of Mughal troops clashing with any European power was in June-October 1632 when Shah Jahan's army attacked the Portuguese trading settlement at Hooghly. Unhappy with the proximity to the Mughal port of Satgaon, an all-out attack was launched and escape routes along the river were cut off

Rani Karnavati was the wife of Mahipat Shah who ruled over Tehri Garhwal between 1622-31. After his death at a relatively young age, his wife took over the reins on behalf of her seven-year-old son, Prithvipati Shah. (Garhwal Regimental Centre Museum, Lansdowne) ►

Rani Karnavati

1640 CE

Raja Mahipat Shah was a warrior and a skilled military leader. After his passing, the responsibility of running Tehri Garhwal's affairs and securing the kingdom fell on his wife, Rani Karnavati. Her husband's frequent military campaigns had given her some exposure to managing the affairs in his absence and that experience now came in handy.

Rani Karnavati assured Najabat Khan that they would be spared if his men cut off their noses and fled! The Mughal army had no other option. She earned the moniker 'Naak Kati Rani' after this peculiar occurrence.

Hampered by a hostile neighbour in Kumaon, her biggest threat, however, came from the powerful Mughal Emperor Shah Jahan, who had been lured by stories of riches like silver, copper and gold mines in the region. It was widely believed that the royals dined in goldware.

In 1640, Shah Jahan sent a massive force of 30,000 soldiers led by General Najabat Khan to conquer the Garhwal region. When news of the arrival of the Mughals near Rishikesh reached the Rani, against the advice of many, she decided to fight and not surrender. Manucci, an Italian chronicler, claims that the Rani allowed Najabat Khan's forces to advance and enter the highlands until a certain point before cutting off their rear. They could not turn around, nor could they fight effectively because of a lack of knowledge of the terrain, the language as also the art of fighting in the rugged mountainous terrain. The Mughals had been trapped. The general filed for peace after realising that his soldiers were in an impossible situation. Despite being in a position to annihilate the entire body of troops, Rani Karnavati offered them another option. She assured Najabat Khan that they would be spared if his men cut off their noses and fled! The Mughal army had no other option. She earned the moniker '*Naak Kati Rani*' after this peculiar occurrence.

Rani Karnavati was more than just a warrior queen. She was a visionary credited for developing Karanpur, building monuments at Navada in Dehradun, and also building the Rajpur Canal. She is also a permanent part of folklore.

King Louis XIV, the reigning monarch ▶

The French Arrival

In 1604, King Henry IV of France authorised the establishment of the *Compagnie des Indes Orientales* (East India Company), granting the new firm a 15-year monopoly on French trade with the East Indies. This company was a precursor to a firm of the same name founded by Jean-Baptiste Colbert, though the first business was not a joint-stock company and was funded by the French Crown.

The seventeenth century saw several French efforts to trade with the East Indies. They were influenced by the successful

business ventures of the Dutch East India Company. Between the 1630s and early 1660s, French efforts were smaller in scale, but they enjoyed some success. French merchant ships traversed the Persian Gulf, the Red Sea, and the northwestern coast of the Indian subcontinent. These accomplishments paled France in comparison with England and the Dutch Republic. France's Atlantic ports pursued to compete and amalgamate with each other. The commercial and capital expertise was dispersed around the coastal regions of Brittany and Normandy.

◄ Army and camp followers breaking camp, returning to the country road, with two women on horseback, one breastfeeding, another woman seated in the right foreground with a basket

The Mughal Emperor Aurangzeb ▸

Aurangzeb

1658–1707 CE

Muhī al-Dīn Muhammad, better known as Emperor Aurangzeb and holding the title of Alamgir, was the third son of the Emperor Shah Jahān and Mumtaz Mahal. Born on 3 November 1618, in Dahod, Malwa (present-day Madhya Pradesh), he became the sixth emperor of the Mughal Dynasty in 1658. During his rule, the Mughal Empire reached its zenith before embarking on a path of slow decline, meeting its end 150 years later. He ruled for over 49 years.

He was raised as a serious-minded, devoted young man who was committed to the Muslim orthodoxy of the time and free of the sensuality and inebriation that were characteristic of the regal Mughals. Early on, he demonstrated military and leadership prowess. These traits, coupled with a hunger for power, led him to compete with his eldest brother, the bright and erratic Dara Shikoh, who was chosen by their father to succeed him as emperor. Aurangzeb served in a variety of significant positions beginning in 1636, excelling in each one. He led troops with distinction in battles against the Uzbeks and the Persians (1646–47) and during his two spells as viceroy of the Deccan provinces (1636–44, 1654–58), Aurangzeb brought the two Muslim Deccan kingdoms to the brink of submission.

The rivalry between the two brothers made the struggle for succession a foregone conclusion when Shah Jahan became very sick in 1657. By the time Shah Jahan unexpectedly recovered, the situation was extremely

Emperor Shah Jahan receiving Prince Aurangzeb in happeir times; Dara Shikoh, the eldest son of Aurangzeb was decisively defeated in 1658 by Aurangzeb who was supported by Prince Murad in the Battle of Samugarh (near Agra) and put to death the following year

serious, with neither son willing to back down. Aurangzeb demonstrated excellent tactical and strategic military competence, great dissimulation abilities, and relentless determination in his quest for power. In May 1658, after decisively defeating Dara at Samugarh, he imprisoned his father in his own palace in Agra. The bloody succession war ended after the killing of three of his brothers and two nephews.

The reign of Aurangzeb saw two distinct phases of governance. For the first 22 years, till 1680, he was seen as a skilled Muslim ruler of a Hindu-Muslim empire, though he was primarily despised for his harshness but feared and revered for his vigour and brilliance. He spent most of this time protecting the northwest against Central Asian and Persian Turks, while he also dealt with the Maratha chief, Shivaji, who twice pillaged Surat's important port in 1664 and 1670. In order to conquer the Deccan, Aurangzeb followed his great-grandfather Akbar's strategy: vanquish your foes, make peace with them, and enlist their assistance. This policy brought him control of large chunks of territories but failed to have a settled peace with Shivaji who continued to rule as an independent sovereign till his death in 1680.

Around that time, a marked change in Aurangzeb's style of handling affairs of state began to emerge. A very high

▲ Aurangzeb's brothers, Prince Shah Shuja and Prince Murad Bakhsh

Sultan Ibrahim Adil Shah II of the Bijapur Sultanate who was overthrown by Aurangzeb in 1686; Mir Jumla, who was the governor of Bengal, was defeated by the Ahoms at Saraighat ▶

The second half of Aurangzeb's rule made him come across as an intolerant, orthodox Sunni Muslim ruler; he enacted more and more puritanical laws.

degree of intolerance marked this phase of his life. Suddenly, Hindus became subordinates rather than colleagues; the Marathas, like the southern Muslim kingdoms, were targeted for annexation rather than containment; and the pious ruler of an Islamic state replaced the experienced politician of a mixed kingdom. The reimposition of the *jizya*, or toll tax on non-Muslims in 1679 (a tax that had been eliminated by Akbar), was the first overt indication of change. This was then followed by a Rajput uprising in 1680–1681 that was encouraged by Akbar, Aurangzeb's third son. Hindus continued to serve the empire, but they were no longer willing accomplices.

After the Deccan kingdoms of Bijapur and Golconda were overthrown in 1686–1687, however, the ensuing unrest sparked a long-brewing economic crisis, which was then made worse by war with the Marathas. Sambhaji, the son of Shivaji, had his empire dispersed in 1689 after being kidnapped and put to death. However, the Marathas thereafter turned to guerrilla warfare and advanced across southern India amidst a supportive populace. Aurangzeb spent the remainder of his life waging exhausting and futile sieges on Maratha hill forts.

Due to his absence in the south, Aurangzeb was unable to keep the north under strict control. Religious movements

◂Durbar of Aurangzeb

frequently grew out of agrarian unrest, as was the case in the Punjab with the Satnamis and Sikhs. Guru Tegh Bahadur, a Sikh guru who had refused to convert to Islam, was captured and put to death by Aurangzeb in 1675; his successor, Guru Gobind Singh, was in open rebellion for the remainder of Aurangzeb's rule. While he adopted a frugal lifestyle, his intolerance towards other faiths became his hallmark.

It was the second half of his rule that made him come across as an intolerant, orthodox Sunni Muslim ruler; he enacted more and more puritanical laws that were zealously upheld by *muhtasibs*, or moral censors. Many Hindu temples, shrines, and figurines were frequently demolished on his orders. Rajput backing was weakened, and Hindu sentiment was alienated by the new Islamic agenda. The Sikh and Jat rebellion was bad news for the northern kingdom. The entire administrative system was stressed due to the financial burden on the land. After nearly 49 years in power, Aurangzeb passed away in 1707, leaving behind an empire that was not yet doomed but was facing a number of grave issues.

Bent with age, Aurangzeb during the seige of Golconda. The Golconda Sultanate (later Hyderabad) was famous for its fort, palaces, factories, and diamond mines. Aurangzeb was Sunni, while the rulers of the Deccan Sultanates were Shia and accepted the suzerainity of the Shah of Persia and resisted the Mughals. Under the direction of the emperor, the city was besieged for eight months. It fell in October 1687 as the result of a bribe

Bombay 1661 CE

Bombay's strategic importance had been evident to one and all. The Delhi Sultanate had established control in 1347–48 and the sultans of the Gujarat Sultanate had governed on their behalf before transferring power to themselves.

Around the time of the Mughal Emperor Humayun, Sultan Bahadur Shah of Gujarat was obliged to sign the Treaty of Bassein with the Portuguese on 23 December 1534 and hand over the seven islands and the town of Bassein that made up Bombay. As the Portuguese, the Dutch, and the British jostled with each other to establish a hold on the west coast, in a bizarre development, the islands of Bombay were given to King Charles II in 1662 as a dowry for marrying Princess Catherine de Braganza of Portugal.

This marked the beginning of the decline in Portugal's fortunes in India. The British however, ran into considerable trouble as Shivaji's Maratha forces made it difficult for them to take control of Bombay.

Aurangzeb, following the age-old dictum that 'the enemy of my enemy is my friend', was extremely pleased with the British fighting the Marathas, and he, in turn, would issue *firmans* in their favour.

In a bizarre development, the islands of Bombay were given to King Charles II in 1662 as a dowry for marrying Princess Catherine de Braganza of Portugal.

◄ sketches of the villages that made up Bombay ▼

A Dutch Squadron under the Command of Cornelis Simonsz van der Veer launched a surprise attack on three Portuguese galleons in the Bay of Goa, Velha on 30 September 1639 ▼

▲ In 1663 the Dutch easily captured St Angelo's Fort in Kannur from the Portuguese

The capture of Cochin by VOC ships in 1682. The Dutch, who were equally hostile towards the Portuguese, also shared with them interests in Sri Lanka. Having lost control of Bombay, the Portuguese could only watch in dismay as the British Navy got more and more powerful ▼

▲ With no love lost for each other, the Dutch, the Portuguese and the British rarely missed an opportunity to attack each other

Portrait of Sir Henry Oxenden (1643-1709), Governor of Bombay and President of the East India Company ►

A portrait of Lachit Bhorphukan at the Indian Military Academy Museum ▶

Lachit Borphukan

1671 CE

On 24 November 1622, Momai Tamuli Borbarua, the supreme commander of the Ahom army, was blessed with a son—Lachit Borphukan. The Ahom kingdom in the Brahmaputra Valley of eastern India was repeatedly attacked by Turkic and Afghan kings of the Delhi Sultanate and also the Mughal Empire. This was the environment in which Lachit was raised. Young Lachit was assigned to serve as a scarf-bearer to the Ahom king. Before being named the leader of the Ahom army, he had already held other significant appointments, such as superintendent of the Royal Horse Stable and superintendent of the Royal Household Guards.

Lachit Borphukan was appointed commander soon after the Mughals, under Mir Jumla, gained control over Guwahati and compelled the Ahoms to sign the humiliating Treaty of Ghilajharighat, which was heavily biased against and restricted the Ahom kingdom. Lachit Borphukan would carry out King Chakradhwaj Singha's directive to free the entire territory from Mughal control. That was to be his mission in his life.

By the summer of 1667, Lachit had reorganised and trained the army for guerrilla warfare. Guwahati was successfully recaptured by his army from the Mughals after a series of smaller battles. As a response, Emperor Aurangzeb dispatched an additional force from Dhaka led by Ram Singh. In 1671, Ram Singh led a naval fleet along the Brahmaputra River. In the vicinity of Saraighat, they came across the Ahom boats commanded by Lachit Borphukan that were waiting for them.

The spectacle of the advancing Mughal flotilla was a daunting sight and the Ahom warriors started to waver because they were vastly outnumbered and outgunned on the open expanse of the Brahmaputra River. Lachit, who was very ill, led from the front while declaring that he would die carrying out his duty to his king

At the National Defence Academy at Khadakwasla, he Assamese general's bust dorns a corner of the parade ground ►

and country, even if it meant doing it alone. The Ahoms were inspired and came together to fight valiantly on the Brahmaputra. Closing in and grappling with the larger Mughal boats, Lachit Borphukan's men triumphed, and the Mughals were forced to flee across the Manas River, the western limit of the Ahom kingdom. The brave warrior passed away at Jorhat the next year.

At the National Defence Academy at Khadakwasla, the Assamese general's bust adorns a corner of the parade ground ▸

▴ The Battle of Saraighat. The Brahmaputra River is at its narrowest at Saraighat, narrowing down to just a kilometer in width

Ruins and sculptures of the Ahom kingdom near Sibsagar. After the Battle of Saraighat the Mughals once again reoccupied Guwahati but were subsequently defeated by Gadadhar Singa, one of the many Ahom generals who distinguished themselves during that period

Guru Gobind Singh
1675 CE

The tenth Guru of the Sikhs, Guru Gobind Singh, was born on 5 January 1667 CE, in Patna Sahib, Bihar. He was a divine messenger, warrior, poet, and philosopher who helped develop the Sikh religion into what it is today by creating the Khalsa fraternity, completing the Guru Granth Sahib, and designating the Granth Sahib as the Sikhs' next and eternal Guru.

A group of Kashmiri Brahmins came to Anandpur in 1675 to consult with Guru Tegh Bahadur because they were being driven insane by the religious extremism of

▲ Khalsa warriors, the purified and reconstituted Sikh community instituted by Guru Gobind Singh

the Mughals, who had given them six months to convert. Young Gobind Rai, who had arrived there with his playmates, questioned the Guru as he sat contemplating what to do. 'Grave are the burdens that the earth bears,' the father answered. 'Only if a truly deserving individual steps up to lay down his head will she be saved.' Gobind Rai said innocently, 'None could be worthier than you to make such a sacrifice.' Guru Tegh Bahadur urged the Brahmins to return to their village and inform the authorities that they would adopt Islam if Guru Tegh Bahadur could be persuaded to do so first. Soon after, the Guru travelled to Delhi, where he publically refused to accept Islam and was decapitated.

Following the martyrdom of his father, Gobind Rai became the tenth Guru and he decided to establish a community that would oppose the tyrannical rulers to restore justice, equality, and peace for all of mankind. He imbued his disciples with the dual spirit of a saint and a soldier through the formation of the Khalsa in 1699. The new surname of the community was now changed to Singh, meaning lion. The creation of the Khalsa created

Guru Gobind Singh (IMA) ►

a sense of unity among the Sikhs. Guru Gobind Singh then led his men in numerous battles against the powerful Mughals, ultimately leading to reconciliation. However, a lobby in the Mughal court didn't like such a development and plotted to assassinate him. Though he survived the attempt on his life, his wounds finally claimed his human form on 21 October 1708. He was only 41.

Guru Teg Bahadur (1664 –1675) was the ninth Sikh guru ▸

Sahibzadas Ajit Singh
nd Jujhar Singh, the guru's
ons were martyred in a
attle with the Mughals at
hamkaur

▲ Baba Deep Singh

◄The guru at Nanaki Chak with his trademark white hawk which earned him the sobriquet 'Chitian Bajan Valla'

A portrait of Chhatrapati Shivaji at the Indian Military Academy Museum ▸

Shivaji 1674 CE

Chhatrapati Shivaji, regarded as one of India's greatest warriors, founded the Maratha Empire in western India. He carved away an enclave from the waning Adil Shahi Bijapur Sultanate with his bravery and excellent administrative abilities. His formal coronation gave rise to the Maratha Empire. After taking control, he put in place a capable and forward-thinking government and developed an administrative structure. With the aid of well-trained troops, it is commonly known that Chhatrapati Shivaji used unconventional military strategies to defeat significantly stronger foes by taking advantage of variables such as terrain, mobility, and surprise.

Shahaji Bhosle and Jijabai welcomed a baby boy, Shivaji Bhosle, on 19 February 1630, in Shivneri Fort, situated close to Junnar in the Poona area. Shahaji served as a general in the Bijapur Sultanate. He owned an estate near Poona. He had a close relationship with his devoutly religious mother, who gave him a strong sense of right and wrong. Since Shahaji would spend most of his time away from home, a small council of ministers, which included a *peshwa* (Shamrao Nilkanth), *mazumdar* (Balkrishna Pant), *sabnis* (Raghunath Ballal), *dabir* (Sonopant), and a chief teacher (Dadoji Konddeo), were given the responsibility of overseeing Chhatrapati Shivaji's education. Baji Pasalkar and Kanhoji Jedhe were in charge of imparting military and martial arts training to the young lad who had, by then, honed his leadership skills even further. He was an avid outdoorsman who explored the Sahayadri Mountains surrounding the Shivneri Fort and became well-versed in the region. He had gathered a band of

The coronation of Shivaji at Raigad Fort on 6 June 1674 ▾

The rugged terrain of the Sahyadri Ranges that was Shivaji's home ground; formidable Maratha forts dominated the region

devoted men from the Maval District by the age of 15, and they later helped him in his early conquests.

By 1645, he had taken over the Bijapur Sultanate's vital possessions in and around Poona, including Singhagarh and Purandar as well as Torna from Inayat Khan, Chakan from Firangoji Narsala, and Kondana from the Adil Shahi governor. After his success, he became a threat to Mohammed Adil Shah who, in 1648, ordered Shahaji to be imprisoned. Shahaji was freed on the proviso that her son maintain a low profile and refrain from making any more conquests. After Shahaji's demise, Chhatrapati Shivaji resumed his conquests. Afzal Khan, a general under Mohammed Adil Shah's command, was ordered to capture him. On 10 November 1659, Chhatrapati Shivaji agreed to Afzal's proposal to hold a secret rendezvous to discuss the conditions of the bargain.

Chhatrapati Shivaji came prepared with body armour on and a metal tiger claw hidden since he anticipated it to be a trap. He was defended by his armour when Afzal Khan struck him with a dagger. Chhatrapati Shivaji then struck Afzal Khan with the tiger's claw, wounding him fatally. He then ordered his troops to attack the Bijapuri force. In the Battle of Pratapgarh, when the Maratha forces slaughtered almost 3,000 Bijapuri soldiers, Chhatrapati Shivaji easily prevailed. An upset Adil Shah then sent a large force under General Rustam Zaman who fought and lost to Chhatrapati Shivaji in the Battle of Kolhapur. On 22 September 1660, Mohammed Adil Shah's general, Siddi Jauhar, successfully besieged the Panhala Fort, giving him his long-awaited triumph. However, in 1673, Chhatrapati Shivaji re-took control of the Panhal Fort.

Due to his battles with the Bijapur Sultanate and his ongoing triumphs, Chhatrapati Shivaji caught the attention of Mughal Emperor Aurangzeb, who focused his efforts on eliminating the nascent Maratha threat. Conflicts started after raids and looting by Chhatrapati Shivaji's generals near Ahmednagar and Junnar. Shaista Khan, the governor of the Deccan and Aurangzeb's maternal uncle, was ordered to subdue Chhatrapati Shivaji. In a huge assault against him, Shaista Khan took control of his city, Poona, and several forts. He became the victim of a covert attack by Chhatrapati Shivaji in retaliation, which led to his injury and his expulsion from Poona. Later, Shaista Khan planned numerous assaults against Chhatrapati Shivaji, greatly weakening his control over the forts in the Konkan region. Chhatrapati Shivaji stormed and looted Surat, a significant Mughal commerce hub, to replenish his depleted finances. An enraged Aurangzeb sent Jai Singh I, his chief general, with a 150,000-strong army. The Mughal forces inflicted serious damage by besieging Chhatrapati Shivaji's forts, robbing them of their treasure, and killing warriors. To stop more casualties, Chhatrapati Shivaji agreed to reach a settlement with Aurangzeb. On 11 June 1665, Chhatrapati Shivaji and Jai Singh signed the Treaty of Purandar. Chhatrapati Shivaji consented to give up 23 forts in exchange for a substantial payment. To leverage Chhatrapati Shivaji's military skills to strengthen Mughal powers in Afghanistan, Aurangzeb invited him to Agra. Chhatrapati Shivaji travelled to Agra with his eight-year-old son Sambhaji but was offended by Aurangzeb's attitude. Aurangzeb put him under house arrest after he stormed out of court. However, Chhatrapati Shivaji managed to free himself from prison by using deceit. He set up the delivery of sweet baskets to the temple as offerings for prayer while feigning a serious sickness. He escaped by disguising himself as one of the bearers and placing his son in one of the baskets. Subsequently, the Mughal commander Sardar Jaswant Singh's intercession greatly contributed to the pacification of the Mughal and Maratha wars. Peace persisted until 1670 when Chhatrapati Shivaji resumed attacks on the Mughals and, within four months, had reclaimed the majority of the besieged provinces.

After gaining significant authority over areas bordering Poona and the Konkan, Shivaji decided to assume a kingly title and found the first Hindu sovereignty in the South, which was previously ruled by Muslim rulers. On 6 June 1674, in Raigadh, he was installed as the Maratha king in a lavish coronation ceremony. Pandit Gaga Bhatt presided over the coronation in front of a crowd of about 50,000 spectators. He adopted a number of names, including Haindava Dharmodhhaarak (one who elevates the sanctity of Hinduism), Kshatriya Kulavantas (leader of Kshatriyas), Shakakarta (creator of an era), Chhatrapati (paramount sovereign), and Shakakarta (founder of an era). Chhatrapati Shivaji died at the age of 52 on 3 April 1680 at the Raigad Fort, after a sudden illness.

Originally captioned 'Severndroog' (Suvarnadurg), this photo features Vijayadurg Fort in Devgad, Maharashtra. A 12th-century fort later expanded by Shivaji, Vijayadurg was an important naval stronghold for the Marathas ▼

Kanhoji Angre

1698–1729 CE

Kanhoji Angre's remarkable journey began within the walls of Sindhudurg Fort, his birthplace, where he emerged from humble origins to ascend as one of the most formidable naval commanders on the west coast of India. The foundation for Kanhoji's coastal domination was, however, laid by Chhatrapati Shivaji, who was a rare Indian monarch who understood the potential of maritime power.

◀ Except for a few pockets on the west coast, the Mughals had abdicated control to the Marathas. While the four primary European powers continued to jostle for dominance, the coastal waters were being ruled by Kanhoji Angre, perhaps the most successful Indian naval commander of all times. Between 1717 and 1720, the EIC made at least two attempts to defeat the Maratha Navy but were unsuccessful. In response to a British ship being captured by Kanhoji's men, the British attempted to capture Vijaydurg and Khanderi, but these attempts were unsuccessful

During his reign, Chhatrapati Shivaji went through various phases, his military tactics evolving with him as he metamorphosed the Marathas into a composite kingdom. After his coronation in 1674, the Maratha Army, in its shape and structure, began to operate along a defined organisational triad that centred around the infantry, cavalry, and artillery. That the Maratha forces under Chhatrapati Shivaji had kept pace with the latest techniques in warfare can be gauged by the fact that the Maratha army systematically captured English and Dutch forts in their march and subsequently in the sacking of Surat in 1664.

By then the Maratha Navy held control of the coastline from Tarapur in North Konkan to Karwar in North Karnataka, barring the regions of Bombay, Janjira and Goa. Chhatrapati Shivaji was well aware of the importance of naval warfare. He also knew that the sea-borne Portuguese were as much a threat to him as were the Mughals. By 1659, he had a fleet of 20 warships, which grew steadily in number. Since the Portuguese were more advanced in maritime tactics, he invited Portuguese mercenaries to join the Maratha Navy, even going so far as to appoint Rui Leitao Viegas as the commander of his navy. However, the Portuguese authorities were increasingly uncomfortable with these developments, for they feared the Maratha Navy would neutralise the Siddis who controlled the Janjira region. After a series of covert negotiations with the Viceroy of Goa, Joao Nunes da Cunha, Rui Viegas and 300 Portuguese sailors 'returned' to the Portuguese colours in 1668.

When Chhatrapati Shivaji was succeeded by Sambhaji in 1680,

Kanhoji Angre was barely 13 years old. His father, Tukoji had served at Suvarnadurg under Chhatrapati Shivaji with a command of 200 posts. In 1685, the commander of Suvranadurg tried to defect to the Siddis of Janjira who continued to be aligned with the Mughals, but he was thwarted by Kanhoji, which brought him to the notice of Sambhaji. After the death of Admiral Sidhoji Gujar in 1698, Kanhoji was appointed the *Sarkhel* or *Darya-Saranga* (admiral) of the Maratha Navy.

Under the command of Kanhoji, the Maratha Navy started attacking merchant ships of the EIC and began to dominate all the European fleets. He positioned his naval base at Vijaydurg, which also featured a dockyard with facilities for building vessels, using the teak grown in the Western Ghats. The Maratha naval fleet consisted of *gurabs* (warships) that weighed up to 400 tons and *gallivats* (warboats) that were lighter in displacement at around 100-120 tons. Another ship type developed

An aerial view of the sea fortress of Vijaydurg, that would become the major stronghold of the Maratha Navy that earned its fighting spurs under Kanhoji Angre. In 1653, Chhatrapati Shivaji captured the Gheria Fort from Adil Shah of Bijapur and renamed it 'Vijaydurg'. The first fortification is believed to have been constructed in 1200 CE during the reign of Raja Bhoj II. It was during Sambhaji's reign that Kanhoji Angre, alias Conajee Angria, became the admiral of the Maratha Navy. In 1698, Kanhoji made Vijaydurg the capital of his territory ▼

for coastal waters was the *pal* (man-of-war), which was a three-masted vessel armed with cannons. After the Marathas signed a treaty of friendship with the Portuguese and another with the Siddis in 1703, they began to concentrate all their forces against the EIC. Any European ship (British, Dutch, or Portuguese) sailing through Maratha territorial waters at the time was to pay a levy called *chouth*, which underlined Kanhoji's complete dominance.

Remanents of monuments at Arcot, which was strategically very well situated on the banks of the Pallar River ►

Subedars of Arcot 1692–1710 CE

Aurangzeb's policy that 'my enemy's enemy is my friend', as had been the case with the British and Shivaji vis a vis Bombay, resulted in the setting up of the Arcot Dynasty. The Mughal emperor's armies were being challenged by Marathas in the Deccan and the south and by the end of the seventeenth century, he invited Zulfikar Ali Khan to take on the Marathas. At that time, the Marathas were dominating south Carnatic from Gingee Fort, but Zulfikar Ali Khan gave a decisive blow to the power of Rajaram, their king. In 1690 the siege of Jinji was assigned to him and would continue for eight years. Though Aurangzeb was unhappy with Zulfikar Ali Khan for failing to capture Rajaram, his political fortunes continued to grow as he was promoted.

In 1692, he was appointed by Aurangzeb as the *faujdar* of the Carnatic with his seat at Arcot, and he was no longer under the legal purview of the Nizam of Hyderabad as the Carnatic had, until then, been a part of the Golconda Sultanate. Post 1703, Aurangzeb sent Zulfikar Ali Khan on various assignments to combat the Maratha insurgency, during which time his subordinate, Daud Khan Panni, an Afghan nobleman and military commander of the Mughal Empire, served as the deputy *faujdar*. In 1705, after the Siege of Wagingera, Zulfikar came under a cloud for he had let Pidia Nayak escape.

In 1710, Saadatullah Khan I was appointed the Mughal governor of the Carnatic after Daud Khan Panni moved to Gujarat as the governor. Belonging to the Navaiyit family, a subgroup of Konkani Muslims who were considered to be of Arab descent, Saadatullah Khan I would go on to become the first Nawab of the Carnatic, with active support from Daud Khan Panni.

▲ Muhammad Ismail, better known by his title Zulfikar Khan, was the son of Asad Khan, who was Aurangzeb's wazir. Appointed the first faujdar of the Carnatic by the Mughal emperor in 1692, he was a key player in the Mughal battles with the Marathas

Nader Shah

1739 CE

Nader Shah justified his invasion of India in 1739 on the grounds that the Mughal Emperor Muhammad Shah had insulted the Persian envoy at the Delhi Imperial Court. The governor of Punjab asked to strengthen the defences after Nader Shah crossed the Khyber Pass, but the Mughal emperor disregarded his appeal. Meeting perfunctory opposition, Nader Shah swept through the Mughal Empire's western frontiers capturing Ghazni, Kabul, and Lahore.

With the Persian, also known as Alexander the Second, easily running through Punjab, Muhammad Shah, along with a few allies, finally confronted him at Karnal. The two armies collided head-on, but the Mughal Army was soon surrounded and routed. Saadat Khan, the Nawab of Awadh, was captured, and there was disarray within the Mughal army's ranks.

Muhammad Shah's general, Nizam-ul-Mulk, convinced Nadir Shah to return to Persia in exchange for 20 million rupees, acting as a go-between. Pleased with Nizam's diplomatic skills, the Mughal emperor named him *Amir-ul-Umra* and made him the *wazir*. The envious Saadat Khan, who was being held prisoner, told Nader Shah not to be content with such a trifling amount, which even a province governor could provide. The fabled wealth of the Mughals was his for the asking, and the Persian king arrived in Delhi accompanied by the humbled Mughal Emperor. The keys of the Delhi Fort and treasure had already been surrendered. Nader Shah had already been paid the earlier agreed amount in exchange for his return. However, a rumour spread that Nader Shah had passed away. A few Persian soldiers were killed in the Delhi riots that were set off by this news. A furious Nader Shah issued an order for the widespread killing of the populace in any area where Persian soldier corpses had been discovered. Consequently, the citizens of Delhi were massacred and pillaged, resulting in the death of two lakh people. In addition to the war booty, he made sure to add about 100 elephants, 7,000 craftsmen, 200 carpenters, and 100 stonecutters to his train, totalling over 700 million rupees in loot.

◄ After killing and robbing the people of Delhi for 57 days, Nader Shah returned to Persia with the Koh-i-Noor diamond, the Peacock Throne, 600 million rupees worth of looted jewellery, and another six million rupees in cash

Battle of Colachel
1741 CE

Vattakottai is an elaborate sea fort designed and constructed by the Dutch Commander Eustachius De Lannoy after he was defeated by the Travancore Army at Colachel in 1741. A captive of Marthanda Varma, Lannoy was asked to continue as the Maharaja's commander and reorganise the Travancore Army using modern European techniques. His success over the next four decades earned him the Tamil name, *Dillanai, Valiya Kappithaan* or the Great Captain. In addition to the fortress, he also created a long defensive wall extending from Nedumkotta in the north up to the Western Ghats to prevent land and sea attacks. These defences would subsequently come in handy against the English, the Dutch, and later against Tipu Sultan's Mysorean Army. In *The First Firangis* J.G. Harris writes 'With the strong encouragement of Marthanda Varma, *Dillana*i had introduced specific Dutch technologies – especially artillery and gunpowder – to the reorganised Travancore army, which helped make his new country a bulwark of 'Indian' resistance to foreign invasion and colonial rule'. *Dillanai*'s was largely responsible for the spice trade remaining in Indian control. His grave at Udaygiri Fort bears an inscription, both in Latin and Tamil, noting that 'for 37 years he served the king with utmost fidelity'.

◀ The Battle of Colachel (or The Battle of Kulachal) was fought on 10 August 1741 between the kingdom of Travancore and the Dutch East India Company. Marthanda Varma's forces, led by Ananthapadmanabhan Nadar, defeated the Dutch led by Admiral Eustachius De Lannoy. The Dutch never recovered from the defeat and no longer posed a large colonial threat to India ▼

▲ Marthanda Varma

▲A stone pillar marks the spot (top right); The sea fort of Vattakottai that was subsequently built by De Lannoy

Dupleix's arrival on 15 January 1742 at Pondicherry would mark the beginning of a new phase as the French would become a lot more aggressive and take on the British for supremacy on the East Coast of the subcontinent ▼

Muscle-flexing by the French 1742 CE

Just as the Dutch were being handed one of their worst defeats on the west coast of India by Marthanda Varma's army, Joseph François Dupleix's arrival at Pondicherry as the new governor-general of all French territories was a clear sign that the French wished to consolidate their position further and intended to challenge the Portuguese, the Dutch, and the British in a no-holds-barred contest. Ever since the French governor, François Martin, had set up a trading post at Pondicherry in 1674, the French had made it their main settlement even though they briefly lost it to the Dutch.

Dupleix's reputation matched that of Robert Clive, and he too saw in the constant succession disputes an opportunity to advance the interests of the French in India and for this purpose he entered into relations with various native princes and adopted a style of oriental grandeur in his dress and surroundings. He too built an army of native sepoys, who were trained as infantrymen.

▲French sepoy

Dupleix was at the helm of affairs when the city of Madras capitulated to the French in 1746. Dupleix opposed that the town be returned under British rule, thus violating the treaty signed by La Bourdonnais. He then sent an expedition against Fort St David, and won over the Nawab of Arcot, until then a staunch ally of the British. Dupleix once again captured Fort St David, and in 1748 besieged Calcutta. Dupleix's next task was the subjugation of southern India. where the two claimants were the Nawab of Carnatic and the Deccan Sultanates, the French choosing to side with the latter. Six years after Dupleix left Pondicherry, the British captured Pondicherry but would return it later.

Dupleix's reputation matched that of Robert Clive, and he too saw in the constant succession disputes an opportunity to advance the interests of the French in India.

A multilayered tableau depicting the successful 1760–61 English siege of Pondicherry. The EIC forces (under a stylised Union Jack) are shown fighting alongside allied local soldiers, which indicates the web of regional alliances forged by the Europeans

Carnatic Wars

1744–63 CE

Global events had a major impact on India in the mid-eighteenth century, with fortunes swinging one way or the other between the British and the French. Fought between 1744 and 1763, the three Carnatic Wars

were a reflection of the same struggle for supremacy. In 1740, the War of the Austrian Succession broke out in Europe and the British were drawn into the war in 1744. Although French company officials were ordered to avoid conflict, British officials were not under any such compulsion. Emboldened by the news that a Royal Navy fleet was en route, the British initially captured a few French merchant ships. The French governor general, Joseph François Dupliex, immediately called for backup from Mauritius, which made the situation even more volatile. In July 1746, French commander Bertrand-François Mahé de La Bourdonnais and the British fleet under Commodore Curtis Barnett, and subsequently under Commodore Edward Peyton, fought an indecisive action off Negapatam where both sides incurred damage to their ships. La Bourdonnais withdrew to Pondicherry for repairs and to embark on additional guns, while Peyton pulled back to Trincomalee. The two fleets met again in August 1746, but the British refused battle and retreated to Bengal while La Bourdonnais then proceeded to lead the successful attack on Madras in September.

Nawab Muhammad Anwaruddin had cautioned both sides from attacking each other, but the French had disregarded his warning, and Joseph François Dupleix, the French governor general, had placated the Nawab by

The Carnatic Wars involved numerous nominally independent rulers and their vassals, and their struggles for succession and territory. The third conflict spread to Bengal as well ▼

promising him Fort Saint George. However, after the fort was taken by the French, Dupleix went back on his word as La Bourdonnais had promised to return it to the British. A furious Anwaruddin sent an army of 10,000 men under his son Mahfuz Khan. They were up against the 300-man French force in the Battle of Adyar and lost. The defeat sent shock waves through the country for it demonstrated the effectiveness of well-trained European forces in combating poorly trained Indian troops.

After Dupliex's volte-face, Muhammad Anwaruddin started supporting the EIC openly. The French then decided to support Husayn Dost Khan, alias Chanda Sahib, as the rightful Nawab of

Mohamed Ali Khan Wallajah was the Nawab of Carnatic after having declared himself the Nawab in 1749 and being recognised by the Mughal emperor Shah Alam II. Before him, his predecessor, Nawab Muhammad Anwaruddin (1744–1749) had supported the French. Chanda Sahib had become the Nawab, even though Wallajah had also staked his claim. After Chanda Sahib had been defeated by Clive at Arcot in 1751 he was captured by the Nayaks of Thanjavur and executed. Mohammed Ali Wallajah, after several clashes, expelled Chanda Sahib's forces and his French allies from Arcot and became an ardent ally of the EIC ▾

the Carnatic against Muhammad Anwaruddin. The French made several attempts to capture Fort Saint David at Cuddalore, but the timely arrivals of reinforcements halted these and eventually turned the tables on the French. Admiral

Edward Boscawen then besieged Pondicherry in the later months of 1748 but lifted the siege with the advent of the monsoon rains in October.

The war concluded with the signing of the Treaty of Paris in 1763, which returned Chandernagore and Pondicherry to France, but also effectively ended the French challenge.

Though a state of war did not exist in Europe, the proxy war continued, spreading inland to the Deccan as well. On one side was Nasir Jung, the Nizam, and his protege, Muhammad Ali, supported by the British, and on the other was Chanda Sahib and Muzaffar Jung, supported by the French, vying to become the Nawab of Arcot. Muzaffar Jung and Chanda Sahib were able to capture Arcot while Nasir Jung's subsequent death allowed Muzaffar Jung to take control of Hyderabad. Muzaffar's reign was short as he was soon killed, and Salabat Jung became

Nizam. In 1751, however, Robert Clive led British troops to capture Arcot, and successfully defended it. The war ended with the Treaty of Pondicherry, signed in 1754, which recognised Muhammad Ali Khan Walajah as the Nawab of the Carnatic.

The outbreak of the Seven Years' War expanded the French-British conflict and became known as the Third Carnatic War, which was fought between 1756–1763 CE. The conflict spread beyond Southern India and into Bengal where British forces captured the French settlement of Chandernagore in 1757 and also successfully defended Madras. Sir Eyre Coote defeated the French, commanded by the Comte de Lally, at the Battle of Wandiwash in 1760, after which, the French capital of Pondicherry fell to the British in 1761. The war concluded with the signing of the Treaty of Paris in 1763, which returned Chandernagore and Pondicherry to France, but also effectively ended the French challenge.

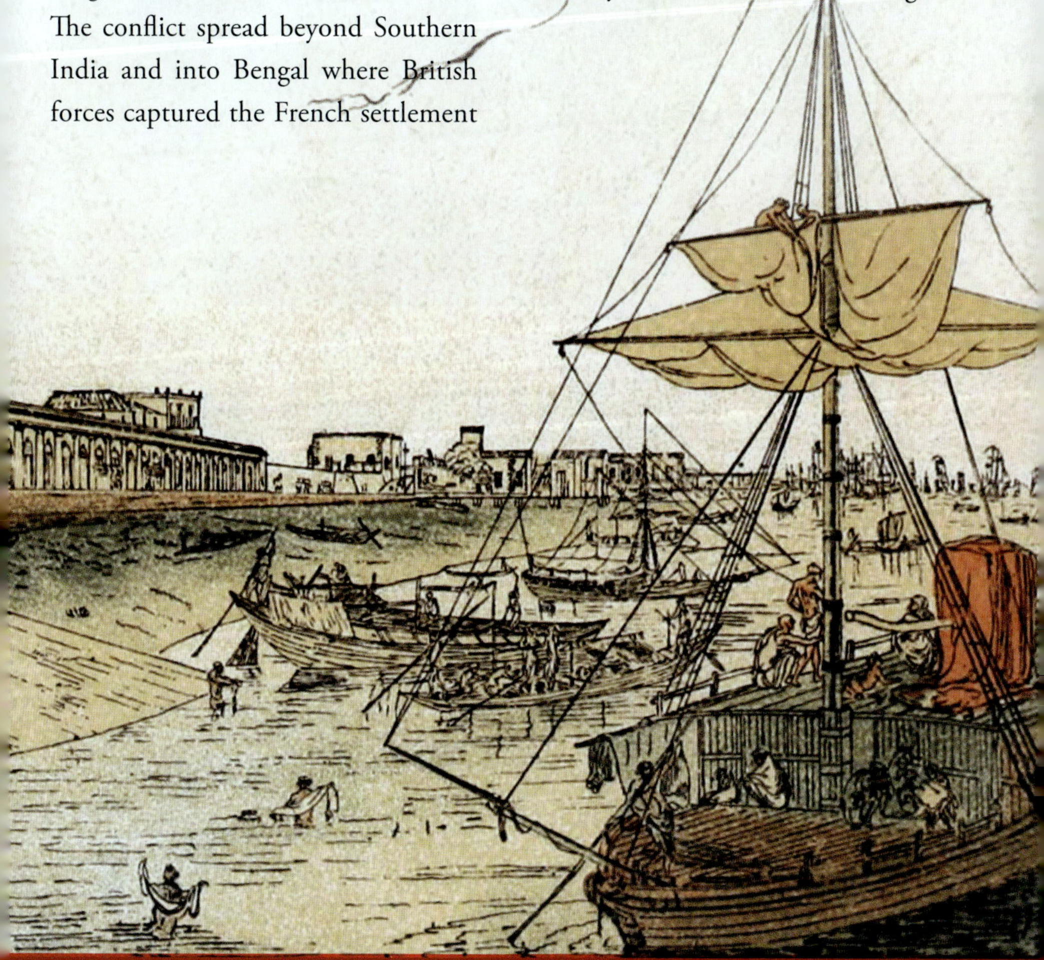

Sambhaji, whose capture and execution by Aurangzeb temporarily checked the dominance of the Maratha Empire ▶

Balaji Baji Rao

1749 CE

Shivaji took the title of *Chhatrapati* in 1672. This also marked a transformation of his army, which began to reflect, in its structure, more and more the Mughal Army, which, by then, was the Maratha's principal fore. The Marathas started to not only dominate the Western Ghats but also the Bijapur and Golconda Sultanates, which were their main source of revenue. Their deployment of *pindaris,* who were organised gangs of looters, and their tendency to adopt a scorched earth policy made them an unconventional and deadly foe, which constantly had the Mughals on the run. But after the death of Chhatrapati Shivaji in 1680, his son Chhatrapati Sambaji, after initial successes, began to lose his grip and in 1689, he was caught, tortured, and executed by Aurangzeb. Immediately thereafter, the Mughals started to recapture most of the territories which they had lost to Shivaji, and the Maratha's powerful empire began to shrink rapidly.

Along with the execution of Sambaji, his son Shahu, then aged seven, was taken hostage by the Mughals. After Aurangzebs's death, Shahu made his way back to Maharashtra and after

◂ Chhatrapati Shahu and Nana Saheb, who led the Maratha resurgence

the Battle of Jhaju, he was recognised as the rightful heir to Shivaji's throne. Balaji Vishwanath assisted Shahu in consolidating his grip on a kingdom that had been racked by civil war and persistently intruded on by the Mughals under Aurangzeb. In April 1720, after the death of Baji Vishwanath, Shahu appointed his 19-year-old son, Balaji Baji Rao, as Peshwa. During his 20-year tenure as the Peshwa, he engaged in several military conflicts such as the Nizam's Carnatic campaigns (1725–27) and the Maratha invasion of the Deccan (1739). He was also responsible for the Maratha raid on Delhi in 1737.

Nana Saheb, as the Peshwa, was also largely responsible for the debacle during the Third Battle of Panipat.

Balaji Baji Rao, also known by the sobriquet 'Nana', later became 'Nana Saheb'. Just after becoming Peshwa, his position was challenged by other Maratha chieftains such as Tulaji, the son of Kanhoji Angre, and Raghoji Bhosale. Raghoji's resentment stemmed from his desire to be the Peshwa himself. Apart from having to sporadically fight the Portuguese, Baji Rao also had to deal with the Nizam of Hyderabad and his successors who were not willing to fulfil their treaty obligations. In Karnataka, the Muslims were challenging the Maratha sovereignty, while to their immediate north, the Gaikwad of Baroda and the Rajput rulers were also dissatisfied with them. To make matters worse, there was also an internal dispute within the Marathas as Scindia and Holkar were jostling for power. The financial condition of the Marathas was deplorable.

Nana Saheb first had to pay attention to the royal treasury, which gradually recovered during his 20-year reign. However, his career saw the best and worst moments as the Maratha power in India reached its peak under his watch. Chimaji Appa, the younger brother of Vishwanath Balaji, and his cousin, Sadashivrao Bhau, along with Nana Saheb's younger brother, Raghunath Rao, were successful in establishing and consolidating Maratha dominance in India. During Nader Shah's invasion, the Mughal emperor Muhammad Shah summoned the Nizam of Hyderabad, Asaf Jah, to Delhi. Accepting the emperor's request, Asaf Jah mobilised his army and marched to

Delhi in a bid to resist the invasion. In the absence of the Nizam, Nana Saheb launched an attack on Hyderabad with the aim of capturing the six provinces of the Deccan. Having already secured Malwa through the Battle of Bhopal from Jai Singh II, Nana Saheb sought to expand the Maratha influence by targeting Hyderabad in the absence of the Nizam. Then again in 1756, Nana Saheb aligned with the British and helped defeat Tulaji at Vijanagar in order to place Manaji at the head of the Maratha Navy. This was, perhaps, one of his greatest blunders for it ended Maratha maritime dominance and allowed the British to consolidate their hold. As the Peshwa, he was also largely responsible for the debacle during the Third Battle of Panipat.

Adil Shah of Bijapur who helped the Mughals fight against the Ahmednagar Sultanate. Aurangzeb's all-consuming fascination with the Deccan led to endless wars and sieges ►

Decline of the Mughals

An old proverb, 'Delhi is distant' has guided the geopolitics of the Deccan over centuries. The lands of the peninsula were fertile and their wealth in gold and diamonds was legendary, catching the attention of every ruler from the north. However, most baulked at the thought of the logistics involved in mounting an invasion, and it was left to the eccentric Muhammad bin Tughlaq to first defy conventional wisdom and bring the area south of the Vindhyas and Satpuras under the control of Delhi. His passing ended the North's brief flirtation with the South, and it was left to the Afghani Dynasty of the Bahmani kings to take possession of the region. Their subsequent splitting into five sultanates gave the region a semi-autonomous status, which was never too far from the radar of the Mughal Emperors. Akbar, Jehangir, and Shah Jahan had set about mounting forays but were too wise to get sucked into the politics of the region full-time. Emperor Aurangzeb, however, was drawn to the Deccan like a moth to a flame and, in the process, literally reduced his empire to a pale shadow of itself.

Aurangzeb had been appointed the viceroy of the Deccan on 10 May 1636 by Shah Jahan at the age of 18, and right from the start, along with his trusted Mir Jumla, had been on a trail of destruction, reaping in vast riches, including the Kohinoor diamond from the Kollur Mines on the Kistna River, which later allowed him to defeat Dara Shikoh is his own war of succession.

At the age of 63, Aurangzeb returned to the Deccan, but he had a deadlier foe on his flank, for the Marathas had, by then, emerged as a potent fighting force

Abul Hasan Qutb Shah was the eighth and the last ruler of the Qutb Shahi Dynasty ▼

◄ Bahadur Shah I, who succeeded Aurangzeb, reigned from 1707 to 1712 but could do little to arrest the decline of the Mughal Empire that had set in with his father

under Shivaji. Aurangzeb could hardly, at the time, have realised he would never see Delhi again or, for that matter, he would still be fighting in the Deccan a quarter of a century later.

Both Bijapur and Golconda Sultanates, when attacked by Aurangzeb, had learnt from the Marathas and laid to waste the entire countryside. Even though the Mughals were the ones laying siege, their own armies were on the brink of starvation. Bijapur succumbed in November 1686, while Golconda, led by Abul Hassan Tana Shah, surrendered in June 1687 following a prolonged and intense struggle. The Mughal army, grappling with famine and a devastated landscape, reached a critical state by that time. Aurangzeb had conquered Bijapur and Golkonda, and wiped out the Adil Shahi and Qutub Shahi dynasties, but in the process, the direct result of his destructive zeal was to eliminate the only powers that at the time made for some sort of settled order in the peninsula. This greatly strengthened the hands of the Marathas and laid the foundation for the decline of the Mughal Empire.

The quagmire of the Deccan not only sucked in Aurangzeb, but he took with him his three principal sons, Bahadur Muhammad, Azam Shah, and Muhammad Kam Bakhsh. The Mughal armies were huge, and, invariably, would win the battle or see each siege invariably succeed. However, in the long term, the Mughals were bleeding slowly. The Rajputs, their most loyal allies of earlier Mughal Emperors, had been alienated by Aurangzeb and, in any case, could hardly be expected to exterminate the Marathas who were, like them, also Hindus.

The crop of generals under Aurangzeb soldiers was not as hardy as those of his predecessors and none of their generals could be trusted. In addition, three or four generations of court life had ruined their ancient manliness. According to the British writer Stanley Lane Poole, Babur would have scorned to command such officers as those that surrounded Aurangzeb in his gigantic camp at Bairampur. Instead of hardy swordsmen, they had

Ever since the Sikhs sided with Dara Shikoh during the war of succession, Aurangzeb was furious with them and there were constant skirmishes. Mai Bhago depicted riding a white stallion, battling Mughal soldiers ▼

become padded dandies. They wore wadding under their heavy armour, and instead of plain soldierly bearing, they luxuriated in comfortable saddles, velvet housings, and bells and ornaments on their charges. They were adorned for a procession when they should have been in rough camping outfits. Their camp was as splendid and luxurious as if they were on guard at the palace in Delhi. The very rank and file grumbled if their tents were not furnished as comfortably as in quarters at Agra, and their requirements attracted an immense crowd of camp followers, 20 times as numerous as their effective strength. An eyewitness described Aurangzeb's camp at Galgala in 1695 as having 60,000 cavalry and 100,000 infantry for whose upkeep there were 50,000 camels and 3,000 elephants, in addition to sutlers, merchants, and artificers who were much more numerous. The whole camp was a moving city containing five million souls, abounding not only in provisions but in all things that could be desired. There were 250 bazaars, every amir or general having one to serve him and his men. The royal tents alone were spread across a distance of three miles!

The alienation of the Rajputs and the persecution of the Sikhs would also have serious long-term repercussions and contribute to the disintegration of the Mughal Empire. Though the Sikhs had been in conflict with the Mughals even earlier, relations remained sour throughout Aurangzeb's long tenure. After Guru Gobind Singh's passing in 1708, the leadership of the Khalsa Fauj passed on to the newly-converted Sikh, Banda Singh Bahadur, who continued to fight further battles against the Mughals and established the first Khalsa Rule in 1710. However, he was captured in 1715 and put to death a year later. Subsequently, the Sikhs reorganised themselves into *misls* creating the Dal Khalsa, which fought further battles against the Mughals under the leadership of Jassa Singh Ahluwalia and other *misl* leaders. The weakened Mughal hold in Punjab would create a vacuum that would be filled by the northward -thrusting Marathas.

From the Mughal perspective, Aurangzeb's handling of the Rajputs had been nothing short of suicidal. The peace established during the time of Emperor Akbar was broken by the religious intolerant policies of Aurangzeb, and in 1679 the states of Mewar and Marwar rebelled against the Mughal Emperor. Even after Aurangzeb's death, the Mughal Empire was further weakened by ruinous wars of succession in the following three decades. Most Muslim nobles had asserted their independence whilst the Marathas had by then captured vast swathes of territory in central and northern India. In the South, the British and the French were jostling to emerge as the dominant European power.

As lesser kingdoms, until then subservient to the Mughals, began to assert themselves, the situation became worse. Muazzam, who took the title of Bahadur Shah after winning the war of succession, tried to adopt an appeasement policy with the Rajputs by granting independence to Mewar and Marwar, but this failed to bring the Rajputs back into the Mughal fold. The Marathas, despite the release of Shahu, continued to fight amongst themselves and also the Mughals.

In the Punjab, even though Guru Gobind Singh was given a high *mansab*, the rebellion by Banda Singh

◄ Ajit Singh, who ruled Mewar between 1679 and 1724. The Mughals were forced to accept humiliating peace terms with the Rajput rajas in 1710

A pale shadow of what he had inherited, the Mughal Empire a few decades after Aurangzeb's death

carried the fight with the Sikhs forward as well. After Bahadur Shah's demise, the Mughal court became a virtual den of 'kingmakers' and the subsequent emperors were 'lame ducks'. Jahandar Shah was the first puppet ruler, as the real power lay in the hands of the *wazir*, Zulfiqar Khan.

The thirteenth Mughal Emperor, Muhammad Shah (1719–48), could not stop the disintegration of the empire despite the fact that the imperial court administration was corrupt and weak whereas the surrounding countryside continued to be extremely rich. The Mughal Empire suffered irreversible harm from Nader Shah's invasion. The Persians gained control of Mughal provinces spread all along the Indus. Ahmad Shah, Nadir Shah's successor, also invaded India several times between 1748 and 1767 while the hapless Mughals could do little to check them.

The Raja of Mandi, Raja Sidh Sen, ruled his state between 1628 and 1727. The geographical location of the Himalayan princely states allowed them to exist in relative peace and quiet ►

Vijaydurg 1756 CE

Kanhoji Angre's success as a naval commander had been spectacular and by the time of his death, in 1729, he had carved out a virtual maritime kingdom for himself. He controlled the entire coastline from Sawantwadi to Bombay, which is the entire coastal belt of Maharashtra. He built coastal fortifications on almost all creeks, coves, and harbours. Extending south from Surat to Goa, the main Maratha naval bases were at Bankot, Anjanvel, Jaygad, Vijaydurg, and Sindhudurg. The East India Company (EIC) ships, virtual floating flotillas by themselves, were challenged by the Maratha *ghurabs* who themselves had a fair amount of firepower. They had broadsides of six and nine-pounder guns and carried two nine or 12-pounders on their main decks that pointed forward through port holes cut in the bulkheads. The *gallivats* were mostly armed with light swivel guns, but some also mounted six or eight cannons, either two or four-pounders. These boats were propelled by 40 to 50 oars. Having somewhat ironically branded Kanhoji a 'pirate', the EIC first ran into him in 1702 when Kanhoji abducted a merchant vessel from Calicut with six English sailors and took it to his harbour. Five years later, he attacked the East Indiaman *Bombay* which blew up during the fight. Only the heaviest European merchant vessels that were heavily armed seemed immune from attack.

During Sambhaji's seven-year reign, he had been at loggerheads with not just the Mughals but had also engaged in battles with the Siddis and the Portuguese, invading Goa in 1683. In the constant game of musical chairs, to sustain his fight against the Portuguese who were in an alliance with the Mughals, Sambaji had to sign a treaty with the EIC a year later. In 1687, Sambaji's luck ran out as the Mughals closed in on him from the north and the south. Humiliated and tortured by the Mughal imperial army, he was asked to convert to Islam, but refused to do so and was, thus, executed. As the Maratha kingdom went into a state of turmoil and a virtual war of succession, Kanhoji held firm along the coast, giving his support to Tarabhai, Shivaji's daughter-in-law, who continued the fight against Aurangzeb's Mughal armies camping in the Deccan.

When Chhatrapati Shahu ascended the leadership of the Maratha Empire, he appointed Balaji Viswanath Bhat as his *senakarta* (military commander) and negotiated an agreement with Angre in 1707 wherein Angre retained his apex position as the head of the Maratha Navy.

Kanhoji's complete domination of the coastal waters resulted in his intensifying attacks on European ships on the western coast of India. In 1712, his navy captured the yacht HCS *Algerine* that belonged to the Governor of Bombay, and in the process killed the chief of their Karwar factory and took his wife hostage. The East Indiamen *Somers* and *Grantham* were intercepted near Goa as these vessels were on their voyage from England to Bombay. At around the same time, Kanhoji disabled a 30-gun man-of-war, which was conveying Portuguese 'armado' and captured it. After a short-lived armistice with the British in 1715, the Governor of Bombay, Charles Boone, teamed up with the Portuguese and tried to capture Khanoji, but instead met with even more reverses.

Kanhoji died in 1729, and after his demise, two of his illegitimate sons, Manaji and Tulaji, laid their claim to be the *sarkhel*. With the Peshwa having to intervene, Manaji had control of the northern coastal belt with his headquarters at Kulba while Tulaji held the southern half and Vijaydurg. Extremely aggressive and an equally skilful seaman, Tulaji ran riot and captured more English ships than his illustrious father. *Charlotte, William, Svern, Darby, Restoration, Pilot, Augusta,* and *Dadabhoi* were captured in quick succession. Tulaji also captured Anjanvel from the Siddis. To make matters worse for himself, he also aligned with the Portuguese and went against the Maratha Confederation.

Under Commodore Sir James Watson's command, the British first attacked Suvarnadurg in 1755 while the Peshwa, Balaji Baji Rao, attacked from the east. After a fierce and bloody battle, the fort fell, after which Watson withdrew to Bombay to sit out the monsoon. In February 1756, Watson converged on Vijaydurg and started to bombard the fortress. He had with him Colonel Clive with 500 *topasses* (mainly Goan) and other troops. The Maratha ships were anchored at the mouth of the creek and bunched up, almost hull to hull. Under bombardment from the EIC ships, the entire Angre fleet was sunk while the bombardment of the fort caused considerable damage as the magazine had been blown up. On 11 February, Clive delivered the *coup de grace* when his marines landed and captured Vijaydurg. Tulaji had tried to negotiate with the Peshwa camp but was promptly arrested. A huge amount of booty was captured. 250 pieces of cannons, stores and ammunition, 100,000 Rupees and 30,000 invaluable items fell into English hands.

Under bombardment from the EIC ships, the entire Angre fleet was sunk while the bombardment of the fort caused considerable damage as the magazine had been blown up.

British Expansion I

Among the first European forts in India, Fort Emmanuel was built in 1503 by the Portuguese. Situated at Fort Kochi, it was once a symbol of the alliance between the ruler of Kochi and the monarch of Portugal. Fort Aguada in Goa was next, for it not only secured the Portuguese position but also had within it the only source of fresh spring water. The British built Fort Saint George in Madras between 1639–

▲ After the Battle of Vijaydurg, the Maratha Peshwa, Balaji Baji Rao, aligned with the British and replaced Tulaji with Manaji as the Maratha naval commander. This 'self goal' effectively ended the Maratha domination in the coastal waters, and allowed the European ships to run unhindered. As the British and the French fought various campaigns on the land to establish their supremacy, their ships were quick to attack each other on the seas as well. English ships, referred to as 'Indiamen' were, by then, superior to what the Portuguese, Dutch, and French had to offer. The fleet of merchantmen of the EIC, which was their lifeline between England and India, were among the best-built ships with extremely good seamen on board

1644 and only felt confident enough to challenge the Portuguese and Dutch domination on the west coast in the early eighteenth century.

▲ The British, in order to safeguard their trade activities in the Malabar region and counter the French who were established at Mahe by 1725, built a fort around the outlying hills of Tellicherry with the support of the Kolathiri Raja. From 1776 to 1784, the fort was garrisoned with a strong military force, which made the British the most powerful player on the Malabar Coast, virtually checkmating any thoughts of Portuguese, French, or Dutch expansion ▶

English ships, referred to as 'Indiamen' were, by then, superior to what the Portuguese, Dutch, and French had to offer. The fleet of merchantmen of the EIC, which was their lifeline between England and India, were among the best-built ships with extremely good seamen on board

Plassey 1757 CE

The struggle between the Nawabs of Bengal and the EIC grew intense in the early 1700s. Following Aurangzeb's demise, the Nawabs declared their independence from the imperial Mughals like other regional powers at the time. Murshid Quli Khan and Alivardi Khan, who preceded Siraj ud Daulah, were powerful rulers and they refused to make any concessions for the EIC, which also prevented the British from building any further defences at Fort William on the eastern bank of the Hooghly. The Nawabs demanded hefty tributes in exchange for granting the EIC permission to trade and refused the Company the right to mint currency. There was further bad blood, with the Nawabs accusing the Company of lying, weakening their authority and sabotaging the Bengal government's revenue stream. The British were not sticking to tax payments and, instead, sent nasty letters and attempted to make the Nawab and his officials look foolish.

On its part, the Company stated that the EIC's trade was being severely hampered by the demands of the local officials, and trade could only recover if the duties were eliminated. It was also argued that to increase trade, the British needed to strengthen their fortifications, purchase villages and repair their settlements. Finally, the mounting tensions led to the Battle of Plassey, which gained notoriety as the first significant victory won by the British, opening the door into the Indian hinterland.

Following Alivardi Khan's death, Siraj ud Daulah became the Nawab of the Bengal Subah in 1756. It was expected that he would not deviate from the policies of his predecessors. On the other hand, eager to install a puppet leader who would voluntarily grant other benefits and concessions in trade to the EIC, the British made an unsuccessful attempt to prop up Murad ud Daula, one of Siraj ud Daulah's adversaries, as the new nawab. An enraged Nawab demanded that the Company cease fortification, stop interfering in his dominion's political affairs, and pay the due revenues.

Citing the example of Cuddalore, where the French had attacked Fort St

Robert Clive, then a lieutenant colonel, had, the previous year, fought Vijaydurg ▼

David, the English refused to stop work saying war with France was imminent. Following the failure of negotiations, the Nawab marched to the English factory at Kasimbazar with 30,000 soldiers, seized the executives of the EIC, closed the warehouse, disarmed all Englishmen, and blockaded English ships. To take command of the EIC's assets in Calcutta, Siraj ud Daulah marched against the fort. John Zephaniah Holwell, who was taken captive, subsequently wrote a questionable account about the 'Black hole of Calcutta', in which he claimed over a hundred Englishmen and sepoys died of suffocation.

Upon learning of the disaster at Calcutta, EIC officials dispatched an army of 900 Europeans and 1,500 Indian sepoys under the command of Colonel Robert Clive on 16 October 1756, supported by a small naval fleet. Ironically, after Siraj ud Daulah became the Nawab, he replaced most of his father's ministers, including the wazir and the minister in charge of his household troops. Mir Jaffar, his key general, had retained his post but since then had let British emissaries know he was willing to hold back his troops and as the paymaster, siphon off two crores in exchange for being made the Nawab.

At Palashi with Mir Jafar's help, Clive would defeat Siraj ud Daulah's army for the loss of 23 dead ▼

The battle took place at Palashi on the banks of the Hooghly River, about 150 km north of Calcutta and south of Murshidabad, the then-capital of the Bengal Subah. Clive's artillery combined with Mir Jaffar's treachery, who simply sat back and watched the carnage unfold in front of him, carried the day for the British, who were then quick to capture and execute Siraj ud Daulah. The Battle of Plassey (the anglicised version of Palashi) would become a watershed in the subcontinent's subsequent history.

Great Britain and France had been struggling for control in India for several years. In 1746, Fort Saint George at Madras had been captured by the French led by Bertrand-Francois Mahe de La Bourdonnaix, as both countries found themselves on opposite sides during the War of the Austrian Succession. It was returned to the British in 1748 as per the Treaty of Aix-la-Chapelle. Following the fresh outbreak of war in Europe, both sides were soon in conflict again. By 1757, Britain held the upper hand in India after several victories by Robert Clive.

In 1756, when Siraj ud Daulah took over the Bengal Subah, despite agreements to the contrary, the British started to fortify the original Fort William, which they had started to construct in 1696 after Aurangzeb gave them permission to do so. Sir Charles Eyre started construction near the bank of the Hooghly River with the southeast bastion and the adjacent walls. In 1700, it was named after King William III. John Beard, Eyre's successor, added the northeast bastion in 1701 and, in 1702, started the construction of the Government House at the centre of the fort. Construction ended in 1706 but once Fort Saint George fell to the French, the British began to further fortify their positions. After it fell to Siraj ud Daulah, the British built another fort and also named it Fort William.

Saadat Ali Khan, despite being of Persian origin and belonging to the Shia faith, was the first Nawab of Awadh, having initially been appointed the governor in 1722 ▸

Nawabs of Awadh

Prior to the Iron Age in 1200 BCE, Awadh's history, also known as Oudh, relied on oral traditions aligning with the Puranas and Ramayan texts. It narrates tales of kings and kingdoms around Hastinapur and Ayodhya. The earliest recorded history talks of a widely extended monarchy, the Raghuvamsa Dynasty, whose authority over the region was limited. The land, covered by forest, was hardly explored or cultivated, and many basic kinds of cereals were not yet known. There existed a thinly-spread population of Ahirs and other pastoral tribes.

The Islamic conquest of India is dated to the invasion of Mahmoud Ghazni in 1000 CE. His nephew, Masood, entered Awadh with a large army and penetrated to the furthest corners, but failed to establish himself. The kingdom of Kanauj established itself in Ayodhya around the same time. Through the eleventh and twelfth centuries CE, the region was ruled by various clans of Rajputs. In 1192 CE, Shihab ad-Din Ghori founded the Delhi Sultanate by defeating Prithviraj Chauhan and the king of Kanauj, Raja Jaichand. There followed vigorous attacks in all directions as important Rajput cities were put to the sword. Mount Abu, Anhilpur-Patan, Gwalior, Benaras, Gaya, and Ajmer fell in quick succession.

Most of the subjugated Rajput clans migrated en masse southward across the Vindhyas, northward into Kumaon, westward to Rajasthan, and towards Ayodhya, the old capital. This vacuum was filled by Rajput clans who were at ease with the entrenched Mohommadan and Mughal powers in the region, and they took service in the armies of the conqueror, gradually forming the backbone of the Mughal army. Both Jehangir and Shah Jahan were sons of Rajput mothers. Awadh's strategic location between the Mughals and Bengal allowed it to control the Gangetic Doab. It was the granary of India, making it an extremely wealthy region.

From 1394 to 1478, Awadh became a part of the Sharqi Sultanate of Jaunpur and, in 1555, Emperor Humayun made it a part of the Mughal Empire. Jehangir then allowed Sheik Abdul Rahim and his descendants, the *Sheikhzadas,* to control the region. In the post-Aurangzeb period, pleased with Saadat Ali Khan, the Mughal Emperor appointed him the governor of Agra where he fought and defeated the Jats. He was then recalled and given charge of Awadh where he fought and defeated the *Sheikhzadas*. Despite being Shias, Nawab Saadat Ali Khan's successors became the rulers of Awadh. They would fight wars with the Marathas in the Battle of Bhopal (1737) and against the Maratha Confederacy in the Battle of Karnal (1739). They joined Ahmad Shah Durrani during the Third Battle of Panipat (1761) and played a role in the restoration of Shah Alam II to the imperial throne. The Nawab of Awadh also fought the Battle of Buxar (1764) and continued to play a pivotal role in the political landscape.

Asaf-ud-Dowlah, the fourth Nawab of Awadh, who shifted the capital of Awadh from Faizabad to Lucknow ▶

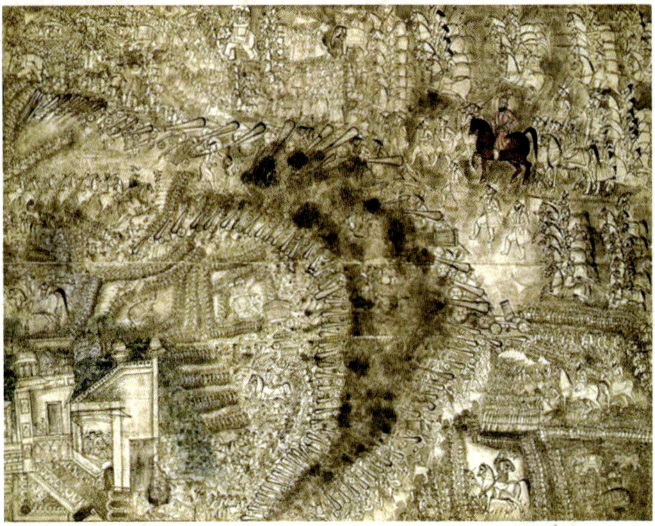

Third Battle of Panipat 1761 CE

After Plassey, while the British were consolidating their hold from the east, the Maratha Empire's northern expeditionary force, under Sadhashiv Rao Bhao, clashed with the Ahmad Shah Durrani (or Abdali) in the Third Battle of Panipat, on 14 January 1761. Durrani was supported by the Rohilla Afghans of the Gangetic Doab who were led by Najib-ud-Daulah and Shuja-ud-Daula, the Nawab of Awadh, plus a Mughal force under Prince Mirza Jawan Bakht and some others. On the battlefield, Durrani and Najib-ud-Daulah, both Pashtun Afghans, led the heavy cavalry and mounted artillery (*zamburak and jizail*) against the Marathas, who were using French tactics. The conflict is regarded as one of the biggest and bloodiest of the eighteenth century, and it may have resulted in the maximum number of deaths in a single day.

The Mughal Empire's 27-year-old war of attrition had taken a toll and the Marathas, under Peshwa Baji Rao, had pushed the Mughals back northwards and extended their grip over Gujarat and Malwa. After finally defeating the Mughals in 1737, on the outskirts of Delhi, Baji Rao had control of the erstwhile Mughal lands south of Delhi. By conquering Punjab in 1758, Baji Rao's son, Balaji Baji Rao, also referred to as Nana Saheb, came into direct conflict with Durrani.

He organised an army from the Pashtun tribes in 1759 and defeated the weaker Maratha garrisons stationed in Punjab. Durrani's grand alliance then clashed with the Marathas under the leadership of Sadashiv Rao Bhau. The Marathas had mobilised an army of 45,000–60,000 soldiers and some 200,000 civilians, many of whom were pilgrims on their way to Hindu sacred sites in North India. On 14 March 1760, the Marathas left Patdur and began their northward march. Shuja-ud-Daulah kept his options open but, finally, in July, decided to join the Afghan-Rohilla coalition. For the Marathas, this was a major strategic setback in the long run because Shuja supplied crucial funding for the subsequent extended Afghan stay in North India.

◄ Sadhashiv Rao Bhao, the Maratha commander during the Third Battle of Panipat

▲ Prince Mirza Jawan Bakht, the grandson of Aurangzeb who commanded the Mughal Army that fought alongside what was termed the 'Grand Muslim Alliance'

◄ Ahmad Shah Durrani

Sir Hector Monro, the commander of the East India Company forces ▶

Battle of Buxar

1764 CE

If the Battle of Plassey had opened the gates for the British into the hinterland, the Battle of Buxar, seven years later, set the stage for the British Raj to further make inroads into the subcontinent. The battle was fought between the British, with their English and sepoy troops, and the army of the Mughal Emperor, Shah Alam II. The East India Company's colonialist aspirations and the Nawab of Bengal's alleged misuse of trade privileges are said to be the main causes of the clash between the two sides. Buxar was the culmination of a series of clashes between the Mughals, the Nawab of Awadh, and the Sultan of Bengal who had come together to fight the expanding influence of the East India Company.

▲ Nawab Suja-ud-Daula, the Nawab of Oudh

The genesis of the conflict went back to when Mir Jaffar was instated as the Nawab of Bengal in place of Siraj ud-Daulah by the British after the Battle of Plassey. However, he detested the English interference and attempted to plot against them by allying with the Mughal Emperor Shah Alam II and also the Dutch whose ships were seen on the Hooghly. In 1760, Mir Jaffar was replaced by Mir Qasim, his son-in-law. In 1762, to avoid British interference, Qasim moved his capital from Murshidabad to Munger Fort. He also employed foreign specialists, some of whom were at odds with the British. Furthermore, English merchants were not given any preferential treatment, being treated at par with their Indian counterparts. These elements provided the impetus for the English to want to depose him, and in 1763, hostilities broke out between the British and Mir Qasim and his two allies.

▼ Mir Qazim Khan, the Sultan of Bengal

In this conflict, the English forces emerged victorious at Katwah, Murshidabad, Giria, Sooty, and Munger. Having failed to dislodge the British from Patna, Emperor Shah

◄ The Mughal Emperor Shah Alam II who was captured and forced into exile as per the Treaty of Allahabad

Alam, assembled a well-trained army and marched towards Bengal. By the time he set up camp at Buxar, on the Awadh-Bengal border, he had been joined by Shuja-ud-Daula and Mir Qasim, swelling his numbers to around 50,000. His infantry was commanded by the Frenchman, Jean Baptiste Gentil. Strategically, Shah Alam's position was a good one—protected on his left side by the Ganges River and on his right by the Torah Nulla, while the front had defensive earthworks.

As news arrived in Calcutta of the advancing triple alliance, Major Hector Munro was selected to lead a force consisting of a mere 4,200 men (3,000 of which were sepoys or native troops) plus a 1,000-strong cavalry group. Munro left Bankipur on 9 October and headed for Buxar, where he arrived on 22 October. Shah Alam could hardly believe that such an inferior force had been sent to take him on, and though Gentil implored the Mughal Emperor to launch an attack before the British could offload their equipment from the boats, he waffled, By the time the attack started, Munro had managed to get his troops into a defensive position, from where they could take on the advancing Mughal cavalry.

The Battle of Buxar was won by the British in large part due to the unwavering performance of the native sepoys, who literally turned the battle on its head with their disciplined performance, maintaining their defensive square formations even when the situation looked so hopeless that Shah Alam was convinced he had already won the battle. After the Mughal artillery was neutralised by the smaller and more mobile British cannons, British infantry marched forward in columns and smashed their opponents into disarray. There was a chaotic retreat of men, camels, bullocks, and elephants. Shah Alam fled across the Torah Nulla, using a temporary bridge of boats, while the retreating Mughals who managed to get to the river and wade across it were shot dead by accurate fire from British

Robert Clive, Governor General of Bengal and representative of the East India Company, meeting the Mughal emperor Shah Alam II in 1765 to gain tax collecting rights

muskets so that the waters became choked with bodies. Hector Munro had snatched victory from the jaws of defeat, or to be more accurate, Shah Alam had managed to lose a battle he should have won with ease.

After the Battle of Buxar, Mir Qasim fled to the west, while Shuja-ud-Daula recognised the supremacy of the British. Shah Alam, recognising the fact that the British were the rising dominant power, switched his loyalty to them, and on 12 August 1765, he signed the Treaty of Allahabad with the East India Company.

The terms of the treaty were virtually dictated by the British, though as a face-saving, the emperor was allowed to make it look like he was giving a gift rather than a concession to the East India Company. The British now had the perpetual right to collect land revenue (*dewani*) in Bengal, Bihar, and Orissa, which meant that the East India Company now had vast resources to develop and protect its trade with secure bases, while simultaneously expanding its sepoy armies and an armada of boats that dominated the inland waterways as well. In return for the Mughal emperor's concessions, the British guaranteed that the state of Bengal would pay him an annual fee of 26 lakh rupees. However, the Treaty of Allahabad had also stipulated that the East India Company be paid the incredible sum of 53 lakh rupees to cover the expenses of the recently concluded war.

Robert Clive, the governor general, now held all the aces, for not only were all three neutralised, but also the foundations of the British Raj had been laid.

Mir Qasim was replaced by Nazim ud-Daulah, a British puppet, which meant the control of Bengal was now completely in the hands of the East India Company. Awadh, too, had to sign a subsidiary treaty by virtue of which Shuja ud-Daula had to give up both Kara and Allahabad, two cities on the Ganges, to the Mughal Emperor. It was also decided that Shah Alam II would not return to Delhi but would reside in Allahabad. In addition, Shuja ud-Daula would pay the East India Company 50 lakh rupees as war damages and cede all of his personal estate to Balwant Singh, the Zamindar of Banaras. The only reason the British did not take over Bengal and Awadh at the time was that they simply did not have the resources to govern these large regions. As per the Treaty of Allahabad, military defence, police, and administration of justice were now in the hands of the British in these areas. Robert Clive, the governor-general, now held all the aces, for not only were all three neutralised, but also the foundations of the British Raj had been laid. The Battle of Buxar and its aftermath ensured that the entire Gangetic Plain was under British control. Smaller states in the region, like Sardhana, were not going to be a threat to them and they were left to themselves and allowed to maintain small forces for their pomp and show. To the north were the Gorkhas, and to the south the Marathas, who would next be tackled by the Bengal Army of sepoys.

Mahadji Scindia

1768 CE

Mahadji Shinde, later known as Mahadji Scindia or Madhava Rao Scindia, born on 3 December 1730, was the fifth child of Ranoji Rao Scindia, the founder of the Scindia Dynasty, who governed Malwa following the Marathas' conquest of the region from the Mughal Empire. He was inducted into the military at a young age. When he led his first military expedition against the Nizam of Hyderabad, at Berur in 1742, he was just 12 years old. He would launch numerous campaigns in Northern India during the next two decades and through these conquests, the Maratha Empire would expand to include the regions of Malwa, Rajputana, Rohilkhand, Bundelkhand, and so on.

Mathura, which was under Mughal rule, was conquered by Mahadji in 1755, where he reconstructed old temples and established a centre for Sanskrit learning. In January 1758, Mahadji established Ujjain as his headquarters.

In 1761, he took part in the Third Battle of Panipat and, despite his injuries, made it through the fight. His continued existence would be essential to the future success of the Maratha clan. Having burnt their fingers badly against the Afghans, most established Maratha leaders were reluctant to spend their resources on standing armies and in the accepted Maratha tradition, huge numbers of *pindaris* were retained by them for a percentage of the plunder. The exception was Mahadji Scindia who saw the pindaris as a major threat to law and order and the economic stability of the region. He systematically then went about rebuilding and creating a standing army for Gwalior.

Panipat had been carnage and, with the virtual loss of a generation, Mahandji opened his doors to European mercenaries as well. He had two objectives in mind—the first was to stop any further Afghan incursions into North India and the second was to tap the great revenue potential of the Ganga/Yamuna doab. Looking well

beyond the horizon of his state for the recruitment of the new-look Gwalior army, he concentrated on obtaining various types of soldiers from different areas. Not only did the Gwalior state become the biggest employer in the region, but also individual growth in the new heterogeneous army was not necessarily based on caste or religious groupings since men were given equal opportunities to prove their worth. Flocking to Mahadji's colours were the Gosseins from Bundlekand, Brahmns from Bihar, Muslims from Bengal, Deccani and Pathan recruits for the cavalry, Europeans who had fought in a few campaigns earlier, and soldiers of mixed race from Goa, Agra, and even Calcutta.

As the Marathas once again steadied their ship, Mahadaji would become a dependable lieutenant of Peshwa Madhav Rao I. He became the Maratha Confederacy's regent after travelling to Delhi with Shah Alam II in 1771 and restored the Mughals to power, thereby making the Marathas the power behind the throne. He then defeated the Jats of Mathura, and in 1772–1773 overthrew the Pashtun Rohillas in Rohilkhand and captured Najibabad.

Mahadji was one of his side's most important players in the First Anglo-Maratha War that was fought between 1775 and 1782 wherein his disciplined troops defeated the EIC Bombay troops, leading to the Treaty of Wadgaon. Mahadji also acted as a

mediator in Central India, between the Peshwa and the British.

In 1784, the Mughals appointed Mahadji as deputy regent of Mughal affairs and bestowed upon him the title of *Amir-ul-Umara*, meaning 'head of the amirs'. Mahadji's victory in a battle against the troops of the Nizam of Hyderabad was another accomplishment. After this fight, the Nizam Empire largely withdrew to the Deccan and ceased to be a political force in North Indian affairs. Ironically, the Marathas would align with the Nizam in 1786 during the siege of Adoni, which was one of Tipu Sultan's earliest campaigns.

Mahadji's military power, however, soon began to develop problems of its own, for despite having the best fighting force in the region, the Gwalior state could not quite tap the revenue

◄ Painting of the Battle of Adoni, 1786. Tipu Sultan is in green, riding inside a tiger skin howdah, on an elephant

The royal procession of the Mughal emperor Shah Alam II (ca.1759–1806) making its return to Delhi after a forced exile of 12 years when the British East India Company had forced the emperor to reside in Allahabad and not in the imperial capital of Delhi. Reduced to being a titular head, in 1772 the emperor returned to Delhi after an absence of 12 years

potential of the Gangetic Doab. In 1787, as the *Naib Vakil-i-Mutlaq* of the Mughal Empire, Mahadji asked Sawai Pratap Singh of Jaipur to pay his outstanding taxes.

When Pratap Singh refused, Mahadji marched against the kingdoms of Jaipur and Marwar. In command of his mixed Gwalior and Mughal Army, the Gwalior army was under the command of the French General de Boigne while the Mughal elements were under Muhammad Beg Hamadani and Ismail Beg Hamadani. The Mughal and the Gwalior state forces were owed arrears as the troops had not been paid for months and a major section of Mahadji's forces defected to the Rajputs, resulting in a humiliating loss. This also marked the rise of de Boigne, who would play an important role later.

The Nizam of Hyderabad and the Marathas faced a setback during the siege of Adoni in 1786, where they were defeated by the emerging Tipu Sultan. After this defeat, the Deccan Sultanates stayed within their own domains and had little or no role in the Gangetic Doab ▼

While the British were fast becoming a force to reckon with in northern India, the Marathas were the only other players in the region who could challenge them, as was amplified by the emergence of Mahadji and the Holkars. To the south of Gwalior and Indore, the Deccan Sultanates were

▲ Akbar Shah II, who succeeded his father Shah Alam II, receiving the British Resident

▲ Mughal Emperor Akbar II with his four sons

The Mughal Empire more or less confined to the Red Fort in Delhi, an idyllic scene on the Jamuna with sepoys in the service of the East India Company along with a British officer also in the vicinity ▼

existing in a time warp, jostling among themselves for domination especially as the Mughal power waned. Ever since 1565, when they had rallied together to effectively end the Vijayanagar Empire, they had been either fighting among themselves or battling the Mughals. During the critical phase between the Battle of Plassey (in 1757) and the Second Maratha War, the political spectrum went through a sea change. The Mughals, except for a spark here and there in the post-Aurangzeb era, were reduced to a caricature of themselves, while the Deccan Sultanates, with the Nizam of Hyderabad emerging as the most powerful, continued to be silent spectators as the fighting around them

raged for supremacy and control of the subcontinent.

Mahadji died in 1794 but the army he had created and then allowed de Boigne to run helped the Marathas remain a dominant power in the Gangetic Doab. The Mughals were more and more confined to their immediate forts, and though the pomp and regalia continued, they were a spent force by then. Mahadji was temporarily succeeded by Nana Farnavis, but eventually, Daulat Rao Scindia, Mahadji's grand nephew, took charge. Not very experienced in military matters, de Boigne's continued steadfast loyalty to him soon allowed him to settle down.

A Mughal procession in Lucknow ▼

A miniature portrait of Hyder Ali (1720–82), born Hyder Naik. Having drawn the attention of Krishnaraja Wodeyar II, the Mysore ruler, due to his military skills, he rose to the post of ***dalwai***, or commander-in-chief, and came to dominate the titular monarch and the Mysore government, eventually seizing the reins of power. He expanded the kingdom's borders at the expense of the Maratha Empire and the Nizam of Hyderabad and effectively blunted the military advances of the British EIC during two wars. In the First and Second Anglo-Mysore Wars, he came within striking distance of the British outpost at Madras. He was given a number of honorific titles and was referred to as Sultan Hyder Ali Khan or Hyder Ali Sahib ▸

Hyder Ali

Hyder Ali's exact date of birth is not known. However, most observers agree that he was born sometime between 1717 and 1722 CE. His father, Fath Muhammad, was a Kolar native who commanded 50 soldiers in the Nawab of Carnatic's bamboo rocket artillery. Eventually, Fath Muhammad went to work for the Wodeyar Rajas of the Kingdom of Mysore, where he advanced to become a formidable military leader. He was given Budikote as a jagir (land gift) by the Wodeyars, where he later held the position of Naik. It was in Budikote that Hyder Ali was born and spent his formative years.

Not much is known about his early life. However, after his father was killed in a battle, he enlisted in the military. Initially, he served under the Arcot kings for several years before joining the forces of Srirangapatnam. By 1755, his force comprised 1,500 cavalry and 3,000 men. He was named Dindigul's *faujdar* (military commander) in that same year. To organise and train his artillery companies, Hyder Ali hired French experts. He became the king of Mysore in 1761 after overthrowing the prime minister and making King Krishnaraja Wodeyar II a prisoner in his own palace. Thereafter, he assumed the title of sultan. Among his numerous subsequent campaigns, during the Maratha-Mysore wars, Anglo-Mysore wars, and the Carnatic wars, his performance stands out. He also maintained a fleet consisting of eight dhows and 20 larger ketches in the Indian Ocean. He used his navy to conquer and dominate islands in the Indian Ocean. He died of a cancerous growth in December 1782 and was succeeded by his son, Tipu Sultan.

British and French ships clash off Cuddalore ▶

Battle of Cuddalore
1783 CE

Following the demise of Hyder Ali in December 1782, the British commanders at Fort Saint George decided to attempt the recapture of Cuddalore. The army, under Major-General James Stuart, marched south from Madras, making slow progress and taking almost a month before encamping south of Cuddalore, which lay a mile and a half away from the ruins of Fort Saint David. The army consisted of three European regiments and a considerable body of sepoys and was subsequently reinforced by a detachment of two Hanoverian regiments from the King's German possessions, commanded by Colonel Christoph August von Wangenheim.

Major General James Stuart, the commander-in-chief of the Madras Army; the Marquis de Bussy-Casteinau, the governor-general of Pondicherry, who commanded the French-Mysore troops

On 6 June, Stuart took up a position on the sandy ground two miles from the garrison, with the coast on the right and the Bandipollum hills on the left. The French and Mysore troops, commanded by Marquis de Bussy-Castelnau, took an intermediate and parallel position half a mile in front of the fort walls. In the ground-fighting that followed, neither side could dominate the other. British losses, as the attacking force, were higher and James Stuart was suspended from command by George Macartney, the governor.

The Battle of Cuddalore, fought simultaneously on land and sea, is seen as a continuation of the American Revolutionary War and the naval clashes between 20 June and 29 June are seen as the final engagements of that war. The British fleet, 18 ships of the line under Admiral Sir Edward Hughes, had been anchored to the south of Cuddalore, to protect the army and its supply ships during the siege of Cuddalore. Hughes' ships, at the time, had been hit by a severe bout of scurvy, and the arrival of Admiral Pierre André de Suffren's French fleet. News then arrived that the Treaty of Paris had ended all hostilities between the two sides. However, the seeds for the subsequent Mysore Wars between the French-backed Tipu Sultan and the British had been sown.

◄ British and German troops clash with French and Mysorean troops

Tipu Sultan's portrait at the Indian Military Academy Also called the 'Tiger of Mysore', he was perpetually at war with almost all his neighbouring states ►

Tipu Sultan

Sultan Fateh Ali Sahab Tipu (Tipu Sultan) was born on 1 December 1751. The king of the south Indian kingdom of Mysore, he was also known as Sher-e-Mysore or the 'Tiger of Mysore'. Hyder Ali was still in the saddle when Tipu first came into prominence. In 1780, he virtually annihilated a British force of 4,000 sepoys and a regiment of the Highland scouts at Pollilur some 35 miles south of Madras. The British troops were under the command of Colonel William Baillie and his deputy, David Baird. Out of 86 British officers, 36 were killed, 34 were wounded and taken prisoner, and only 16 of the captured were unwounded. Baillie himself received a back and head wound, in addition to losing a leg, while Baird received two sabre cuts on the head and a pike wound in the arm.

Such was the ferocity of the Mysorean attack that the English were on the verge of being wiped out in India. But Hyder Ali, unfortunately, did not follow up on the success that he had attained at Pollilur, for, with his son Tipu, he had inflicted on the EIC the most crushing defeat the Company would ever receive. The French connection at this stage played a negative role, for they hesitated to aggressively support Hyder Ali while, at the same time, the Maratha Confederation also dithered and adopted a 'wait and watch' policy. Had the father/son duo been able to push the envelope further, in all probability they would have taken Fort St George in Madras as well. Fortunately for the EIC, despite the severity of the reverses, the British could keep their toehold in the south only due to the lack of confidence shown by their adversaries.

The summer palace at Seringapatnam, which was the capital of the Mysore state ▼

The southern gate of the Bangalore Fort

Indian 'demons' shooting arrows at British soldiers, while other soldiers and musicians who are smaller in scale are inside the fort. The painting has a caption in Persian—Anne SK Brown Collection. After victories in the first two wars, Mysore, led by Tipu Sultan, invaded the nearby coastal state of Travancore, which was a British ally. This led to the Third Mysore War, where the British turned the tide

Tipu Sultan succeeded his father in December 1782, and in 1784 he concluded peace with the British and assumed the title of the Sultan of Mysore. However, he inherited his father's idealogy of keeping his alliance with the French intact so as to use the latest fighting techniques to take on his enemies, which were plenty. He had the farsightedness to realise that the British

Kodava officials of Coorg in their traditional attire. The Kodava kingdom of Coorg bitterly opposed the expansionist Mysore state first under Haidar Ali and subsequently under his son, Tipu Sultan, resulting in one of the most violent rivalries in South Indian history. After decades of resistance, Coorg was finally annexed by Tipu Sultan, but the Kodavas never forgot the excessive cruelty meted out to them. Tipu's belligerent stance towards the Travancore kingdom also weakened his position vis-a-vis the British with whom he would violently clash in subsequent years ▼

The Battle of Pollilur, which took place on 10 September 1780, as part of the Second Anglo-Mysore War, saw the EIC army under Colonel William Baillie suffer a major defeat

were the biggest threat not just to the Mysore state but also to the entire southern peninsula.

Administratively, during his reign, he instituted several far-reaching reforms, such as a new calendar and coinage system as well as a new land revenue system that sparked the expansion of the Mysore silk industry. At the same time, Tipu Sultan also had to contend with the Marathas' offensive manoeuvres. The Marathas and the Nizam of Hyderabad had formed a military alliance with the aim of regaining the territories that they had both lost to Hyder Ali in earlier battles. Tipu participated in several significant battles against the Marathas, such as the Siege of Badami in May 1786, the Siege of

To commemorate his victory, Tipu Sultan commissioned a painting of the Battle of Pollilur as part of a large mural for the newly built Daria Daulat Bagh in Seringapatam in 1784

Nargund in February 1785, the Siege of Adoni in June 1786, the Battle of Gajendragad in June 1786, the Battle of Savanur in October 1786, and the Siege of Bahaḍur Benda in January 1787. The Marathas and Tipu Sultan engaged in combat in the Battle of Gajendragadh, which took place between March 1786 and March 1787. The Marathas emerged victorious, extending their territory's boundary to the Tungabhadra River. The treaty stipulated that Tipu Sultan had to return all of the territory that Hyder Ali had taken and pay the Marathas an annual tribute of 1.2 million rupees and 4.8 million rupees as a one-time war cost.

With a growing sense of paranoia, London believed one of the main reasons why Napoleon Bonaparte invaded Egypt in 1794 was to link up with Tipu and drive the English out of India.

Apart from his battles with the Marathas, Tipu also fought with the Sira Province, Malabar, Kodagu, Bednore, Carnatic, and Travancore. Though not at war with the British, Tipu continued to be a fierce adversary of the British EIC, and finally, in 1789, the gloves were off when he attacked Travancore, a British ally. As a result, a combined force of 20,000, comprising British EIC troops, Marathas, and the Nizam of Hyderabad's cavalry, assembled at Savendroog in January 1792 under the command of Lord Cornwallis who had recently arrived in India after having fought in the American War of Independence. By the first week of February, this combined force had reached Seringapatam, a fortified fortress-city that was situated on an island on the Kaveri River. Strangely enough, Tipu chose not to harass the advancing army with his cavalry, letting them get within a few miles before he bombarded Cornwallis's army with his arsenal of Mysorean rockets. On 6/7 February, the two sides clashed in combat, and though the British suffered serious initial reverses, they managed to surround Seringapatam. With more troops from Malabar under General Robert Abercromby

The gap in the wall created by Mir Sadiq allowed the British troops to breach the formidable fortress ▼

British troops surge forward in a three-pronged attack (top), and the death of Tipu Sultan (bottom)

also reaching Seringapatam, Tipu was compelled to sign the Treaty of Seringapatam which cost him several previously conquered lands, including Malabar and Mangalore. Cornwallis also took two of Tipu's sons, aged 11 and 7, as hostages. Though he was left with Seringapatam, almost half of Tipu's Mysore Empire was gone with the EIC, with the Nizam and the Marathas sharing in the spoils.

Though reduced in his fighting ability, Tipu continued to further hone the use of the iron-cased Mysorean rockets and put the military treatise, Fathul Mujahidin, into service. He remained implacable toward the British, and he reached out to several foreign nations, including Afghanistan, France, and the Ottoman Empire to continue the fight against the British. With a growing sense of paranoia, London believed one of the main reasons why Napoleon Bonaparte invaded Egypt in 1794 was to link up with Tipu and drive the English out of India. This development, combined with the fact that Tipu had given the British a bloody nose earlier, triggered a vilification campaign where Tipu Sultan became the target of British propaganda.

In a missive to the Nizam of Hyderabad in 1796, Tipu would write in vain to the Nizam of Hyderabad who had been aligned against him: 'Know you not the custom of the English? Wherever they fix their talons they contrive little by little to work themselves into the whole management of affairs'. The British, on their part, were also aware that Tipu had also evolved into an extremely able administrator, for, unlike his father who functioned within established Mughal practices, his style of functioning had made the Mysore state one of the best-run kingdoms in the country. This made him a marked man in the eyes of Lord Wellesley, the governor-general, who began a deliberate campaign to vilify Tipu, after which he put together

In the desperate fighting that followed on 4 May 1799, Tipu had the option of escaping but he famously chose to stay, saying it is 'better to live one day as a tiger than a thousand years as a sheep.

the largest army the EIC ever gathered. Once again, the Nizam of Hyderabad and the Marathas became bit players in the events that followed.

Tipu's streak of cruelty, be it the torture of British prisoners at the end of the Second Anglo-Mysore War or the barbaric treatment of populations in the Malabar, Travancore, and Coorg regions, made it easy for Wellesley and other British writers of the time to paint a picture of a Muslim tyrant who was running amuck unchecked, converting, killing, and abducting the women of non-Muslim populations of these regions. Most historians now agree that though Mysore under Tipu was indeed a Muslim kingdom, his administration was almost entirely Hindu as was a major portion of the Mysorean Army.

The Policy of Expansion was Wellesley's brainchild, and he introduced the Subsidiary Alliance System that would ensure the British would become the sovereign power in India. Tipu Sultan was the obvious target and a massive army of 50,000 men was raised to capture or kill him. The Fourth Anglo-Mysore War had all the ingredients that were, by then, typical of the British. David Baird, who had been Tipu's prisoner a decade previously, was to lead the assault on Seringapatnam, which was being defended by 30,000 well-trained soldiers on the Kaveri River. However, as was their style of functioning, the British had been in communication with Mir Sadiq, a minister in Tipu's cabinet, and he had agreed to betray his own people by withdrawing the defending troops from a critical part of the fort's defences. Having abandoned his post and, in the process, killed Ghazi Khan, who tried to stop him, Mir Sadiq gave the pre-determined signal to the British officers to advance. In the desperate fighting that followed on 4 May 1799, Tipu had the option of escaping but he famously chose to stay, saying it is 'better to live one day as a tiger than a thousand years as a sheep'. Mir Sadiq, as he came forward to greet the British, was killed by Tipu's loyal troops. Once the Sultan's body had been identified later that evening, a British officer is believed to have acclaimed, 'Now India is ours!'

Tipu's family identifying his corpse (top), and Tipu's sons being taken hostage (bottom)

Arthur Wellesley, the first Duke of Wellington would eventually be known for his famous victory over Napolean 12 years later ▸

Second Maratha War
1803 CE

In 1802, the Maratha Confederacy consisted of five major chiefs—the Peshwa, Baji Rao II, at the capital city of Poona, Anand Rao Gaekwad of Baroda, Daulat Rao Scindia of Gwalior, Yashwant Rao Holkar of Indore, and Raghuji Bhonsle II of Nagpur. Unfortunately, at the time, all the Maratha chiefs were at loggerheads among themselves.

Extremely quick to smell and exploit any fault lines that existed, the British once again cosied up to Baji Rao II from the very outset of the Second Maratha War, ensuring that the Marathas remained divided. In February 1799, Yashwantrao Holkar replaced his brother Kashi Rao as the Raja of the Holkars. He immediately captured Ujjain and started campaigning towards the north to expand his empire in that region. Yashwant Rao rebelled against the policies of Peshwa Baji Rao II. In May 1802, he marched towards Poona, the seat of the Peshwa. This resulted in the Battle of Poona, which was fought at Baramati, just 40 miles from the city, in which the Peshwa's forces were easily defeated.

After the battle in which Baji Rao escaped with his life, Yashwantrao appointed Amrutrao as the Peshwa and tried to settle the differences within the Maratha state. However, by virtue of an independent treaty signed with the EIC in July 1802, the Gaikwad of Baroda accepted British protection and continued to oppose the new Maratha administration. The British were in the thick of the action, recognising

▲ The Battle of Assaye was fought on 23 September 1803 between Major General Arthur Wellesley and Daulatrao Scindia and the Bhonsle Raja of Berar

Yashwantrao Holkar of Indore who was the last man standing on the Maratha side. Holkar would repeatedly keep asking other kingdoms to unite with him so as to throw the British out of India, but almost everyone in the northern half of India had signed some treaty or the other with the British. Yashwantrao even knocked at the doors of Maharaja Ranjit Singh, who initially seemed inclined to fight with the Marathas, but then held himself back. With each passing day, the British, especially Wellesley and Drake, got more and more desperate to defeat Holkar, but that was not to be ▶

◄General Lake at Laswari

Nawab Sadat Ali Khan (ca. 1798–1814) seated with his son in a box-like ***takht*** (throne) at a durbar, surrounded by the important people, Indian and European, in Lucknow at the end of the eighteenth century. Among those present are the British Resident Colonel William Scott seated left next to the nawab, the chief minister, Tafuzzai Hussein Khan (1727–1800) seated right next to the nawab and Major General Claude Martin (1735–1800) ▼

◀ Maharaja Krishnaraja Wadiar III (ca. 1799–1831) had been brought back by the British after the defeat of Tipu

the independence of Baroda from the Maratha Empire in exchange for Anand Rao Gaekwad's acknowledging British Paramountcy. Baji Rao, though out of power, also signed a similar Treaty of Bassein with the British, which sent shock waves through the Maratha Confederacy.

With the Marathas divided and baying for each other's blood, the EIC put Marquis Richard Wellesley's plans of empire-building into action. The Bengal governor-general's strategy was for his brother, Major General Arthur Wellesley, to secure the Deccan Plateau, while Lieutenant General Gerard Lake would take control of the Gangetic Doab and then Delhi. Powell was to subdue Bundelkhand, Colonel Murray was to take Gujarat, and Lieutenant Colonel Harcourt was to neutralise Orissa and Bihar. Wellesley's objective was to strike a decisive blow and, in a massive effort, to strike at every corner of the Maratha Confederacy at the same time. He had, at that time, 50,000 troops available to him, and they were assembled in different quarters.

Deployed in the Deccan and Gujarat, Arthur Wellesley had 8,930 men, while 7,826 formed a covering army under General Stuart. 3,596 men were left to garrison and protect Hyderabad and Poona, leaving 7,352 men in Gujarat under Colonel Murray, subject to the overall control of Arthur Wellesley. Lake had 10,500 men at his command as he approached Delhi along the southern bank of the Jamuna, while another 3,500 men were assembled at Allahabad to act on the side of Bundelkhand, and finally, 5,216 men were earmarked for the invasion of Raghujee Bhonslays districts in Cuttack.

The first to fall was the Ahmadnagar Fort on 12 August after an infantry attack exploited an artillery-made breach in the wall. With the fort in British hands, they were able to extend control southwards to the River Godavari. On 11 September 1803, the Battle of Patparganj was fought between troops of the Bombay Army under General Gerad Lake and the Marathas of Scindia's army under General Louis Bourquin and Sardar Ravsaheb Wable. Shortly thereafter, in September, Scindia's forces lost to Lake at Delhi and Arthur Wellesley at Assaye. On 18 October, British forces took the pettah of Asirgarh Fort with a loss of two killed and five wounded. The fort's garrison subsequently surrendered on the 21st after the attackers had erected a battery. On 1 November, Lake defeated another Scindia force at Laswari, near Alwar in Rajasthan, and this was followed by Wellesley's victory over Bhonsle forces at Argaon on 29 November 1803.

On 17 December 1803, Raghuji Bhonsale agreed to the Treaty of Deogaon in Orissa after the Battle of Argaon. This treaty meant giving up Cuttack province (which included Mughal and the coastal part of Orissa, Garjat/the princely states of Orissa, Balasore Port, and parts of Midnapore district of West Bengal). On 30 December 1803, Daulat Scindia signed the Treaty of Surji-Anjangaon with the British, after the Battle of Assaye and Battle of Laswari, and ceded to the British, Hisar, Panipat, Rohtak, Rewari, Gurgaon, Ganges-Jumna Doab, the Delhi-Agra region, parts of Bundelkhand, Broach, some districts of Gujarat, and the fort of Ahmadnagar. Given the numbers—Scindia had 100,000 men including 40,000 horses at Delhi itself—the scale of the British victory was nothing short of a miracle, but battle after battle had been won as much by bribing officials and dangling carrots, which left the British virtually holding most of the country. And yet, the Second Maratha War was not decisive, for the British had failed to pin down Yashwant Rao Holkar. With all the other Maratha chiefs having signed treaties with the British, Wellesley had to defeat Holkar in order to bring the Second Maratha War to a successful conclusion.

General Lake was on Holkar's heels but the Marathas were far from finished. A British force, led by Colonel Fawcett, was defeated at Konch, in Bundelkhand in June 1804, the defeat sending shockwaves through the rest of the country. In July, in another engagement, Colonel William Monson came across a cropper at the Mukandwara Pass, approximately 30 miles south of Kota. Monson had extended his rear lines, which then got attacked by Holkar, forcing the British to abandon their guns on the banks of the Chambal River. Monson's losses had been heavy; twelve British officers had been killed, two were drowned and two were missing. Five other officers were wounded. Half of the five battalions under Monson's command had been lost. In the next couple of months, the British kept getting defeated at different locations.

Wellesley changed tactics in August, occupied both Indore and Ujjain and with Baji Rao's army in tow, Lake closed in on Mathura. Holkar decided, instead, to take Delhi, and he defeated a screening defensive force, commanded by Colonel David Ochterlony, who had been the British Resident in the Mughal Court after Mahadji Scindia's defeat in the Battle of Patparganj. Holkar then laid a siege on Delhi, which he lifted after a week as Lake was too close for comfort and there was a danger of getting caught in a pincer between the British forces commanded by Lake and Ochterlony. Holkar's plea to Indian rulers to stand up and fight drew a response from the besieged Mughal Emperor Shah Alam II who, though himself reduced to a British puppet, hailed Holkar as *Maharajadhiraja Raj Rajeshwar Alija Bahadur*. In an engagement at Farrukhabad, Lake managed to engage Holkar's forces but couldn't stop the Marathas from proceeding towards Deeg where the Jat king, Ranjit Singh, decided to throw in his lot with Holkar. Lake, with his entire force, then attacked Bharatpur on 13 January 1805 where the Jats and Holkar fought them off in one of the bloodiest battles fought in the subcontinent. General Lake, the Marquis Wellesley and the British, despite having comprehensively defeated the formidable Marathas, not only lost face but the governor-general was recalled to England. Yashwant Rao Holkar eventually retained all his territory but, unfortunately, died at the age of 36.

Holkar notwithstanding, almost all princely states were happy to align with the British at the beginning of the nineteenth century. Individuals like the Anglo-Indian James Skinner began to make an impact by the raising of irregular cavalry units. Owing to his Indian heritage from his mother's side, Skinner was unable to serve like his Scottish father in the EIC army, so as a 16-year-old, he entered the Gwalior army as an ensign under Benoît de Boigne. Skinner remained in service until the outbreak of the Second Anglo-Maratha War when all Anglo-Indians were dismissed from Scindia's Maratha service.

At that stage, in February 1803, he was welcomed into the EIC's Bengal Army where he raised a regiment of irregular cavalry that would bear his name—Skinner's Horse. Commanding

his regiment, Colonel James Skinner would be a part of the siege of Bharatpur in 1805. During this period, various states began to adopt the European model and started organising their own state forces on the de Boigne model. The three British armies—Madras, Bombay, and Bengal—were reinforced by the state troops should they be required. Yashwant Holkar's plea to various rulers was: 'First country, and then religion. We will have to rise above caste, religion, and our states in the interest of our country. You, too, must wage a war against the British, like me.' His appeal fell on deaf ears! At this stage, it was game and set to the British, for the march was yet to come!

◂ The EIC with control over various parts of India, began to transform into a formidable army

▲ Either Colonel James Skinner or his son as the commanding officer

◄ Building on their military successes, various British cavalry units started to establish themselves. An Indian officer, a kettle drummer, a trumpeter, and a trooper, from Skinner's Horse. These paintings depict the costumes and weapons in 1802

The fort at Vellore, built by the Vijaynagara rulers in the 16th century, where the sons of Tipu Sultan were also kept by the British after 1799 ▸

Vellore Mutiny

1806 CE

Ever since British troops killed Tipu Sultan in the Fourth Anglo-Mysore War and restored the Wodeyar Dynasty to power in Mysore, the soldiers, families, and children of Tipu Sultan were banished to Vellore. The local populace despised the British for the looting of the sultan's harem and the subsequent treatment meted out to the sons of the former ruler. This factor is seen by many commentators as the main trigger for the mutiny.

The commander-in-chief of the Madras Presidency, Sir John Cradock, enforced military regulations in 1805 that were suggested by the then governor, William Cavendish Bentinck. The Indian sepoys were issued new uniforms and weapons, and rigorous discipline was enforced as part of the new military regulations. The order in which the sepoys had to shave their facial hair hurt the Muslims' religious feelings. Similarly, Hindu sepoys were prohibited from donning any religious symbols on their foreheads. It was forbidden to wear earrings. To complicate matters further, in June 1806, the Adjutant General Patrick Agnew mandated that soldiers wear the Agnew turban rather than their customary headgear. It was a round hat with a cross emblem on it, similar to the European hats of the time. The order, in a stroke of brilliance, managed to alienate both Muslim and Hindu soldiers alike who opposed the order because they believed they were being converted to Christianity. Those who refused to wear them faced harsh penalties.

The mutiny began when the Vellore fort was attacked on 10 July 1806 by native sepoys from the 1st and 23rd Regiments of the Madras Native Infantry. They killed 14 officers and another 115 British soldiers when they raided the barracks of the 69th Regiment. The Indian soldiers proclaimed Fettah Hyder, Tipu Sultan's elder son, to be their ruler and replaced the British flag in the Vellore Fort

Madras sepoys of the era whose dress and headgear differed considerably from that worn by the British soldiers

with the tiger-striped flag of the erstwhile sultan.

However, word had reached Colonel Robert Rollo Gillespie stationed at nearby Arcot, and within hours and some hard riding the Colonel promptly wrested back the fort. His galloper guns blew the gates away and 350 sepoys were killed by gunfire during the British counter-offensive. The mutiny was subdued and another hundred sepoys, along with the chief offenders, were immediately executed. Another six were blown from cannons, five were shot by the firing squad, and eight were hung, while the surviving members of Tipu's family were subsequently moved to Calcutta. Most importantly, the new regulations were withdrawn.

The Vellore Mutiny, or the Vellore Revolution, was the first instance of a large-scale and violent mutiny by Indian sepoys against the British East India Company, predating the Indian Uprising of 1857 by half a century. The revolt, which took place in the Indian city of Vellore, lasted one full day, during which mutineers seized the Vellore Fort and killed or wounded 200 British troops.

Earlier, Arcot had been the scene of a strategic battle between the British led by Robert Clive and the forces of Chanda Sahib in 1751. This was the first major victory of Clive wherein he captured and then succeeded in defending Arcot, the then capital of Carnatic. The outpost at the time of the Vellore Mutiny was garrisoned by the 19th Light Dragoons under Gillespie.

◂ Twelve miles from Vellore, the small fortified outpost at Arcot that dominated the Palar River and the main trade route between Madras and Bangalore

▴ William Bentick, the first governor general to be recalled after the Vellore Mutiny. British officers had warned of the simmering discontent, but Bentick had refused to budge, ordering lashings instead

Rajputana

Rajputana was the term used collectively for the group of princely states that inhabited northwestern India. The vast 343,328 square km consisted of 23 princely states, one chiefdom, one estate, and the Bengal Presidency district of Ajmer-Merwar that was ceded to the EIC by Daulat Rao Sindhia by the treaty on 25 June 1818. These kingdoms were spread across two distinct geographic regions—the area northwest of the Aravalli Range, which was mostly sandy and unproductive and included a part of the Thar Desert, and the area to the southeast of the range, which was generally higher and more fertile. The whole area, together, formed a compact block occupying the hill and plateau country between the northern Indian plains and the main plateau of peninsular India.

The majority of the ruling families were Rajput clans, the warrior class of Rajputana, who began to enter the area in the seventh century. Their loyalty to their clans and constant conflicts among themselves did not allow them to function as a cohesive unit, even though they had held the Islamic invaders at bay until Mohammad Bin Qasim's conquest of Sindh in 712 CE. Even then, after he captured Multan, he was not allowed to make further gains and among those who opposed him were the Bappa Rawal rulers of the Guhila dynasty that, at the time, ruled Merwar.

The largest states were Jaisalmer, Bikaner, Jaipur, Kota, Udaipur (Mewar region), and Jodhpur (Marwar region). The state of Jodhpur was founded in the thirteenth century by the Rathore clan of Rajputs. After the sacking of Kannauj by Muhammad of Ghor in 1194, and its capture by the Delhi Sultanate in the early thirteenth century, the Rathores migrated west and, after a long struggle, wrested control of Marwar from the Turks. The city of Jodhpur, the capital of the Rathore state, was founded in 1459 by Rao Jodha. In 1561, the kingdom was invaded by the Mughal Emperor Akbar. Parganas of Jaitaran and Merta were captured by the Mughals. After a war for almost two decades and the death of Rao Chandrasen Rathore in 1581, Marwar was brought under direct Mughal administration and remained so till its administration was handed back to Raja Udai Singh in 1583.

◄ Kota became an independent state in 1631 when Rao Madho Singh, the second son of Rao Ratan of Bundi was made the ruler, by the Mughal Emperor Jehangir. Soon Kota outgrew its parent state to become bigger in area, richer in revenue, and more powerful; Zalim Singh, a diplomat, and statesman, emerged as another prominent figure of the state in the eighteenth century. In 1817, a treaty of friendship was signed between him and the British on his condition of carving out part of the existing state for his descendants, resulting in Jhalawar coming into existence

The state of Udaipur, also known as Mewar, was established around the seventh century by the Sisodia clan. In 1303, the kingdom was invaded by the Delhi Sultanate and its capital fort, Chittorgarh, was besieged and taken by Alauddin Khalji. The mass extermination of the entire main branch of the ruling family resulted in the Ranas coming to power two decades later, and under them, the kingdom became the most powerful state in northern India. The kingdom was engaged in multiple battles against the sultanates of Gujarat, Malwa, Nagor, and Delhi. After Maharana Pratap's defeat, Mewar was constantly in a struggle with the Rajputs accepting Mughal suzerainty in 1615. It became independent in 1707 when Aurangzeb died, and in 1818, it accepted British suzerainty.

The expansionist nature of both Marwar and Mewar initially had most other Rajput kingdoms turn to the Mughals for protection, and eventually, the Rajputs became the biggest allies of the Mughal Empire. The Kachhwaha clan (Jaipur) established their kingdom in the Dhundhar region of Rajputana in the eleventh century. They would fight alongside Prithviraj Chauhan and Rana Sanga, but under the rule of Raja Bharmal (1498–1574), the kingdom

◄ Raja Bharmal of Amer (Jaipur) who aligned with the Mughals; his daughter, Jodhabai, also known as Mariam uz Zamani, who was Akbar's chief consort, and his grandson, Raja Man Singh I ▼

▲ Chandrasen of Merwar reigned from 1562 to 1581 and fought against Akbar

Raja Bhim Singh of Mewar and Raja Surat Singh of Bikaner, who along with most Rajput and Jat kingdoms aligned with the EIC in 1818

would align itself completely with the Mughals. Bharmal's daughter was Jodha Bai (Mariam-us-Zamani) the chief consort of Akbar and the mother of Jehangir. Bharmal, along with his successor, Raja Bhagwant Das, and his grandson, Raja Man Singh I, would become the highest *mansabdars* in the imperial Mughal court. Man Singh also served as the *subahdar* of Bengal for three terms—from 1595 to 1606—and the *subahdar* of Kabul from 1585 to 1586. He served in the imperial Mughal army under Emperor Akbar. Man Singh fought 67 important battles in Kabul, Balkh, Bukhara, Bengal, and central and southern India. He was well-versed in the battle tactics of both the Rajputs as well as the Mughals. He was considered to be one of the *navaratnas*, or the nine gems of the royal court of Akbar.

In 1488, Rao Bika, the eldest son of Maharaja Rao Jodha of Jodhpur, wanting to establish a kingdom of his own, occupied the arid country in the north of Rajasthan that was known as Jangladesh. Though it was in the Thar Desert, Bikaner was considered an oasis on the trade route between Central Asia and the Gujarat coast as it had adequate spring water. Around a century after Rao Bika founded Bikaner, Raja Rai Singhji, who ruled from 1571 to 1611, accepted the suzerainty of the Mughals and held a high rank as an army general in the court of Akbar and Jehangir. Rai Singh's successful military exploits, which involved winning half of the Mewar kingdom for the Empire, won him accolades and rewards from the

Mughal Emperors. He was given the *jagirs* (lands) of Gujarat and Burhanpur.

After the Third Maratha War, the British government offered its protection to the Rajput rulers, offering to protect them from the roving bands of Pindaris and remnants of the defeated Maratha armies. After the British defeated Amir Khan at the Pindari War, in 1817, they gave the possession of Tonk to him and made him its nawab. Amir Khan then signed a treaty with the British, making him the ruler of Tonk. By the end of 1818, similar treaties had been executed between the other Rajput states and Britain. The Maratha, Daulat Rao Scindia, the ruler of Gwalior, gave up the district of Ajmer-Merwar to the British, and the Maratha influence in Rajasthan came to an end.

The British continued to have issues with the Rajput states, in some cases even leading to conflicts. By 1800, the British had eradicated the threat of the French, not only in India but on the global stage as well. With their victory over the Marathas, they were the masters of North and Western India, and the Rajputs, having allowed the Mughals to dominate them, turned their face towards the new rising sun. For the British, this period was a critical one, for having consolidated their position, the EIC was transforming itself from a commercial entity to a governing organisation. With the Crown beginning to play a more active role in Indian affairs, this period coincided with their growing interest in Rajputana, an area that had not, until then, overly featured in their plans.

Earlier, In 1810, two British officers disguised as Indian horse traders explored the Sindh-Balochistan-Persian region. They returned with sketches of Sindhi foot soldiers who were manning the western frontier with Balochistan. With Rajputana aligned with them, the British could now look beyond the Sutlej and the Indus Rivers. The systematic subjugation of what was then Hindoostan was complete ▼

Tibet (Shangrila)

With its deep azure skies, low wispy clouds and strong sunshine, rolling grasslands interspersed with grazing yaks, flat snow-mottled deserts, and distant yellow, grey, and rusty moonscapes with snowy peaks, Tibet is an otherworldly place that is more intense than beautiful. It's also a harsh, unforgiving holy land, dotted with monasteries and inhabited mostly by nomads as well as clans of various sub-ethnic identities.

Tibet, even then, was known as the 'Land of the Snows' and the 'Roof of the World', and at the time very little was known about it. The mystique surrounding Tibet stemmed from the fact that it had historically been extremely difficult to access from any direction. Tibet was referred to as Bod Qiang or Bod for centuries and it had been a religious state with varying degrees of autonomy and control, coexisting with Mongolia and China for the majority of its history. The majority of Tibet is the Tibetan-Qinghai Plateau, a high, wind-swept plateau that gets little rain and is extremely cold in the winter. Himalayan nations, including Nepal, Sikkim, Bhutan, and Burma, are on the southern side of the Great Himalayan Range, which practically isolates Tibet from all of them. Similarly, even though Tibet shared its borders with the Qinghai province to the northeast, Xinjiang (now the Xinjiang Uyghur Autonomous Region, XUAR) to the north and Ladakh to its west, the intervening terrain is vast, arid and largely uninhabited.

The lack of communication in most parts of Tibet during these times ensured that the populace remained isolated not only from the rest of the world but also within themselves in this vast region. As a result, there was minimal interaction between the inhabitants of its different geographical regions. As the decades rolled by, outsiders made a few attempts to gain a foothold in Tibet.

In the seventeenth century, the senior lama of the Gelug school, the Dalai Lama, became the head of state with the aid of the Khoshut Khanate.

There is plenty of archaeological evidence that suggests that the Tibetan plateau has been inhabited since prehistoric times. However, as is the case with India, most of Tibet's early history went unrecorded. While mythical accounts of early rulers of the Yarlung Dynasty exist, historical accounts begin with the introduction of Buddhism from India in the sixth century and the appearance of envoys from the unified Tibetan Empire in the seventh century. Tibetan texts initially refer to the kingdom of Zhangzhung (ca. 500 BCE–625 CE) as the precursor of the later Tibetan kingdoms and the originators of the Bon religion. Following the dissolution of the empire and a period of fragmentation in the ninth to the tenth centuries, a Buddhist revival in the tenth to the

twelfth centuries saw the development of three of the four major schools of Tibetan Buddhism.

After a period of control by the Mongol Empire and Yuan Dynasty, Tibet became effectively independent in the fourteenth century and was ruled by a succession of noble houses for the next 300 years. In the seventeenth century, the senior lama of the Gelug school, the Dalai Lama, became the head of state with the aid of the Khoshut Khanate. The Ladakhi Gyalpo invaded and controlled Western Tibet for a few decades in the eighteenth century after which the Dzungar Khanate occupied Tibet. In 1720, a Qing dynasty expeditionary force attacked them and took control of Tibet, and it would remain Qing territory until the fall of the dynasty.

◂ The epic of the legendary King Gesar originated between 600 and 200 BCE. Like the Indian and Greek epics, the heroic deeds of the kingdom of Ling continues to be recited by Tibetan, Mongolian, Buryat, Balti, Ladakhi, and Monguor singers; Tibetan Buddhism spread outside of Tibet primarily due to the influence of the Mongol Yuan dynasty (1271–1368), founded by Kublai Khan, which had ruled China, Mongolia, and parts of Siberia ▾

In Tibetan Buddhism, especially in the early period of Sarma schools, Arya Achala is the wrathful tutelary deity who not only protects but is also the remover of obstacles ▾

British troops advance through the Kherigarh Pass in Kumaon

Gorkha Wars
1814–15 CE

The unexpected success of the East India Company in the Battle of Buxar in 1764 gave them the Crown's permission to collect taxes in Orissa, Bihar, and Bengal. Later, the acquisition of Gorakhpur and parts of Awadh by the English brought them into direct contact with the Kingdom of Nepal. The English, with their eyes on Tibet, wanted a passage through Nepal, but the Nepalese, wary of the British, refused to cooperate. The tension between the two then acquired a more significant

▲ Girvan Yuddhavikram Shah, the boy-king of Nepal

proportion by the beginning of the eighteenth century. Matters came to a head when Nepal captured the Terai of Butwal and Sheoraj, prompting Lord Hasting to order an invasion of Nepal in 1814.

Over the next two years, several bloody clashes were fought by the two sides, with fortune often switching sides. As the Nepalese progressively kept on losing ground, the English were awed by their opponent's raw gallantry and taken aback by the losses they suffered at the hands of the Nepalese. After a few notable battles of Nalapani, Jaithak, and Malaon, the Nepalese finally conceded defeat and signed the Treaty of Sugauli in 1816.

As a result of the treaty, the English took away the Terai region and the hilly areas of Garhwal, Kumaon, and Sikkim from Nepal. However, they agreed to pay an annual grant of two lakh rupees to compensate Nepal and started recruiting Gorkha soldiers. Such an outcome of the treaty was unprecedented, wherein a vanquished army had been treated very honourably by the victor, who was in awe of the warriors of the Himalayas. A resident was stationed in Kathmandu, but the king was left free to rule his land with some conditions.

While the series of battles, collectively known as Gorkha or Anglo-Gorkha Wars, did add to the territory and revenue of the East India

▲ The Nepalese Prime Minister Bhim Sen Thapa

◀ Nepalese troops

▼ A Nepalese sepoy

▲ The Battle of Jaithk, fought off Nahan on 26 December, would see another bloody encounter between the East India Company's 53rd Division and the Nepalese forces marshalled by Ranajor Singh Thapa

Indian soldiers fighting for the British ▶

Company, the victory was to have long-term implications as the Great Game began unfolding some two and a half decades later. With Garhwal and Kumaon under their control, the English made sure that no liaison between the powerful Sikh Empire and the warrior Hindu Kingdom of

British cavalry and infantry marching to attack the fortress of Kalanga, 1814. On behalf of the East india Company, Francis Edward Rawdon, Marquess of Hastings, Governor-General of India took a loan of 2 Crore rupees from the Nawab of Awadh and was also supported by the kingdoms of Sikkim and Patiala ▼

Nepal was ever allowed to develop, thus, preventing the formation of any formidable alliance against their designs in the subcontinent. Later, around the onset of the twentieth century, the British were able to send their forces to Tibet via Sikkim, which they had retained as part of their war booty.

Third Maratha War

1817–1818 CE

Most historians view the Third Maratha War as a virtual continuation of the earlier conflict. Wanting to seal their absolute supremacy on the Indian subcontinent, the British assembled an army that was twice as large as what Marquis Wellesley had put together a decade and a half previously. The Bengal Army, supported by troops in the Deccan numbered 120,000 men that apart from the British Regiments, had close to 60 battalions of native infantry, various

◄ The Battle of Sitabuldi was fought in November 1817 on these hillocks between the forces of Appa Saheb Bhonsle of Nagpur and the British

▼ Thalner Fort on the banks of the Tapi River

sections of irregular and regular cavalry, elephant and horse-drawn artillery units, and rocket troops—each with well organised logistical lines. The army was under the command of Robert Francis Hastings and he was being supported by Lieutenant General Thomas Hislop.

The Marathas had lost major chunks of territory in the previous clash with the British, but they still remained the only obstacle to complete British domination of the Gangetic Doab and Central India. Peshwa Baji Rao II was supported by Mudhoji II Bhonsle of Nagpur and Malharrao Holkar III of Indore. Daulatrao Shinde of Gwalior chose to remain neutral even though he lost control of Rajputana.

The British Indian Army had honed its battle drills and the conflicts that

An East India merchantman ***Castle Eden*** with plenty of cannons approaching Madras harbour in 1824. This was an 818-ton ship, which besides transporting goods to the UK, also allowed the British a reach into areas that were otherwise not easily accessible, for example, Burma, the route they took to eventually extend their influence on the northeast as well

British Expansion II

started with a clash with the Pindaris and the Battle of Khadki saw successive victories for the British against the numerically superior Maratha forces that were clinical, resulting in the complete breakup of the Maratha Empire and the loss of Maratha independence. British domination

▼ An East India merchantmen entering Madras Harbour

▲ Boats tackle the surf of the Bay of Bengal to ferry the passengers and cargo ashore

on the seas was now reflected on the land as well. Wellesley's master plan had been given the final flourish by Harding. The Peshwa was exiled to Kanpur and his territory was annexed by the Bombay Presidency. Satara was given the status of a princely state. Bhonsle was defeated in the Battle of Sitabuldi and his dominions in and around Nagpur became a part

◄ Major General Sir Thomas Munro was appointed governor of Madras in 1820, where he founded systems of revenue assessment and general administration which substantially persisted into the twentieth century. The EIC, at this stage, was well into governing and administering its large land acquisitions

Ghulam Ghouse Khan was the last nawab, for after the British annexed the Carnatic, his successors were called the Prince of Arcot. After having been aligned with the French, the Carnatic rulers became staunch allies of the British ▼

▲ Nawab Azim ud Daula (1801–1819) who succeeded his father, Umdat ul-Umara, as the Nawab of Arcot

of British India. Malharrao Holkar lost the battle of Mahidpur, which resulted in the acquisition of the Maratha kingdoms of Nagpur and Indore. Gwalior and Jhansi became princely states acknowledging British control. The British could now look at expanding the frontiers even further.

Madhav Rao Narayan was made the Peshwa in 1792, after the end of the First Maratha War. However, the real power in the Maratha Confederacy was wielded by his ministers, which included Fadnavis, who is seated to the Peshwa's right ▸

Decline of the Marathas

After the British loss in 1782 in the First Anglo-Maratha War, Mahadji Scindia got Madhavrao recognised as the Peshwa by the British. However, in reality, all powers of the Peshwa were in the hands of ministers like Nana Fadnavis, Mahadji Scindia himself, and others. After the Treaty of Salbai was signed in May 1782, wherein the British accepted Narayanrao's son Madhavrao II as the rightful Peshwa and pensioned off Raghunathrao, the First Anglo-Maratha War ended. The treaty also restored the status quo and established peace between the East India Company (EIC) and the Marathas for the next two decades.

However, just like the Rajputs could not get together as a single cohesive force, the multiple power centres that emerged among the Maratha Confederacy resulted in multiple faultlines that were then exploited by their enemies, especially the British, who were past masters in exploiting any weakness. Like the Rajput, the Maratha was a fierce warrior, and both had their repeated moments in the sun.

Shivaji had established a strong military system with an elaborate intelligence network and well-structured financial and treasury systems. However, once the Maratha Empire became a confederacy and came under the direct administration of the Peshwas, who then subsequently served as rulers of the Maratha territory, most Maratha holdings were feudal possessions ruled by zamindars. Apart from the fact that the leadership of the Marathas was working at cross purposes with each other, most military history analysts concur that by the time the Marathas faced Durrani in the Third Battle of Panipat, the discipline that was required to defeat the Afghans and then the British sepoys was lacking, resulting in multiple defeats.

Maharaja Daulat Rao Scindia, who ruled from 1794 to 1827; Amir Khan Pindari, the mercenary Afghan, who had been loosely attached to the Maratha army but sided with whoever gave him the most money. After he was expelled from Jodhpur in 1818, he was given the title of Nawab of Tonk by the EIC ▼

Sayyid Mubarak Ali Khan II, popularly known as Humayun Jah, was the Nawab of Bengal between 1824 and 1838 ▸

Bengal Sultanate II

The East India Company's (EIC's) first factory was established at Surat on the west coast of India in 1612, and another settlement was established at Madras on the east coast in 1640. In the same year, the first expedition was sent to Dacca in Bengal and was so well received by the Mughal governor, Islam Khan Mashhadi, that it was decided to establish a trading post on the Hooghly River, which already had, at the time, Portuguese and Danish factories established there. At the end of the eighteenth century, Bengal had become one of the wealthiest and most important presidencies, but in 1756, the military establishment amounted to a little more than 150 men, most of whom were Dutch or Eurasian mercenaries. Most of them had been killed in the subsequent defence of Calcutta in June that year, and when Robert Clive first arrived at Fulta some months later, all that he found was a single volunteer company, largely put together by Captain Alexander Grant from the surviving civilians. This gave Clive an opportunity to put into practice some innovative methods, and by largely enlisting sepoys from Awadh, he built up an entirely new army by 1763, wherein the strength of the Bengal Army had dramatically gone up to 6,680 all ranks. By 1782, the Bengal Army had a strength of 52,400 men, and by 1805, it had further increased to 64,000 men and was still expanding.

Ruins in the Sunderbans ▾

A soldier from the 1st European Bengal Regiment (left), and native troops of the East India Company (1791–98)—Bengal Army Sepoy (right)

Trade in Bengal was flourishing, and substantial quantities of treasure was being earned by merchants in exchange for goods locally manufactured for export. As early as 1415, there are records of Chinese trade missions bringing gold and silver, in addition to satins, silks, and porcelain. Although textiles were already prominent among locally manufactured goods at the dawn of the Muslim encounter in the tenth century, the volume and variety of textiles produced and exported increased dramatically after the conquest. According to some Chinese records, the *tanka* was accepted as the currency to settle accounts by them.

A century later, the Italian traveller Ludovico di Varthema, who was in Gaur between 1503 and 1508, noted in his diary: 'Fifty ships are laden every year in this place with cotton and silk stuffs. These same stuffs go through all Turkey, through Syria, through Persia, through Arabia Felix, through Ethiopia, and through all India.' A few years later, Tome Pires described the export of Bengali textiles to ports in the eastern half of the Indian Ocean. Clearly, Bengal had become a major centre of Asian trade and manufacture.

The Mughal conquest of Bengal started with Akbar defeating Daud Khan Karrani in a series of battles between 1572 and 1576. Although on the face of it, the entry of imperial forces into the Bengali capital in September 1574 would appear to have been decisive, the full conquest of the Bengal Province actually took three-quarters of a century to accomplish, commencing as far back as 1537 and continuing until 1612. Significantly, the Mughals also abandoned Gaur and preferred to establish their hub at Dacca. From their perspective, even though Bengal was a wealthy province, it was but one of the twelve provinces that made up the vast Mughal Empire.

1815—Havildar of the Bengal Grenadiers (left), and Bengal Army 'Sipahi' in 1817 (right)

Post the 1765 Treaty of Allahabad, when the EIC was appointed the imperial tax collector on behalf of the Mughal Emperor in Bengal, Bihar, and Orissa, and Awadh had more or less also accepted the British as the main power in the region, Calcutta had been declared a Presidency city and became the de facto headquarters of the East India Company by 1773. Two decades later, the ruling power of the Nawabs was abolished, and the EIC took complete control of the city and the province. By the early nineteenth century, the marshes surrounding the city were drained, and the government area was laid out along the banks of the Hooghly River. Richard Wellesley, governor-general of the Presidency of Fort William between 1797 and 1805, was mainly responsible for the development of the city and its public architecture. Throughout the late eighteenth and nineteenth centuries, the city was also the centre of the EIC's opium trade. After the territorial conquest of Bengal in 1757, the EIC pursued a monopoly on the production and export of opium from India. The company bought opium from local traders and later directly from farmers and sold it at auctions in Calcutta. From there, much of it was smuggled to Canton in China by foreign traders, eventually leading to the First Opium War in 1839–42.

A census in 1837 records the population of Calcutta properly as 229,700, of which the British residents made up only 3,138. The same sources place another 177,000 Indians that resided in the suburbs and neighbouring villages, making the entire population of greater Calcutta 406,700.

Calcutta had been declared a Presidency city and became the de facto headquarters of the East India Company by 1773.

The Nawab of Awadh, who reigned from Lucknow between 1814–27, Ghazi ad-Din Haider. The treaty of 1801 had been signed by his father, Yameen-ud Daula Saadat Ali Khan II Bahadur, by virtue of which, the EIC were able to use Awadh's vast treasuries, repeatedly digging into them for loans at reduced rates. In addition, the revenues from running Awadh's armed forces brought them useful revenues. The Nawabs were ceremonial kings, limited to pomp and show but with little influence over matters of state. By the mid-nineteenth century, however, the British had grown impatient with the arrangement and wanted direct control

Burma 1823–26 CE

After the Ahom victory over the Mughals at Saraighat, Assam and its surrounding areas were annexed by Burma, which was a monarchy ruled by the Konbaung dynasty. As Lord Hastings was handing over the governor general's post to Lord Amherst, the Burmese demanded the 'restoration' of a large part of Bengal. Cut off from the subcontinent by the Naga-Patkai Hills, the Burmese had historically never owned any part of Bengal. To make

▲ The British invading force did not have any troops from the Bengal Army as the soldiers were not willing to cross the sea (Kaala Paani), which would result in their losing their cast

matters worse, the Burmese occupied an island belonging to Chittagong, which was a part of the Bengal Province.

The Burmese invasion proved to be a tedious and costly affair. The terrain was extremely difficult, and climatic conditions ensured that military operations were impracticable for a considerable part of the year. In the war of attrition, the Burmese realised they could not match the combined force of European troops and the sepoys from the Madras Army, and hence, in the Treaty of Yandabo, they ceded the districts of Assam, Arakan, and Tenasserim (bordering Malaysia) to the British.

Bharatpur

1826 CE

Since 1805, when General Lake's army had been defeated by the Jats and Yashwantrao Holkar's Maratha troops, Bharatpur had been a major sore point with the British. The Third Maratha War had come and gone, but the fortress that was 13 km in circumference, and had clay and horse-dung bastions and a dry moat that could be flooded around it was considered impregnable. In 1825, Arthur Wellesley, by

◄ British infantry and artillery in battle with Jats at Bharatpur in December 1826

then the highly celebrated Duke of Wellington, was asked how the one symbol of Indian resistance could be destroyed. Wellesley had recommended Stapleton Cotton. The Directors of the East India Company (EIC) promptly sent Cotton to Calcutta, and he was tasked with the capture of the fort.

The Jat maharaja, Baldeo Singh, died mysteriously, and his five-year-old son, Balwant Singh, was declared his successor. On Cotton's arrival on 10 December, British troops captured the reservoir to prevent flooding the area, as had been the case during the 1805 siege. By the middle of December, the fort was surrounded by British forces, with skirmishes occurring on a daily basis. The siege continued until the night of 18 January, when two breaches were made, and mines exploded so that within two hours, the fort had been stormed and taken by sepoys.

Stapleton Cotton (later Lord Combermere) receiving the surrender of Jat commanders

Cachar Levy

1835 CE

The task assigned to the Cachar Levy immediately after its raising in 1835 was to guard the eastern frontier of Assam from the Brahmaputra River to Cachar and to carry out small-scale punitive expeditions in the hill areas. The pattern of deployment consisted of strong detachments at Nowgong and Silchar with smaller satellite posts all along the frontier. The administrative headquarters was set up at Asaloo

(16 miles from Haflong), which was garrisoned with the Levy's strongest detachment. Initially, the Levy had established twelve stockades all along the 400-km frontier that ran through the great Nambhar Forest on the base of the Naga Hills to the plains of the Surma Valley, east of Silchar.

As per British records, the maintenance of law and order was a whole-time occupation of the Force against unending incidents of violence on the part of tribal warriors, who raided the adjoining tea gardens and murdered British officials, transgressed the recognised boundaries, or hunted human heads in the neighbouring villages.

Technically, western Assam, which was known as the undivided Goalpara district, came under British rule after the transfer of the Deewani from the Mughal Emperor on 12 August 1765. As the region was extremely remote and hard to administer, the area was left more or less alone. British military presence in Assam predated the Burmese invasions. In September 1792, Captain Welsh, with Lieutenants Williams, Macgregor, and Wood, with six companies of Native Infantry, each commanded by a British officer, had moved by boat to Assam and reached Goalpara by early December. The creation of police levies allowed the army the freedom to expand further into the hills, and in subsequent years, vast swathes of land would be brought under tea cultivation.

British Expansion III

Naga-Patkai

The British chose to bring the Naga-Patkai Hills that flanked the eastern extremity of Assam under their control and, in 1839, launched the first of many expeditions into the Naga Hills. In 1845, the British signed a non-aggression pact with several Naga chiefs to bring an end to Naga raids on British-controlled territory in Assam. However, the Nagas violated the agreement and continued to launch raids on British-controlled territories. During the nineteenth century, British attempts to subdue the Naga tribes and abolish traditional Naga practises such as headhunting and intertribal violence were resisted with guerrilla tactics from the Nagas, in particular the Angami Nagas. The colonial authorities responded by launching a series of successive punitive expeditions, which eventually brought this resistance to an end.

The first expedition into the Naga Hills was led by Captain Jenkins and Pemberton in 1832. Despite being no match for the British in terms of weapons, the Nagas used the terrain and the conditions to their advantage. In frustration, all that the British could do was burn the Naga settlements and kill whoever they could lay their hands on. A second expedition was launched seventeen years later, in 1849, when the Angami village of Kohonoma

To control the Naga tribes, the EIC resorted to atrocious acts like brutally killing people and ruthlessly burning entire villages, especially in the Angami-dominated areas ▾

▲ Captain Butler (seated), Major Foquett and other British officers during the 1850 expedition into Nagaland

openly supported the Mezoma village in a rebellion against the British government.

By 1839, the Assam Tea Company had come into being, and by the next year, British residences and churches were coming up in the newly cleared areas that were being planted with tea bushes. A large number of these gardens were along the base of the Naga-

Various Naga tribes spread across the entire Naga Patkai stretch

Patkai. As a result, the punitive expeditions into the Naga Hills were more 'police' than 'army'. British tactics were to try to 'shock and awe' the Nagas and subdue them with their firepower so as to stop Naga raids in the plains. After the 1950 expedition, Captain J Butler would go on to raise the 3rd Battalion of the Assam Rifles.

Maharaja Ranjit Singh (1801–1839) riding a white stallion, his retinue around him carrying spears and a ceremonial fan ▶

The Sikh Empire

In the 1730s, the Sikhs faced multiple threats to their faith and dignity from Mughals, Afghans, and their local Muslim governors, some of whom were notorious for their atrocities on non-Muslims. More out of compulsion than anything else, the Sikh community organised itself into two *jathas* (military groups) to tackle the threat to Sri Darbar Sahab at Amritsar and the community per se. Called the *Taruna Dal* and the *Budha Dal*, their roles were to go on campaigns and protect the Darbar Sahib, respectively. As the military influence of Sikhs increased, and as the confrontation with opposing powers became frequent, many more *jathas* were raised locally by wealthy and influential Sikhs. By 1748, there were 63 such jathas. The senior Sikh leadership then took a call, and all the *jathas* were disbanded for the sake of unity. The new combined force was named Dal Khalsa. Akalis were given the responsibility of protecting the Darbar Sahib, and eleven *jathas* were created with their geographical areas clearly defined. These *jathas* came to be known as *misls*.

All went well for a couple of decades, and *misls* fought unitedly under the Dal Khalsa flag. This period saw Abdali, better known as Ahmad Shah Durrani, invade Punjab multiple times. The Sikhs put up fierce resistance to such campaigns. However, by 1767, while the Afghans still retained the power to interfere in Lahore and Multan,

The fort of Lahore with a cavalcade of Sikh dignitaries approaching it ▼

the Mughals had become ineffective, and the Marathas were content with staying away from Punjab. Most of the territory east of Lahore was now virtually without any central power. At this point, possibly due to the absence of any formidable external threat, the unity within the Dal Khalsa began to unravel, and the *misls* started fighting one another for power.

◄ The court of Maharaja Ranjit Singh

After the demise of Abdali in 1773, the power struggle gained momentum since Sikh *misls* rushed in to fill up the new power vacuum as the Afghans, too, were going through turbulent times. Different *misls* had their areas defined when they were initially organised. However, now it came down to sheer muscle power. While *misls* were slugging it out, the Afghans, too, kept on appearing and reappearing on the scene. Lahore, for example, witnessed a series of flip-flops, wherein Afghan rulers of the Abdali Tribe, Taimur Shah, and Zaman Shah, would come and throw the *Bhangi Misl* out before Sikhs regrouped and regained the same—the cycle continuing for twenty-five long years. During this period, the *Sukerchakia Misl* contributed towards the cause under their chief, Maha Singh. Unfortunately, he was killed during an inter-misl battle in 1792. His son, Ranjit Singh, then rose in power and stature, bringing much of Punjab under his control. He stabilised the state by 1801.

Maharaja Ranjit Singh is depicted seated on a yellow stool with his prime minister, Raja Dhian Singh kneeling in front of him. Maharaja Kharak Singh, his eldest son and heir, is seated to his right on a European-style chair

The rise of Maharaja Ranjit Singh and his consolidation of power in Punjab was a long-drawn process during which there were a couple of flashpoints. The first was when the Maratha warrior, Yashwantrao Holkar, took shelter in Punjab, and the East India Company (EIC) troops under General Lake came all the way to the southern bank of the Sutlej River in pursuit. Finally, on 1 January 1806, the Treaty of Lahore was signed between Sikhs and EIC. The next notable incident was over the Malwa region (between the Sutlej and the Yamuna) but the Treaty of

Amritsar of 25 April 1809 brought to an end a confrontation that could have escalated into a full-blown war. While at the end of it all, Ranjit Singh's dream of ruling over complete Punjab remained a dream unfulfilled, he was now free to expand except in the south, across the Sutlej River, which became the de facto boundary between the British and the Sikhs.

After assuming the title of Maharaja, Ranjit Singh made Lahore the capital of the Sikh Empire. The monarchy was well-known for both its secularism and wealth. It was a significant era in South Asian history and the Sikh Empire's golden age.

During this period, the Afghans were engaged in their own internal conflicts. The Gorkhas, defeated by

The Ahluwalia Misl was led by the legendary general Jassa Singh Ahluwalia (1718–1783), also addressed as Sultan-ul-Qaum. As the first commander of the newly formed Dal Khalsa, he led the Sikhs to victory in numerous battles against the Mughals and Afghans, capturing the forts of Lahore (1762) and Delhi (1783) ▼

the British, could no longer oppose Ranjit's dominance in the Punjab Hills. After the English had contained the Marathas, they controlled all of India, with the exception of Sindh and the Punjab.

By 1818, Maharaja Ranjit Singh had vanquished the Pathans of Kasur, captured Multan, Attock, and Peshawar, and subdued the Northwestern Punjab rulers. The Treaty of Amritsar, which was once seen as a setback, came to Ranjit Singh's rescue when he decided to throw the Afghans out of Kashmir. When Azim Khan, the Afghan governor, reached out to the English for help, the English cited the treaty to deny him any assistance.

At the zenith of its glory, the Sikh Empire ruled over a vast geographical swathe between the Sutlej River in the south and Karakorams in the north, the Indus River in the east (Western Tibet), and the Safed Koh mountain (Khyber Pass) in the west. In addition to Lahore, which was Ranjit Singh's capital, Amritsar, Multan, Peshawar, Jammu, Srinagar, Rawalpindi, and Sialkot were other notable towns across his empire. The Khalsa army, as it was known under Ranjit Singh, was upgraded and trained professionally.

◄ The fortress at Attock on the Indus River was built during Akbar's reign. It was captured by the Marathas and then recaptured by Abdali, only for him to lose it to the Sikhs in the Battle of Attock in 1813 ▲

He enlisted soldiers in his army who belonged to many ethnic and socio-economic groups. He improved artillery and infantry capabilities. He brought in brand-new military gear. He also founded establishments to produce weapons, gunpowder, and cannons. His territories had greater wealth as a result of enhanced trade facilities, reduced conflict, and improved security. Maharaja Ranjit Singh is credited with bringing the disparate Sikh groups together to form a thriving empire. The Sikh dominion grew significantly and was safeguarded by a well-trained, independent army.

First Afghan War

1839–42 CE

Just prior to the beginning of the Great Game, fearful of a Russian invasion of India via the Khyber and Bolan passes, the British sent an envoy to the Afghan capital, Kabul, to gain the support of Emir Dost Mohammad Khan in 1837. At first, the emir supported allying with the British. However, when they declined to assist him in regaining Peshawar, which the Sikhs had taken in 1834, he was seen gravitating towards the Russians. Because of this, Governor-General Lord Auckland concluded that Dost Mohammad was anti-British. Further, a Persian army supported by Russia besieged the western Afghan city of Herat during the negotiations. It now appeared very likely that foreign powers would invade India through Afghanistan. Thus, the British chose to replace Dost Mohammad with Shah Shuja.

A 20,000-man British-Indian force crossed the Bolan and Khojak Passes in the spring of 1839 under the command of General Sir John Keane. Although the British faced challenges due to the hostile terrain and harassment from tribesmen during their journey, they faced minimal opposition. The force reached Kabul after capturing Kandahar and Gazni by the end of July 1839. Dost Mohammad fled

Meeting little organised opposition, British troops taking the heights at Khelat on 13 November 1839 ▼

The British diplomats, including Sir William MacNaghten, were murdered, and the garrison was eventually forced to surrender.

▲ Alexander Burnes, disguised as a horse trader(above), and Emir Shah Suhja (below)

The ruler of Afghanistan Emir Dost Mohammad (above), and Sir William Hay Macnaghten (below) ►

from Kabul, and Emir Shah Shuja was installed in August. However, the British could not afford to keep troops in Kabul indefinitely.

The Baluchi Khans of Khelat (Qalat) then inflicted heavy punishment on British troops as they tried to keep the route back to the Indus Valley open. Their persistent attacks on British supply lines were the cause of this.

Back in Kabul, resentment against the British was growing, fanned by the son of Dost Mohammad. A series of sexual scandals, cultural insensitivity, and the perceived haughtiness of the British exacerbated the situation that soon went out of hand. The British diplomats, including Sir William MacNaghten, were murdered, and the garrison was eventually forced to surrender. General Sir William Elphinstone, the British commander, then negotiated a withdrawal. He agreed to give up the majority of his cannon and his reserves of gunpowder in lieu of a safe passage. A force of 4,500 with 12,000 camp followers then left Kabul but was ambushed by Afghans who had gone back on their words. There were hardly any survivors.

Shah Suhja enters Kabul under a military escort in 1841 ▾

▲ British troops from 31 Regular supported by a company each from 33 and 53 Bengal Native Infantry in a skirmish with Shinwari tribesmen at Mazinah in the Nangahar Province of Afghanistan on 24 July 1842. Two days later, a larger British force supported by cavalry and artillery decimated the tribesmen

The Prison of Hadjee Khan ►

◀ Afghan soldiers in the Khyber Pass

Instability continued in 1844 with the assassination of Sir Alexander Burns at the gate of his residence, with a simultaneous attack on and conflagration of Captain Johnson's Treasury and the residences of other British officers ▼

Annexation of Sindh 1843 CE

For most of the second half of the eighteenth century, Baloch Talpur Amirs ruled over Sindh after they descended into the region in the 1760s. By 1785, they controlled the entire area of Sindh under their chief, Mir Fateh Ali Khan. After his demise in 1800, his surviving brothers divided the territory among themselves—Hyderabad, Khairpur, Tando Muhammad Khan, and Mirpur.

◀ The Battle of Miani (or Battle of Meeanee, Sindh) was a battle between forces of the Bombay Army of the East India Company, under the command of Charles Napier and the Baluch army of Talpur Amirs of Sindh, led by Mir Nasir Khan Talpur. The battle took place on 17 February 1843 at Miani, and the subsequent Battle of Hyderabad (24 March 1843) eventually led to the capture and annexation of the Sindh region

Soon thereafter, they started exerting outwards and captured neighbouring areas like Amarkot, Sahikarpur and Bukkar (from the Afghans), and Karachi (from the Khans of Kalat).

By 1807, the Anglo-Russian rivalry took a serious turn in light of the declaration by Napoleon to invade India via Persia. Both in France and in England, it was recognised that there must be a fight to the finish, which included the taking over of the British Empire by the French. This forced the English to embark on a mission to put in place friendship treaties with the buffer territories along the likely routes of ingress, which narrowed down to the Punjab, Persia, and Afghanistan. The governor general, Gilbert Kynynmound, better known as Lord Minto, in the same vein, deputed Nicholas Smith to sign the Treaty of Eternal Friendship with Amirs with the common cause of keeping Napolean out of Sindh. The English had established trading centres in various places in Sindh much earlier. Now, they started putting political pressure on it. In 1820, the Amirs were forced to agree that they would not permit any European to settle in Sindh. A few more treaties were signed in 1832 and 1838. The last treaty, however, came in the wake of the capture of the Rojhan area of Sindh by Maharaja Ranjit Singh. Unlike the previous treaties, the 1838 treaty aimed at stationing the EIC troops inside Sindh to thwart the designs of the Sikhs. The Amirs, initially hesitant, finally signed it. A subsidiary treaty of 1839 meant more EIC soldiers were to be stationed in Sindh at an annual fee of three lakh rupees.

Two other factors affected the English policy towards Sindh. One was their plan to use the Indus River to facilitate trade with Punjab and northwest India. The second was the tussle with the Sikhs. The Sutlej River had been designated as the international border by the English through their treaty with the Sikhs in 1809. However, after two decades, the British began to assert that such a boundary alignment only applied up to the point where the Sutlej and Indus rivers met in the west, despite the Sikhs' belief that it extended all the way to the Arabian Sea. Maharaja Ranjit Singh, instead of getting into a confrontation with the English over Sindh, decided to look the other way after the brief excursion into Rojhan in Sindh.

The First Anglo-Afghan War (1839–42) saw the resentment against the EIC building up in the minds of the Amirs. Even though they served the

Major General Sir Charles James Napier and the then political agent, Major James Outram, who was extremely critical of Napier's approach but played his part in the fighting. The army of the Amirs was scattered, and with the exception of Khairpur, the entire region was absorbed into the Bombay Presidency

British loyally, as the dust over the most humiliating defeat of the English troops in Afghanistan was settling down, the new governor general, Edward Law, the 1st Earl of Ellenborough, chose to put the blame for such a massive reversal on the Amirs. Lord Ellenborough believed that annexing Sindh would be beneficial for boosting English morale and demonstrating to the locals the superiority of British weapons. He asked Major James Outram, the then resident of Sindh (and who had fought in the First Afghan War with distinction), to bring accusations against the Amirs. Ellenborough then asked the Amirs to cede the strategically important areas of Karachi, Thatta, Sakhar, Bakhar, and Robri to the English as compensation for their past behaviour. At that time, Mir Rustam Ali Khan of Khairpur was forced to abdicate in favour of his younger half-brother, Mir Ali Murad, who was more inclined towards the British.

In 1842, Charles Napier was assigned full civil and military authority over Sindh. In addition to endorsing Outram's accusations against the Amirs, Napier also held them accountable for their betrayal of the English. He asked the Amirs to hand over the territories already demanded, provide coal to the English ships sailing on the Indus, and surrender the authority to mint coins to the English.

Napier then asked the three Amirs to meet him on 20 January 1843 so they could sign a new treaty. With the exception of the Amir of Khairpur, all three Amirs consented to sign the new treaty and did so in Sindh's Hyderabad. Even though he had promised Outram via a message that he would sign the treaty, the Amir of Khairpur was unable to arrive in Hyderabad in time. Outram told Napier this and asked him not to lead the army on to Khairpur. But Napier disregarded his counsel. The advance of Napier with a threatening posture resulted in the revolt of the Baluchi soldiers. They attacked the Residency. Outram, however, could save himself and fled. But this then became the cause of a full-fledged war. Napier defeated the Baluchis in the battle of Miani on 17 February 1843 and annexed Sindh. The annexation of Sindh was purely the result of British imperialism. It was criticised even by Englishmen. Arthur Innes would write in *A History of England and the British Empire*: 'If the Afghan episode is the most disastrous in our Indian annals, that of Sindh is morally even less excusable.'

First Anglo-Sikh War 1845–46 CE

Maharaja Ranjit Singh passed away in 1839. Unfortunately, inept successors, palace intrigues, and infighting led to the corrosion of power of the Lahore Court. However, the kingdom saw a rapid rise in the volume of armed men in terms of sheer numbers. Every landlord, religious head, and even panchayat leader now had his own personal army. The idea was to create a commonwealth of Sikhs within the empire, with Lahore having limited control over such forces. From the English perspective, it was seen as a dangerous development, and they started responding by increasing their own forces and creating cantonments hugging the Sutlej River.

The settlement of the state of Punjab after the first war, however, neither fulfilled the imperialistic designs of the English nor did it satisfy the Sikhs.

In December 1845, the Sikhs learned that General Hugh Gough, the commander-in-chief, and Lord Charles Hardinge, the governor-general, were headed for Ferozepur. This news had the alarm bells ringing through various factions of the Sikh community. As per the Treaty of 1809, signed between the English and the Sikhs, the Sutlej River was to be the boundary between the two empires. But the Sikhs, distressed by the news of the British moves, decided to take pre-emptive action and crossed the

Sikh Soldiers in 1846 ▼

▲The Battle of Mudki was fought on 18 December 1845. The Battle of Ferozshah was then fought on 21/22 December. At Ferozshah, the Sikh entrenchments had held against repeated British attacks. After an anxious night, the British advanced the next morning only to find the Sikh positions abandoned. Their commander, Lal Singh, had been bought over by the EIC with the promise he would be suitably rewarded. This turned the tide in favour of the British

◄British troops captured the Baddowal Fort in Ludhiana on 21 January 1846

▲Portrait of Sir Henry Oxenden (1643-1709), Governor of Bombay and President of the East India Company

◄The Battle of Aliwal was fought on 28 January 1846

Sutlej River on 11 December 1845. The English professed such a move as a violation of a long-standing treaty and decided to declare war on the Sikhs. Over the next couple of months, a number of battles were fought between the two sides. Out of all such battles, five stand out for their lasting impact on the future of the Sikh Empire. Those battles are mentioned below.

On 18 December, on the southern side of the Sutlej River, the Sikhs and the British engaged in combat for the first time. The Sikhs lost the Battle of Mudki. Three days later, on 21 December, the Battle of Ferozepur was fought just 30 km from Mudki. The

Sikhs were once more vanquished in this battle. However, it was a close call for the English, who succeeded only because of the treacherous behaviour of the Sikh general Lal Singh, who abandoned his position.

After a gap of a month, on 21 January 1846, the Battle of Baddowal was fought less than 13 km from Ludhiana. The English army was routed by the Sikh army led by Ranjodh Singh Majithia. The British, shaken by the ferocity of the Sikh attack, burnt down the Baddowal Fort with civilians tied up inside. The British then regrouped and clashed again with the Sikhs on 28 January at Aliwal, where the tide turned yet again, the British emerging victors this time. Finally, on 10 February, the Battle of Sobraon was fought, and it proved to be a pivotal battle that was decisively won by the British forces.

▲ General Ranjodh Singh Majithia, who attacked the British rear during the Battle of Baddowal

▲ General Sham Singh Attariwala, who was killed during the Battle of Sabraon

The Sikhs lost the First Anglo-Sikh War despite fighting multiple determined engagements against the English. Even though the demise of Maharaja Ranjit Singh and the chaos that followed had weakened the Sikhs militarily, the role played by traitors like Lal Singh and Teja Singh of the Sikh army also played an important part in their defeat. They were in league with the East India Company (EIC) and acted as informers. Another determining factor was the decision taken by the Dogras, led by Raja Gulab Singh, to stay out of the conflict. There were two reasons for such a move. Raja Gulab Singh had lost both his brothers and two of his sons and nephews to the palace intrigues that had followed the death of the Maharaja. Further, seeing the lack of unity within the Sikh army and the overwhelming military superiority of the English, he had advised the Sikh commanders to avoid a direct confrontation with the English and opt for a lightning raid on Delhi to surprise the rear of the English army. However, once his suggestion was not accepted, he opted out of the war before it began.

Ultimately, on 20 February 1846, the British took control of Lahore and on 8 March, the Sikhs and the English signed the Treaty of Lahore, which implied that the British had annexed the area between the Sutlej and Beas Rivers. The EIC was also allowed a war indemnity of 1.5 crore rupees. While the territory was ceded without any issues, the Sikhs didn't have the money to pay the British. While promising to pay fifty lakh rupees in cash soon, the Sikhs

Sir Henry Lawrence, who was appointed Resident with almost unlimited administrative powers ▶

offered the complete hill tract between the Beas River to the south and the Indus River to the north to the English in lieu of the balance. With the British accepting the deal, the whole belt between the Sutlej River and Indus River (Jalandhar Doab, Jammu, Kashmir, Ladakh, and Hazara provinces) was passed on to the British. At that juncture, another issue arose. The ceded territory had many local rajas and chieftains who had been sovereigns of the Lahore Court, and something needed to be done about them. Realising its inability to deal with every such chieftain individually and controlling an underdeveloped mountainous terrain, the EIC agreed to another understanding. Thus, on 11 March 1846, another treaty, again at Lahore, was signed between the EIC and Raja Gulab Singh. Through the Treaty of Amritsar, the EIC, while retaining the territory between the Beas River and Ravi River, handed over the rest of the territory, as ceded by the Sikhs, to Raja Gulab Singh for a consideration of 75 lakh rupees.

Simultaneously, the Sikh army's power was diminished. An almost 80,000-strong Sikh army was disbanded, and only 22,000 soldiers were now allowed to be kept in service. The British acknowledged Daleep Singh as the ruler and Rani Jindan as the regent, while Lal Singh was appointed the *wazir.* The Maharaja also consented to not hire any Europeans into his service without first obtaining British approval.

Henry Lawrence established a British residence in Lahore. The settlement of the state of Punjab after the first war, however, neither fulfilled the imperialistic designs of the English nor did it satisfy the Sikhs. Such a situation, led to an open revolt by the Sikhs against the English a few years later, resulting in the Second Anglo-Sikh War.

Subsequent to the Treaty of Amritsar, the boy-Maharaja Daleep Singh ►

Second Aglo-Sikh War 1849 CE

In January 1848, Lord Hardinge passed the governor general's mantle to Lord Dalhousie, boasting that it should not be necessary to fire a gun in India for some years to come. However, the Sikh refusal to come to terms with their defeat, which they attributed to treachery and their antagonistic attitude towards the Pathans and the Afghans, caused Hardinge's policy of supporting a friendly but subservient

▲ Sikh artillery unit firing from its entrenched positions

▲ British officers observe infantry, artillery, and cavalry advancing to attack across open ground during the Battle of Chillianwallah on 14 January 1849. The battle was one of the bloodiest fought by the British East India Company, and both armies held their positions at the end of the day, severely denting British pride. The siege of Multan that lasted from 19 April 1948 to 22 January 1949 (bottom)

Sikh state as a breakwater against Central Asian Mohammedanism to implode. Dalhousie, all 37 years of age, decided on an aggressive stance, and he advocated grasping all opportunities of acquiring territory or revenue as the opportunity presented itself, as opposed to merely undermining the Sikh state into submissiveness. The opportunity was not long in coming.

The trigger came when two English officers were murdered in Multan by a mob, forcing the governor, Dewan Mulraj to resign. The anti-British sentiment was so intense that in a matter of days, the *Rachna Doab* (area between the Ravi and the Chenab Rivers) and the Doab between the Chenab and the Indus were inundated with Pathan and Baluch swordsmen, eager to join forces with the Sikhs in order to restore a Hindu governor. The banishment of Rani Jindah, the mother of Maharaja Dalip Singh, from Punjab also added fuel to the fire.

The battles of Chillianwala and Gujarat were followed by a surrender by the Sikhs on 11 March 1849, finally

bringing the war to an end. There was a durbar assembled in the fort on 29 March, where a proclamation on behalf of the British government was read out announcing the formal end of the Sikh kingdom. After presenting the Koh-i-Noor diamond to Queen Victoria, Maharajah Dalip Singh abdicated from his father's throne, never to return.

The East India Company army was commanded by Sir Hugh Gough while the Sikhs were being led by Sher Singh Attariwala. Chillianwala was a village situated on the left bank of the Jhelum River, some 147 km north of Lahore. Though the battle itself was inconclusive, the bulk of the British Army consisted of European troops with some relatively few Native sepoys ▼

Gulab Singh was the founder of the Jammu and Kashmir Dynasty, which brought the state under Dogra rule. After the Battle of Shopian in 1819, Kashmir had been annexed by Maharaja Ranjit Singh ▸

Dogra

The most powerful ruler of the Jammu region, Raja Ranjit Dev, had a vast, hilly kingdom that covered the complete province of present-day Jammu. He had a brother, Mian Surat Singh, whose legacy was carried forward by his sons, Mian Zorawar Singh, Mian Mota, and Mian Dulla Bhoola. Mian Zorawar Singh had only one son, Mian Kishore Singh. That family held a small jagir near Jammu and were on good terms with their cousins who descended from Raja Ranjit

Dev. As was the tradition, all such *jagirs* and principalities would unite to resist external threats until family feuds took down the royals of Jammu. However, after the demise of Raja Ranjit Dev, factions in Dogra territories began aligning with opposing forces. Mian Mota, in the meantime, rose to power in Jammu and maintained an excellent familial relationship with Mian Kishore Singh's family.

That relationship saw three young sons of Mian Kishore Singh—Gulab Singh, Dhian Singh, and Suchet Singh—grow up under the patronage of the de facto ruler, Mian Mota Singh. They grew up as skilled warriors and riders.

In 1808, Sardar Hukma Singh Chimni led Maharaja Ranjit Singh's army into the Jammu region. Gulab Singh, barely in his teens, fought bravely in the battle. Though the Dogra army was subdued, his valour and skills were noticed. A positive feedback from Hukma Singh saw Gulab Singh enrol into the Sikh army in 1810. His two brothers soon followed him into the service of the Lahore Durbar. All three brothers slowly gained prominence as soldiers and won the confidence of Maharaja Ranjit Singh.

Unlike his two siblings, Gulab Singh chose to remain in the field, invariably away from the palace at Lahore. His gallantry and battlefield leadership skills saw Gulab Singh being appointed as the commander of the Jamwal Cavalry. In 1815, Maharaja

▲ Buddhism was taken over by Shaivism in the ninth century. In 1339, Shah Mir became the first Muslim ruler of Kashmir. Since then, various kings find mention in Firdausi's *Shahnama* (the Persian epic known as the *Book of Kings)*

Ranjit Singh bestowed all three brothers with *jagirs* in Jammu and in north and western Punjab. By 1820, the three brothers had their combined *jagirs* spread across Jammu, Bhoti, Bandralta, Chenani, Ramgarh, and Reasi. Then came the turning point in 1822 when Gulab Singh was appointed the Raja of Jammu by the Maharaja. Thus, Raja Gulab Singh became a suzerain of the Khalsa Durbar while Dhian Singh rose to be the prime minister, and Suchet Singh was appointed the chamberlain to the royal household.

◀After Shah Mir, for the next five centuries, Muslim monarchs ruled Kashmir, including the Mughal and the Afghan Durrani Empire

Gulab Singh stayed away from palace politics and refused to side with Sikhs after the death of Maharaja Ranjit Singh. His action was dictated by the fact that the Sikh kingdom had been disintegrating due to internal feuds as well as external threats emanating out of the British plans to annexe the Sikh state. After the Sikhs, availing the services of Raja Gulab Singh as their chief negotiator, signed the first treaty at Amritsar on 9 March and surrendered a large chunk of their territory to the English, the second treaty at Amritsar on 16 March 1846 saw the Britishers handing over all hilly tracts between the Indus and the Ravi (and not Beas) rivers to Raja Gulab Singh for a sum of 75 Lakh rupees. He was also elevated to the status of the Maharaja of Jammu & Kashmir, including Poonch. Kashmir was already under the Sikhs, and Ladakh was seen as a forbidden land.

▼ Maharaja Gulab Singh visiting his queen

General Zorawar Singh Kahluria (1786-1841) ▸

Dogra Conquest of Ladakh

Raja Gulab Singh, a man of vision and a great strategist, correctly appreciated the chaotic situation that was likely to emerge after the demise of Maharaja Ranjit Singh. That assessment drove him to plan for the future of his land and his people. He instinctively knew that one day, he would have to create an empire of his own and in the process, sever the umbilical cord with the Lahore Durbar once Maharaja Ranjit

Singh moved to the world beyond. The future relationship with the British, too, merited certain safeguards and would require deft handling. He, therefore, started evaluating his options.

The *jagir* of Jammu had been expanded all the way to the Jhelum in the west, beyond which lay Punjab directly under the control of Lahore. To the east lay Chamba and other principalities, and then beyond were the states of Guler and Kangra. Any expansion in that direction was also not possible because these states had already been absorbed by the Sikh empire in 1809. To the northwest lay Kashmir, which was already under the control of the Sikhs since 1819. Similarly, the area to the south of Jammu was part of Maharaja Ranjit Singh's empire. However, to the northeast lay the forbidden land that had not invited the interest of Maharaja Ranjit Singh and even the British. Hence, for Gulab Singh, that was the only direction he had to expand his kingdom. Gulab Singh also realised that by venturing in that direction, after crossing the Great Himalayan Range, the territory to the east, north, and west lay open for him to exploit and capture. Even for Maharaja Ranjit Singh, after he had made his peace with the British, he had no option but to expand only northwards, an option he chose not to exercise once he had Kashmir.

Politically, events were falling into place for Gulab Singh. The behaviour of Tsepal Dondup Namgyal, the Gyalpo (king) of Ladakh, towards the Sikh governor of Kashmir and the Lahore Court, by implication, created an opportunity for the Dogra ruler. Over the years, Ladakhi *gyalpos* used to pay tribute to the Mughals, Afghans, and then the Sikhs. However, at that point in

The Dogra standard that is preserved in the museum in Leh ▼

Ladakhi soldiers dressed in their traditional attire who fought against the Dogras. The vast region includes Zanskar, with the Zanskar, Suru, and Drass Rivers draining the region, all of them a part of the Indus River system ▼

▲ The mud fort in Leh, the capital of Ladakh, that was built for Zorawar Singh in 1836

A cannon preserved in the well-maintained museum ▶

time, the Ladakhis ceased the tradition and appeared to be defiant. Despite the governor's repeated demands for tribute, the Ladakhis remained unresponsive. When the messages failed to fetch any cash or tribute in kind, Lahore had to seriously think of enforcing its suzerainty. However, Ladakh was a region that required careful planning as the land was, in effect, a high-altitude desert where an army could easily perish to the elements. By then, Gulab Singh had already been preparing for the conquest of Ladakh, and the Sikhs were happy to outsource the same to him.

Since Raja Gulab Singh was a part of the Sikh Empire, it all fitted in. In addition, in the eyes of Maharaja Ranjit Singh, the compulsion to conquer Ladakh and the territory lying to the north of the Kashmir Valley (Baltistan in particular) was extremely tempting. His advisors apprehended that Kashmir could fall to any credible threat from the north. Gulab Singh made the best of the opportunity and tasked his ablest commander, General Zorawar Singh, to subjugate Ladakh.

In 1834, General Zorawar, leading a 4,000-strong army, invaded the Suru Valley in Kargil via Umasi La when a disgruntled local chieftain invited him to do so. Over the next year, the Dogras subjugated the entire stretch between Kargil and Leh, fighting in hostile terrain, surviving the harsh winter and a number of upsets as the Ladakhis fought tenaciously. However, repeated rebellions compelled Zorawar to march into Ladakh three more times to regain control. In 1840, he invaded Baltistan and captured Skardu. When his army

▾ A depiction of the fighting in Ladakh

▲ Situated in the extreme north-western Himalayas, the kingdom was no match for the powerful Dogra army. Between 1834 and 1846, the region was under the suzerainty of the Sikhs, but for all practical purposes, its administration and control were with Gulab Singh. Only in 1846 was it integrated as the 'Ladakh Wazarat' under the Dogras

reached Astor, he was recalled when the Sikh governor of Kashmir prevailed on the Lahore Court to pull the Dogras back.

Not one to rest on his laurels, Zorawar then turned east and led his army into western Tibet in the spring of 1841. The pace of his advance and the defeat of the Tibetans resulted in the capture of Tibetan territory to the west of the Mayum La. Zorawar's campaign in Tibet, however, sent alarm bells ringing not only in Lhasa and Peking but also in the British hierarchy that foresaw a likely liaison between the

powerful Sikh kingdom and the Hindu kingdom of Nepal. The British then prevailed upon the vulnerable Sikh king to recall General Zorawar, whose capture of Western Tibet had also started hurting their ambush-trading model of Pashmina wool. Since it was already December, heavy snow and freezing temperatures had forced the invading army to set up camp.

Before the order could be implemented, a large combined army of Tibetans and Chinese managed to cross into western Tibet during the peak of winter. It attacked the Dogra army that was spread out in the southern part of the region and was caught by surprise since no one was expected to cross Mayum La until the snowmelt the following year. Having cut their supply lines and carried out selective ambushes, the Chinese-Tibetans created a situation for the Dogras, who were left without supplies and war-fighting means. In the final ferocious battle fought amidst a raging snowstorm at Toyo in Tibet, General Zorawar was killed fighting, and the Dogra army was vanquished.

The Chinese-Tibetan army, now beefed up by Ladakhi and Balti survivors of General Zorawar's army, started marching toward Leh to free Ladakh from the Dogras. However, timely reinforcements from Jammu thwarted their plans and defeated them on the bank of the Pangong Tso in Changthang. A treaty was signed between the Dogras and the Tibetans that ended the war, and both sides committed to respecting the traditional boundaries between Tibet and Ladakh.

From the ***Gulabnama***, General Zorawar Singh (seated left) with the Gyalpo and Gyalmo (Queen) of Ladakh. Following his conquest, the Gyalpo agreed to pay 50,000 rupees war indemnity and 20,000 rupees tribute per annum in 1835 ▼

The Shah Hamadan's Mosque in Srinagar ▸

The State of Jammu & Kashmir

Maharaja Gulab Singh became the ruler of the region to the west of the Ravi River in 1846. However, palace intrigues in Lahore created an issue for him when the governor of Kashmir refused to hand over that part of the territory to him. Having overcome the initial hiccups, he focused all his energies towards consolidating his kingdom and enforcing the writ of the state and many stern steps were taken. The British, who wanted to place a resident within the state to control Gulab Singh, were outwitted when, in a departure from the norm, he handed over the reins to his son, Ranbir Singh, in 1856 and appointed himself the governor of Kashmir.

By the time Ranbir Singh became the maharaja, his father had already done most of the groundwork. A profoundly religious man, he restored temples, built schools, encouraged arts and culture, and came across as a progressive king. During his rule, the state became the first princely state to have a written penal code that was aligned with the recently introduced Indian Penal Code in British India. His son, Partap Singh, introduced monumental social reforms after he took over from his father in 1885. His reign was marred by the imposition of a 'central rule' in 1889 when he was relieved of his powers, and a committee was put into place to govern the state. In 1905, he was reinstated. He died issueless in 1925, and after his death, his nephew, Hari Singh, became the fourth ruler of the J&K State.

The Dogra monarch, Maharaja Ranbir Singh, at worship in Jammu ▾

Portrait of Maharaja Ranbir Singh

Maharaja Pratap Singh

Presidency Armies

Richard Wellesley, the governor-general of India, under whose watch the British fought the Second Maratha War, sowed the seeds for the complete military domination of India. The British, like the Portuguese before them, were ruthless in the implementation of their plans, and as the East India Company (EIC) grew in stature and resources, more and more people flocked to their colours.

With the passage of time, each Presidency Army added artillery and cavalry to their increasing foot (infantry)

Madras Horse Artillery, 1844

◀ Another one of Henry A Payne's masterful watercolours, which captures an officer from the Bombay Horse Artillery in 1846 at full gallop

regiments. From the mid-eighteenth century onwards, the Crown began to dispatch regiments of the regular British Army to India to reinforce the three Presidency armies. These troops were referred to as HM's regiments or 'Royal' regiments.

The EIC's army in the mid-nineteenth century had grown by leaps and bounds, and by 1844, the combined strength of the Bengal, Madras, and Bombay armies was 235,446 native and 14,584 European officers and men. A hundred years previously, these very armies were nothing but a collection of watchmen employed in each of the Presidencies of the EIC to protect their trading stations. In 1748, these men were placed under one commander-in-chief, Major-General Stringer Lawrence and each of the three main stations—Calcutta, Madras, and Bombay—began maintaining their own army as well.

Each evolved along different lines, adapting to the requirements of the Presidency, but they all also had a common structure with their own Regiments and a cadre of European officers. All three armies were structured around a few pure European regiments in which both the officers and men were Europeans. These then had a growing number of Native regiments, in which the officers were Europeans and the other ranks were Indians. As the Company's power grew, the face of the British became the Presidency armies. European regiments, with their spit and polish, were the perfect platform to underline the 'majesty of governance'. Indian sepoys, recruited from virtually all parts of the country, became the backbone of the EIC. Every fort that was attacked, or a battle won, resulted in loot and prize money for the European officers, while the sepoys, mostly recruited from among the least educated rural strata, were extolled to fight for the Company because their meagre pay amounted to having eaten the salt of the Company. The average sepoy was well aware that a single word against the *sirkar* would result in ruthless repercussions and the drying up of the fount from where he drew his pension.

The British knew just how fragile the system was and how critical the native troops were for them to stay in contention in India. Sir Thomas Munro, governor of the Madras Presidency, would write: 'The spirit of independence will rise up in this army long before it is thought of among the people. The army will not wait for the slow operation of the instruction of the people and the growth of liberty among them but will hasten to execute their own measures for the overthrow of the government.' The accuracy of Munro's prediction was to be proved correct thirty years later when the Bengal Army would rise in revolt. Had the Bombay and Madras armies also rebelled, the outcome would have been very different.

Mounted and dismounted native soldiers from the 2nd Punjab Cavalry in uniform, outdoors, showing front and rear of Sikh non-commissioned officer and Afghan officer ▼

Crossing the Chambal 1849 CE

An Adi Bobum Bokang warrior near Tuting ▸

Dafla Expedition
1850 CE

Moving cautiously into the hills, the British launched a punitive expedition into what was then known as the Daphla region for the first time only in 1850. Until then, the Ahoms referred to the Nyishi tribes as 'Daflas', and this term was inherited by the British. The Nyishis were mostly settled in the hills north of Nao Duar (nine passes) in Darrang and Che Duar (six passes) in Lakhimpur. To their east was Adi country inhabited by the Galo, Adis, and Hill Miris. The earliest records of conflict between the Nyishis and Ahoms go back to 1614 during the reign of the Ahom king Pratap Singh. After a raid into the plains, Pratap Singh launched the first punitive expedition under Lako Borpatra and Bharali Gohain, but this force was literally decimated by the Nyishis.

The Ahom kings Sutyinpha and Sunyatpha's expeditions against the Nyishi in 1646 and 1672 also met with similar fates, and this resulted in the construction of forts called *daflagarhs* that probably gave the Nyishis the sobriquet of Daflas! Rajendra Singh, who ruled from 1751 to 1769, tried to control the Nyishis with additional forts and market sanctions, but could not stop the periodic Nyishi raids. British control over Assam initially saw them adopt a policy of non-intervention and the entire area, mainly consisting of the Assam Himalaya, was more or less left well alone.

The British initially ignored the northern parts of the Assam Himalayas, but by 1850, had started to send small expeditions to 'punish' maurading Dadplas and Adi tribes that would raid settlements in the plains ▼

Travancore State Forces 1855 CE

While the Deccan and North India continued to be in a state of turmoil in the first half of the nineteenth century, the situation in the Madras Presidency, also known as the Presidency of Fort Saint George, was a lot more settled with the East India Company (EIC) having established a vice-like grip on the region. The French challenge had more or less fizzled out, and the Portuguese were content to

▲ Maharaja Uthram Thirunal Marthanda Varma (1846–60) welcomes General James Outram at the Travancore Royal Court. The British had come to Travancore's aid when Tipu Sultan had attacked them, and as a result, the princely state had good relations with the EIC. After some battalions of the Travancore Army had rebelled in 1805, the army had been disbanded

keep their foothold on Goa and their other bases. By 1765, the British had acquired the Northern Circars. The largest kingdom of the hill-tract region of Visakhapatnam was Jeypore, and the maharaja of Jeypore, Vikram Dev I, had earlier fought with and defeated both the French at Malkangiri and the Marathas at Umerkote. In 1775, Jeypore was conquered by Captain Richard Matthews, and the hill tracts of Ganjam and Visakhapatnam were the last places to be annexed by the British.

The last quarter of the 18th century was a period of rapid expansion. In

addition to the successful wars against Tipu Sultan (1782–99), the British had defeated the Maruthu Pandyars, who were the de facto rulers of Sivagangai; Velu Thampi's rebellion had been put down by 1808, and he had been forced to commit suicide, while the Polygar Wars that had erupted between the Palaiyakkarar of the Madurai region and the EIC, after the demise of the Madurai Nayakas, were kept localised and added vast areas of land

and contributed to the exponential growth of the presidency. Puli Thevar, Veerapandya Kattabomman, the Marudu brothers, Maruthanayagam, Dheeran Chinnamalai, Uyyalawada Narasimha Reddy were Palaiyakkar who kept up their struggle against the British between 1798 and 1847. Despite the disbanding of the Nair units, the Vellore Mutiny in 1807, the annexation of Mysore and then Thanjore, and the constant hanging of the Polygars who fought the British relentlessly, none of these events had any impact on the Bombay or Bengal Army. It was not surprising then that the events of 1857 that were to erupt shortly had little or no impact on the South.

◄ Portrait of Sarabhoji, the last raja of Tanjore and his son Shivaji II Bhonsle (ca. 1832–55), who survived as a titular head. Thanjavur was annexed after his death as he left no male heir

Though the period also witnessed the Vellore Mutiny and a continuous battle by the Polygars against the British, the Madras Presidency would remain relatively calm during the 1857 rebellion ▼

The Uprising

1857 CE

When the execution orders for Mangal Pandey were read on parade on 11 May 1857, the first significant event that marked the beginning of the uprising against British rule in India began in Meerut before quickly spreading to other parts of the country. The regions most affected by what is now known as the First War of Independence extended from Delhi to Barrackpore via Meerut, Kanpur, Gwalior, Jhansi,

◂ Pitched battles... British troops lifting the siege of Lucknow

Siege of the Lucknow Residency in 1857 by the 7th Rajput Regiment ▸

Lucknow, and other parts of Central India. The rebel sepoys' primary goal was to liquidate the East India Company from India.

There were numerous short and long-term factors that contributed significantly to matters coming to a head. Some of the most significant reasons behind the uprising include the following: the Annexation Policy, that allowed the British to take over multiple native states, which infuriated the populace who felt that their basic rights were being usurped; to add to the woes of princely states, the EIC formulated the Doctrine of Lapse, which allowed them to annex any native state whose ruler passed away without a male heir; the British government's economic policies wherein among other issues, heavy taxation was adding to the people's financial suffering that was further compounded by the EIC's monopolistic business model that increased the company's strangle hold on trade, and gave its own people exemption from taxation, even while their own landholdings increased substantially; social policies that included the introduction of Western culture and education systems that were causing a sense of alienation among the populace; the feeling that there was general discrimination against Indians while giving preference to Europeans over Indians in every sphere of life; and finally, the issue of the cartridges for recently introduced rifles that were believed to have been smeared by grease that was made from tallow derived from animal fat. The sepoys, both Muslim and Hindu, became

Later in 1922, Fatehgarh became the Training Centre for the Rajputs ▼

highly agitated because they believed it went against their religious convictions and, in the case of the latter, destroyed their caste. As the uprising then turned violent, the two sides started attacking and slaughtering each other. A lot of blood was shed during the rebellion, which saw most local rulers siding with the sepoys who had mutinied against the English. After a series of protracted and fierce battles, the uprising was finally put down by June 1858. The events of 1857/58 were labelled by the history books from two perspectives—while the British called it a 'Mutiny' or a 'Revolt', many Indian historians, especially during the decades following the exit of the British, have been referring to it as the 'First War of Independence'.

There is little doubt that the uprising caught the British completely off guard. In the final analysis, the factors that played a key role in their eventual quelling of the sepoys was the fact that, by and large, the Madras and

Bombay Presidency armies did not get affected, limiting the uprising to the Gangetic and Indus belts of North India. This allowed the British Empire to divert not only European troops in the subcontinent but also units that were on the way to China.

Unfortunately for the sepoys, three other key reasons for their inability to carry the day despite initial successes was the fact that at no stage did a centralised command structure emerge. A lame-duck Mughal emperor was only a notional head who had little or no role to play in the ad hoc fighting that followed. Begum Hazrat Mahal in Awadh, Babu Kunwar Singh in Bihar, Nana Saheb Peshwa II in Kanpur, and Rani Laxmi Bai in Gwalior could only fight individual battles, but not the war! Tantia Tope, with no formal military training, distinguished himself both at Kanpur with Nana Saheb and then at Gwalior with Laxmi Bai, but neither he nor the others could give the uprising a cohesive shape.

Second, the Sikhs and the Gorkhas, both of whom had been defeated in battle by the sepoy army of Bengal, harboured a deep grudge against the sepoys, and they came to the rescue of the besieged British forces, especially when the fate of Delhi was hanging in the balance. Some key princely states—Patiala, Kapurthala, Nabha, Jodhpur, the Rajputana Agency, Rampur, and the Kingdom of Nepal—actively fought on the British side. The third factor was, ironically, the very cause that acted as a catalyst for the uprising—the greased cartridges! The new Enfield Rifles that used the new ammunition had an effective killing range of a hundred and fifty yards, as against the earlier muskets that were being used by the sepoys that could bring a man down at a maximum range of fifty yards.

The uprising of 1857 significantly influenced the progression of Indian history. The Crown now replaced

Ever since Delhi had fallen to the sepoys in May 1857, the city had become the symbol of resistance. By June over 30,000 sepoys were defending the city while the British managed to garner 9,000 troops of which only a third were English troops while the rest were Sikhs and Gorkhas. Another force of 2,000 plus 32 siege guns had come in from Punjab by September. On the morning of 14 September after a concentrated cannonade, General Wilson gave the order to attack the Kashmere Gate. An Engineer officer and three men then blew up the gate. The dazed defenders were in no position to stop the rush of troops which came through the breach. After some bitter fighting, Delhi was once again in British hands

the EIC as the ruler of India even as Bahadur Shah was exiled, and his sons slaughtered. A Secretary of State for India was appointed, and the Crown's Viceroy became head of the government. However, badly shaken by the uprising, it was decided to revamp the education system and recruit more Indians into the civil service. The British also stopped confiscating rulers' lands and no longer outwardly interfered with religious matters.

The British then reorganised the army and, in the process, created deep fissures in Indian society by introducing the concept of martial races. It impacted the recruitment policy for soldiers over future generations. To safeguard British interests, the ratio of British to Indian soldiers was increased. Indian soldiers were issued with inferior rifles and given limited logistical support as compared to their British counterparts. Artillery, considered to be a battle-

Bahadur Shah Zafar was only a nominal emperor as the Mughal Empire existed only in name and his authority was limited to the walled city of Old Delhi (Shahjahanabad). After he was defeated and captured, his sons were summarily executed. Later, he was exiled to Rangoon, British Burma, where he died in 1862 at the age of 87 ▼

Rani Laxmi Bai of Gwalior was the widow of the Maharaja of Jhansi, Gangadhar Rao. Before his death, the Maharaja adopted a boy as his heir. Lord Dalhousie, the British Governor-general of India, refused to recognise the adopted heir and annexed Jhansi in accordance with the Doctrine of Lapse. The 22-year-old queen refused to cede Jhansi to the British. Joining the uprising against the British, she rapidly organised her troops and assumed charge of the rebel sepoys in the Bundelkhand region. Subsequently, the company's forces surrounded the fort of Jhansi, and a fierce battle raged. Though defeated, she escaped and teamed up with Tantia Tope and mounted a successful assault on the fortress of Gwalior. The treasury and the arsenal were seized, and Nana Saheb was proclaimed as the Peshwa. Lakshmi Bai then marched east to Morar to confront a British counterattack where she was killed in combat ►

◀ Captured Indian sepoys were publically blown from cannons in front of native crowds who were forced to watch the horrific scenes. In places where cannons were not available, the sepoys were hung or simply torn apart. The same techniques had been applied in Vellore by the British who intended to keep the native populations ruthlessly in line

Tantia Tope first emerged at Kanpur as a subordinate of Nana Saheb. He was at the helm of affairs during the Second Battle of Kanpur in November, before he moved to Gwalior to support Laxmi Bai. He continued to fight the British until he was captured and executed ▼

◄ Begum Hazrat Mahal, the second wife of the last Nawab of Awadh Wajid Ali Shah, who was exiled to Calcutta by the EIC in 1856, rallied the sepoys in Lucknow

winning asset, remained in British hands. In effect, the sepoys became auxiliaries to British soldiers. As regards ordinary Indians, the uprising inspired subsequent generations to fight for independence and demonstrated to the Indian populace that they could resist British rule if they could unitedly rise against what once seemed to be an invincible and mighty colonial power.

Babu Kunwar Singh was nearly eighty and in failing health when he assumed command of the soldiers who had revolted at Danapur on 25 July 1857. He was assisted by both his brother, Babu Amar Singh, and his commander-in-chief, Hare Krishna Singh, who fought against the British at Arrah and Jagdishpur. On 23 April 1858, near Jagdispur, the troops under the control of the British East India Company were completely routed by the sepoys. The battle ended when Kunwar Singh brought down the Union Jack from Jagdispur Fort and hoisted his flag. He died on 26 April 1858 in his own palace ▼

◄ Nana Saheb Peshwa II, who led the Sepoys at Kanpur, believed that he was entitled to a pension from the EIC, but was denied recognition under Lord Dalhousie's Doctrine of Lapse. The Peshwa assumed command of the sepoys and forced the British garrison in Kanpur to surrender where the surviving British were put to sword, gaining control of the city for a few days. After a British force recaptured Kanpur, Nana Saheb fled to Nepal, where he died in September 1859 during a tiger hunt

Contributions & Acknowledgments

The two volumes of Yodha are as comprehensive as they could be under the circumstances, and I wish to thank all the known and unknown photographers whose images have helped put together the narrative of the subcontinent's military history. A detailed list of acknowledgements are on the Fauji Days website that can be accessed by scanning the link below.

Apart from Sana Durrani, Asha and Colonel Ajay K Raina who have helped put together this mammoth work, I am also grateful to my friend and publisher, Pankaj P Singh and his editorial and design teams for their valuable contribution in bringing out these two books.

Despite the books extremely large canvas, I expect some readers to revert back to us pointing out important personalities who we may have missed. We welcome such feedback and after due verification, will endeavour to upload the information on the website.

Please scan the QR code below for the complete list of contributors and acknowledgments available on the website faujidays.com/exclusive/yodha/acknowledgments.